INTRODUCTION TO
MISSIOLOGICAL
RESEARCH DESIGN

INTRODUCTION TO
MISSIOLOGICAL
RESEARCH DESIGN

EDGAR J. ELLISTON

WITH
R. DANIEL SHAW, PABLO A. DEIROS, VIGGO SØGGARD,
AND CHARLES E. VAN ENGEN

WILLIAM CAREY
LIBRARY

Dr. Elliston has been teaching research design for a number of years and students like me from all around the world have immensely benefited from the insights and skills generated by this course. Elliston has done a great job in finally putting down his valuable insights on research design in a book form so that students of missiology and other theological disciplines may now have access to this valuable resource. The book not only provides technical and professional insights for developing research design, but also does so from a Christian perspective. I am confident that this book will meet the gap and become a valuable tool for assisting researchers and scholars in undertaking their research effectively.

Atul Y. Aghamkar, PhD, professor and head of Department of Missiology,
South Asia Institute of Advanced Christian Studies, Bangalore, India

Dr. Elliston provides postgraduate missiology students and faculty with an invaluable tool for conducting authentic and reliable research. As a professor of leadership at Thelogocial College in Asia I can testify to the clarity and competence of Elliston's methodology for international students undertaking doctoral degrees through the University of Wales, UK. This book represents decades of successfully mentoring crosscultural students in a wide variety of missiological disciplines. It's a superb contribution to *missio Dei* in today's world.

John Kirkpatrick, DMiss, senior pastor, ICWS Bellagio International Church,
Jakarta, Indonesia

I have studied under Dr. Edgar Elliston during my doctoral program in the School of World Mission/Intercultural Studies, Fuller Theological Seminary from 1994–1998. I have used the material in the book on missiological research as I have developed my PhD research design. I have found it to be very practical and helpful. My experience has shown, while assisting Elliston in his teaching the course and working with master's and doctoral students, that his approach to a wide range of missiological research has helped dozens of US and international students to successfully design and implement their writing projects, theses, and dissertations. Thus, I highly recommend this book to be used by students and teachers of missiological research and design.

Petros G. Malakyan, PhD, associate professor of Leadership Studies,
Center for Life Calling and Leadership, Indiana Wesleyan University

Dr. Edgar Elliston's book, *Introduction to Missiological Research*, has been an effective tool which has shaped the research of hundreds of doctoral students at Fuller Theological Seminary's School of Intercultural Studies. It not only directs the reader step-by-step through the process of missiological research, it also gives the reasoning behind each process. Elliston has also included four essays written by preeminent scholars with each providing their perspective on research in their respective disciplines. In addition, several appendices give instruction on pre- and post-text issues, and common research errors. Exhaustive is the one word that comes to mind when describing the range of material contained in this book.

After almost two decades of development, *Introduction to Missiological Research* is definitive. It will be an invaluable resource and a must-buy for anyone wishing to pursue missiological inquiry.

John Timothy Kauffman, PhD Intercultural Studies, ThM Missiology

Dr. Edgar (Eddie) J. Elliston has recently revised his classic work, *Introduction to Research Design*, which was an invaluable guide to hundreds of us who, over the past fifteen years since its first publication, struggled to understand the inscrutable maze often surrounding missiological research, whether at the MA, ThM, PhD or post-doctorate level. Elliston's book is an invaluable tool in the hands of novice and experienced researchers alike as he leads us through a step-by-step approach to credible research. He provides examples, exercises, checklists, a much-needed glossary of terms, and an up-to-date bibliography for in-depth investigation of specific issues. Perhaps most valuable is Elliston's exploration of the ethical issues and errors that are inherent in missiological research. Elliston's book is a refreshing, much-needed guide for those of us who still see research toward trustworthy findings and conclusions as decidedly necessary to mission integrity and effectiveness.

C. Neal Johnson, JD, PhD, former dean at Belhaven University and currently an international legal and missiological consultant

Introduction to Missiological Research Design
Copyright © 2011 Edgar J. Elliston

Published by
William Carey Library
1605 East Elizabeth Street
Pasadena, CA 91104 | www.missionbooks.org

Francesca Gacho, copyeditor
Hugh Pindur, graphic designer
Jeanne Barrett, indexer

William Carey Library is a ministry of the
U.S. Center for World Mission
Pasadena, CA | www.uscwm.org

Printed in the United States of America
15 14 13 12 11   5 4 3 2 1 BP600

Library of Congress Cataloging-in-Publication Data

Elliston, Edgar J., 1943-
  Introduction to missiological research design / by Edgar J. Elliston with R. Daniel Shaw ... [et al.].
     p. cm.
  Includes bibliographical references and index.
  ISBN 978-0-87808-475-3
  1. Missions--Research. I. Title.
  BV2063.E45 2011
  266.0072'3--dc22
                    2011010979

CONTENTS

FIGURES

TABLES

PREFACE

This text provides an introduction to research in missiology. Missiological research employs single disciplinary methods, multiple disciplinary methods, and multiple methods in a single discipline and may fall along a continuum of qualitative to quantitative research. It may serve to build theory, test theory or serve as action research. Missiology rests on a theological foundation; however, it is always worked out in a human context. Theology with social and behavioral sciences then combine to serve as the basis for missiological research.

This text grew out of teaching "Introduction to Research Design" to master's and doctoral students at Fuller Theological Seminary in the School of Intercultural Studies (formerly School of World Mission). As the author also taught and mentored students at several other colleges, seminaries and universities, it evolved through several delivery methods in interactions with several hundred students. Initially, it was largely a lecture course. It grew into an interactive course with supplements both in an HTML-interactive mode and a video-based mode.

This text addresses missiological research design issues rather than provide instruction about specific research methodologies. The basic design structure addressed includes five basic interactive issues: definition of the central research issue, an evaluation of precedent research, designing an appropriate methodology, reporting the findings from this methodology, and finally, a set of conclusions and recommendations. The text briefly describes other items normally found in a research proposal, thesis or dissertation. Because every research project faces ethical issues, this text also identifies some basic ethical issues related to missiological research.

Edgar J. Elliston, PhD
Seven Hills, Ohio
April 2011

ACKNOWLEDGMENTS

The foundational thinking for this book came from Ted Ward. He taught research design for many years in the College of Education at Michigan State University and then later at Trinity Evangelical Divinity School in Chicago. His imprint appears throughout this text, but he cannot be blamed for weaknesses in this text. He guided research in education, international development, and many related areas for Christian leaders in churches, seminaries, missions, and Christian universities. Since the author studied under him as a mentor in a PhD program, the influence of courses, personal counsel and later professional interaction as we were both leading doctoral programs in seminaries is not possible to fully document in this text except to note at the outset.

Students who studied research design with the author at Fuller Theological Seminary, the Theological College of Asia in Singapore and Daystar University in Nairobi, Kenya, Union Institute of Cincinnati and at a distance from Trinity Evangelical Divinity School, Andrews University, Hope International University, Nova Southeastern University, and the Northwest School of Ministry all contributed to the thinking that emerged through this text. Additionally, the faculties of Fuller Theological Seminary, Andrews University, and others who served on doctoral examination committees sharpened the design issues for the author through their critiques of the hundreds of proposed research projects brought to them.

Pablo Deiros, PhD serves as the President of the International Baptist Theological Seminary in Buenos Aires and is one of the foremost missiological historians in Latin America. His chapter provides key insights about missiological research from a historical perspective.

Viggo Søggard, PhD has long served both as a professor of communication at the School of Intercultural Studies at Fuller Theological Seminary and a consultant to many international agencies about intercultural communication. His research, consulting and mentoring about missiological communication has reached into well over one hundred countries and many more cultures. His personal missionary experience was in Thailand.

Charles E. Van Engen, PhD has continued to be a leading theologian of mission for more than twenty-five years as he has directed master's and doctoral studies in theology. As a professor at Fuller Theological Seminary and the director of a continent-wide doctoral program in South America, his contributions to theological studies and multidisciplinary studies in mission have now influenced multiple generations of missiologists. He is the Arthur F. Glasser Professor of the Biblical Theology of Mission at the Fuller Theological Seminary. He is an ordained minister in the Reformed Church in America (RCA), and spent twelve years as a missionary in Mexico. He is the author or editor of more than a dozen books.

R. Daniel Shaw, PhD, Professor of Anthropology and Translation at Fuller Theological Seminary, served as a Bible translator with Wycliffe Bible Translators for twelve years in Papua New Guinea and has continued to direct missiological research from an anthropological perspective in cultures worldwide. He has authored more than ten books. He has continued to encourage me to revise this text for the students at Fuller Seminary. Georgia Grimes assisted with references and citations.

Francesca Gacho served as the primary editor for this text. Her ongoing dialogue provided encouragement for increased quality while all the while being responsive. Hugh Pindur, the graphic designer, helped with designing graphics which help communicate the key ideas of the book. Thanks also to the WCL team who helped with the countless details to finalize a manuscript.

While many contributed to this text, if weaknesses remain, I take responsibility for them.

INTRODUCTION TO MISSIOLOGICAL RESEARCH DESIGN

The purpose for this text is to introduce the reader to the process of designing missiological research. Missiological research design is an iterative process among five basic components: 1) the central research issue, 2) review of precedent research, 3) research methods, 4) findings, and 5) conclusions and recommendations. Each of these parts cycles again and again back to the central research issue, brings sharper focus to it and then focuses around it. Each of these principal components consists of additional interrelated parts which will be introduced through this text.

This text introduces missiological research in two parts. The first part consists of seven chapters: missiology as a research discipline, central research issue, evaluation of precedent research/literature review, research methods, findings, conclusion and recommendations, and ethics and missiological research. The second part consists of four chapters: Theology of Mission, Education, Anthropology, and Communicational Research. Six appendices provide suggestions for the pre- and post-text sections, as well as checklists to provide a basis for self-evaluation of one's proposed design.

One may ask, "Why is such a book about research design needed?" The answer is simple. Missiological research presents challenges uniquely related to the discipline of missiology. No other single disciplinary approach, or a combination of disciplinary approaches, adequately addresses the issues of missiological research design. This text addresses missiology as an academic discipline to set the stage for missiological research design.

This text aims to serve the designer of missiological research, whether it is local or international in scope, historical, theological, theoretical, or applied in a discipline. The research may focus on documents, surveys, observations, or some other method appropriate to the research context. This research may serve to inform a publication, an agency in its missiological strategy, or apply to a degree program extending up through a doctoral level.

Research provides one important way of discerning what God has done and is doing. It may also help one to discern how to cooperate with Him. Several proverbs illustrate this perspective: "It is not good to have zeal without knowledge, nor to be hasty and miss the way" (Prov 19:2 NIV). "By wisdom a house is built, and through understanding it is established" (Prov 24:3). "The prudent see danger and take refuge, but the simple keep going and suffer for it" (Prov 27:12).

Jesus spoke about the foolishness of the person who had built a house without first counting the cost, or the king who would go into battle without first assessing the enemy. Jesus knew the people he was serving, he knew the situation, and obviously built his messages from an understanding of that situation. Similarly, the Apostle Paul was concerned about understanding and the effectiveness of his communication. Nehemiah did not begin to discuss rebuilding the wall with the people in Jerusalem until he had researched that situation.

Assumptions

First, research does not substitute for the work of the Holy Spirit. Rather, it provides one means to assist in discerning the work of the Spirit, and in preparing a way to work or to explain what has been or currently exists. Second, research is not a substitute for prayer. God's guidance through research is an important part of the process, even as other parts of the work progress. Third, research may provide a systematic means of observation and description of the ministry context. Fourth, research may provide a base for understanding theological perspectives. As an interpretation of the biblical text, it may provide clear insight into authoritative actions that one should take or avoid. Fifth, research may provide a trustworthy means to build a perspective (theory). Finally, missiological research may serve to test existing theory for reliability and validity, trustworthiness, or truthfulness. This theory then may serve as a basis to understand, to act, to predict, and perhaps to give some control over the situation.

Missiological or other church-related research typically requires research from several different approaches because of the complexity of the subject matter. When the complexities of more than one culture and spiritual issues are combined, a reliable perspective requires multiple viewpoints. It is impossible to know what is happening in all the rooms of a multistoried house by looking in a single window. Similarly, missiological research requires one to look through several academic windows to understand both the social and spiritual phenomena that occur in the human household. By definition, missiological research is the process of consilience with the *missio Dei* as its purpose.

Missiological[1] research faces serious challenges. Traditional theological and historical methods simply do not address the full range of questions raised in mis-

---

1   Mission as seen in this text is the crossing of barriers with the good news of the gospel. Missiology is the study of mission. In terms of research, missiology is the process of consilience with *missio Dei* as its purpose.

siology. Like other academic disciplines, research methods emerge out of and reflect the worldview[2] assumptions of their researchers. The social and behavioral sciences, while facing assumption-related limitations, do provide essential complements to extend traditional theological and historical research. However, scientific methods have other significant limitations. One limitation is simply the complexity of the subject matter. Missiologists work in and with intercultural settings. They work in very complex communicational settings and often face difficulties with observation. They may find it difficult to judge motives, values, and attitudes as well as spiritual phenomena.

A missiological researcher faces a challenging range of philosophical approaches to develop valid and reliable research. Cresswell (2003) notes this complexity by describing four schools of thought about how one may know what is knowable: "postpositivism, constructivism, advocacy/participatory and pragmatism" (p. 6). He writes, "Philosophically, researchers make claims about what is knowledge (ontology), how we know it (epistemology), what values go into it (axiology, and how we write about it (rhetoric), and the processes for studying it (methodology)" (2003, p. 6).

Missiological research differs from research in the physical (or hard) sciences in several ways:

- One cannot repeat social and spiritual phenomena for purposes of observation because they are singular events. Total replication is virtually impossible. What is true in Korea may not be replicated either in Korea, Kenya, the Philippines, the Netherlands, or in the US.
- It is difficult to observe what really is happening in the several dimensions about which the researcher is concerned. A given event or process may have spiritual, social system, economic, political, educational, leadership, ecclesial, or other dimensions of interest to the researcher as well as the people in the research context.
- An interaction often occurs between the observer and the subjects. Whether one is collecting data doing a survey, or using questionnaires, interviews, or participant observation, the researcher is often a part of what is happening. Consequently, one may influence

---

2   One's worldview consists of unrecognized assumptions that will affect every dimension of a research design such as assumptions about person-person relations, person-thing relationships, cause/effect, time, space, categorization, and values (Kraft, 1996).

what is happening. This involvement complicates the research, generating issues affecting both validity and reliability.

- If the researcher is studying a historical event, access to trustworthy information, the selection of the information to consider, and the perspectives of the researcher will all certainly play a part.

- Difficulties arise with control. It is impossible to know all that is happening and even if it were possible, no one person could manage it all. One simply cannot control either the social or the spiritual variables as one might control physical variables in a physics or chemistry lab.

- Furthermore, some issues are difficult to measure. For example, it is difficult to measure attitudes. It is difficult to measure worldview change.

- Outsiders find it difficult to interpret what is going on in a community. What is going on in Poona, India may be difficult for someone from the US to perceive, much less to accurately interpret.

- To further complicate missiological research, spiritual matters are often difficult to discern much less research. It is difficult to reliably observe or measure spirituality, spiritual power, or the effects of spiritual power. Researchers and their audiences differ even on the definitions or what would constitute valid and truthful or reliable and trustworthy evidence. That which is not seen is obviously difficult to research. While these matters raise obstacles in research, they are not impossible. Because difficulties arise in observation and measurement, one should not become discouraged about doing research. Both valid and reliable measures can be designed with some limitations.

- One can predict the rise of theological issues because a person's hermeneutic reflects that person's worldview. However, the research subjects may have a different worldview and language affecting their hermeneutic and the ways they may express their understanding of scripture in their context(s).

Missiological Research—What Is It?

Missiology is the study of the *missio Dei*. It involves all that God has done, is doing, and intends to do to accomplish His purpose. The specific focus in missiology is to cross barriers for the communication of the good news of what God has done to reconcile humankind to Himself. Missiological research then takes various forms and employs a wide range of academic disciplinary research methods both singly and jointly.

Some of this variety of approaches is illustrated later in this book. Multidisciplinary or multi-method research commonly serves missiological studies.

Missiological research design typically rests on one of two foundational perspectives: (1) "academic missiology" and (2) "applied missiology." Academic missiology serves to develop theory and/or to test existing theory. "Academic" missiology often focuses on the compilation of historical records, dictionaries, and the development of theology. (See the section "Assumptions" for more consideration of these two approaches.)

Many disciplines commonly undergird missiological research including: anthropology, communications, comparative religion, economics, education, geography, history, leadership, linguistics, management, political science, sociology, and theology. What distinguishes missiological research is the concern about the *missio Dei*. One could turn to subdisciplines in any of these arenas to expand the list.

Overview of the Research Design

The missiological research design process closely weaves interconnecting parts of a proposal. Because these parts are interlinked, a researcher will necessarily cycle back through each one several times with revisions to each before completing a design that has a high level of rigor (validity and reliability or as seen from a theological perspective—trustworthiness and truth). Figure 1 portrays some of these interactions among the parts of a research design.

To understand the research design process, a researcher needs to see the interconnectedness of each part of the design process.

FIGURE 1
Parts of a Proposal

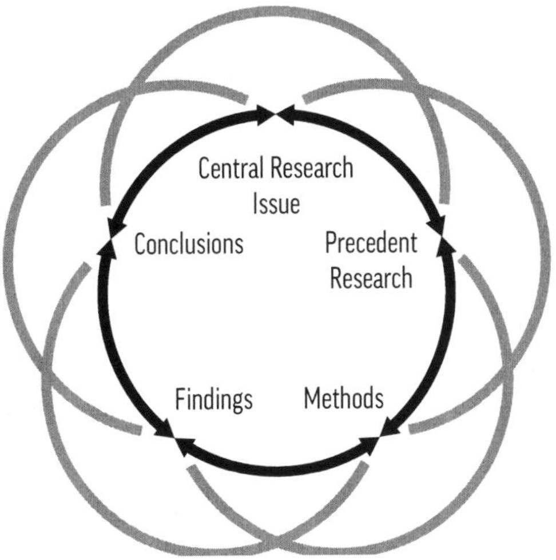

Figure 1 consists of five key interrelated parts of a research design:

- The central research issue;
- The review of the literature or precedent research;
- The methodology;
- The findings; and,
- The conclusions and recommendations.

The central research issue serves as the guiding theme for the whole research project. One may state this central research issue in a variety of ways. The researcher may present the issue as a "problem" to be solved in the form of a statement or a question in which the key variables are noted. Typically, this kind of proposal leads to a qualitative research approach to develop theory. Or, one may pose the central issue as a "thesis statement" which serves as the central proposition to be demonstrated to be true or valid. Typically, this kind of proposed research leads to a quantitative study which aims at testing existing theory. Again, the researcher will relate the key or primary variables in this proposition. A set of questions used to explore the relationships of the variables involved in the primary statement normally follows a "problem" statement. On the other hand, a set of propositions or hypotheses to be tested typically follows a thesis statement. The identification of the central research issue marks the beginning point for a research study and provides focus for the whole study.

The choice among conducting a qualitative, a quantitative, or a mixed study depends in part on the depth of the existing precedent research. If the researcher faces a dearth of information about the subject or culture, then a qualitative research is more clearly indicated to develop the necessary theories or perspectives. On the other hand, if a strong theoretical base exists, wherein the variables are already clearly defined, a quantitative approach would be expected. In many cases a mix of the two sets of approaches may be appropriate to address the research at hand (Creswell, 2009, pp. 98-100).

The review of the literature evaluates precedent research to provide a base for the central research issue. The review of precedent research provides a justification for studying the issue and the theoretical and methodological bases. If the study involves an evaluative dimension, this section typically provides a description of the value bases. A review of the precedent research may also provide a description of the context of the current study. The research questions or hypotheses often provide the organizing base for reviewing precedent literature or research.

After having determined the central research issue, it is time to review research already done about that issue. Hence, a "review of the literature," "library research," or "review of precedent research" follows. Seldom can one engage a topic about which nothing has been written. Often relevant research from disparate disciplines may contribute to an understanding of the context, the current variables, the theoretical perspectives to be considered, or the appropriate mix of research methods. A competent researcher will review and evaluate the literature to learn and evaluate what others have discovered about this particular topic. And, as one reviews what others have written, the next step is to return to the problem and sharpen the focus of the problem and research questions, or the thesis statement and hypotheses. From the review of precedent research one will find the important questions to ask, appropriate theoretical perspectives, the boundaries of what has been done before, values or criteria for evaluative studies, and a range of appropriate (and maybe inappropriate) methods. One begins with the central research issue and moves ahead to the precedent research. Then one goes back and revises the core issue to move forward.

The methodology provides the method(s) one collects, analyzes, and interprets the data. Missiological research depends on a variety of methods and often depends on a multimethodological and/or interdisciplinary approach. Missiological research uses both qualitative and quantitative methods. The methods may aim at building theory, testing a theory, or providing a base for "action-research." Any combination of methods used typically has some limitations or potential threats to reliability or validity so these "limitations" are typically addressed in a researcher's methodological section.

The findings report the data or resulting information, which emerge from the employment of the research methods. These findings may be described in terms of the theories described from the review of precedent research, but should only include information related to the central research issue as it has emerged from the employment of the current methods. These findings should take into account the limitations of the methods used and relate all relevant information.

With a grasp of the literature, one goes on to the methodology necessary to accomplish the research in question. A review of related research foundations (often called a "review of the literature") helps validate the methods to use and to see what others have done. The methodology rests on the research questions or the hypotheses emerging out of the review of precedent research and focusing on the variables of the central research issue. The research questions or hypotheses relate specifically to the central research issues as validated in the review of precedent research to guide in the design of the methodology.

Applying the methodology produces data or the findings, which emerge from an analysis of the data. The findings only report what is relevant to the central research issue and research questions or hypotheses. However, as a matter of ethical research, one should report all that is found whether it is good, bad, supports, or does not support one's position as long as it relates to the central research issue. One does not report other findings, that is, what may have been discovered in another research project (precedent research) or from one's own personal experience. The central research issue and attending research questions with a problem statement or hypotheses with a thesis statement guide what will be reported from using a particular methodology. One then moves to the conclusions and recommendations based on the findings. One may draw either conclusions, recommendations, or both, only from the central research issue-related findings.

The conclusions and recommendations emerge directly from the findings. This section expresses the "so what?" and the "now what?" questions of the findings. The conclusions or recommendations section may be framed on the theoretical base developed from a review of precedent research, but the conclusions and recommendations are only based on the information developed in the findings.

Similarly, one makes recommendations only from the central research issue-related findings. Rather, conclusions come directly out of what has been found from using the methodology and analyzing the data that relate to the central research issue. One may report recommendations and conclusions in the light of values and/or theoretical perspectives identified from the precedent research.

Cresswell (2003) poses nine questions to address this iterative process. These questions may serve as a basic proposal structure. These nine questions require attention through the missiological research process:

1. What is needed to better understand the topic?
2. What is little known or understood about the topic?
3. What does the research propose to study?
4. What is the setting and the people to be studied?
5. What methods will provide the data?
6. How will the data be analyzed?
7. How will the researcher validate the findings?
8. What ethical issues will the study present?
9. What do preliminary results show about the practicability and value of the proposed study (pp. 49-50)?

An overview of the study using these questions before finalizing the proposed design will aid in assuring that one has addressed the key issues. The research designer needs to justify the study in terms of its originality, feasibility, significance, and validity before finalizing a design. Since in virtually every case the researcher will influence the research in terms of his or her worldview, the researcher's assumptions and background must be clarified. In addition to that influence, if the researcher is in the setting, direct influence may occur to change the context where the researcher is aiming to do the research. That potential should be assessed as the design is emerging to be sure the researcher does not unduly skew or bias the results.

No study is complete without the pre- and post-sections such as a prefix, table of contents, tables of figures and tables, index, appendices, glossary, and bibliography or references cited. This text provides an introduction and checklists to evaluate these sections.

Søgaard (1996) described another way to look at the sequential process for survey research. This linear progression depicts the logical sequence through the research process, including some of the key decisions. This research process provides an ideal way to progress through a survey research project. In his explanation of this process he appropriately notes the complexities of working in an intercultural context (pp. 19-21). However, this model does not show the iterative processes that must occur through the design, data collection, reporting, and conclusion/recommendation stages nor does it show the complexities encountered when using a multidisciplinary approach. The complexities of doing intercultural research with a multidisciplinary set of methods will normally require several iterations through the decision-making processes to arrive at an acceptable and feasible design. A researcher may see an advantage in working within a single discipline. The iterations needed for a single disciplinary approach may be simplified to this more linear approach.

Summary Overview of Missiological Research Design

The design of missiological research ideally follows an orderly path through the identification of the central research issue, the identification of precedent research, and the development of a methodology that will produce reliable and valid results, which then serve as the bases for coming to conclusions and recommendations. However, in reality the process seldom works so simply. Multiple disciplines such as theology, history, anthropology, economics, holistic leadership, ecology, politics, and others complicate the picture as one seeks to provide a realistic or reliable picture. In an ideal setting, one would hope for a linear progression through these parts of the design of a research project. However, inevitable changes come either from the ongoing research, the context, the logistics faced by the researcher, the availability of reliable or valid data, or other variables that may enhance, hinder or distract the research. The researcher, however, must keep in mind the issues related to critical thinking whereby the parts of the design and, ultimately, the research projects are inextricably connected and interwoven like a fine tapestry. Each part plays a key role in the integration and the validity of the research project.

Whatever the iterative path one may follow through the research process, the issue of critical thinking is paramount throughout. One may be proposing research in a single community with a view to church planting, evaluating the impact of a relief and development project in a region as to the rate of receptivity to the gospel, or asking what was the message of the early church that contributed to the amazingly rapid spread of the gospel from Spain to Mesopotamia to India and Ethiopia, and around the Mediterranean Basin in the first hundred years. Whatever the case, the complexities of missiological research demand critical thinking. Simplistic answers never suffice critical thinking. Paul and Elder (2006, p. 20) note the complexities of interrelationships of critical thinking issues.

These interrelationships function in critical thinking in dynamic ways. Paul and Elder suggest these research components interact in ways analogous to the functioning of "parts of the human body" (2006, p. 28). Each part has a specific function that contributes to the whole and to the specific functioning of every other individual component. One can neither examine any single part of the body to understand the whole, nor can one look at the whole without recognizing the complex interplay of the parts. One cannot dissect a body and understand what is giving it life just as one cannot, with social science tool alone, examine society-cultural phenomena and explain the spiritual life without recognizing the theological and spiritual dimensions of missiology.

1

MISSIOLOGY AS A RESEARCH DISCIPLINE

This chapter describes "missiology" as a research discipline
by showing the constituent parts of an academic discipline
and how they are being addressed in missiology.

Missiology clearly stands as an academic discipline in its own right. Missiology as an academic discipline both has an "organized body of knowledge" and organized methods of "accumulating and ordering that knowledge" (Dressel and Marcus, 1982). While others have addressed this issue in missiological discussions,[3] this chapter primarily addresses missiology as a research discipline, which serves as a base for designing research. As an academic discipline missiology does not have a unique or distinctive methodology. However, it does embrace components common to other academic disciplines around a theological core. The methods used to support the church in mission are as wide as ethical, valid, and reliable methods permit in other academic disciplines. Any discipline that addresses human behavior may serve missiology for the purpose of providing relevant and valid information and contributing to the growing body of missiological theory. While theological research differs from social science research as it addresses issues of trustworthiness and truth on the basis of sound hermeneutical and exegetical bases, theological research serves a critical and constant role in missiological research. The methods used to research missiological topics often require multidisciplinary perspectives because of the complexities of the subject matter. When the topics

---

3   See also Tippett, (1973, 1974, 1987); Verkuyl, (1991); Scherer, (1985); Shenk, (1987); Scherer, (1987); Forman, (1987); Van Engen, (1987); Whiteman, (1987); Zahnheiser, (1987); Gallagher and Hertig (eds.), (2004); http://www.knowledgerush.com/kr/encyclopedia/Missiology/ (Retrieved 12/31/2009). Pachuau, (Retrieved 12/31/2009); Walker, (2008); Taber, (2000); Skreslet, (2007); Terry, Smith, and Anderson (eds.), (1987); Van Rheenan, (1996); Pocock, Van Rheenen and McConnell, (2005); Moreau, McGee and Corwin, (2004).

cross ecclesial, religious, cultural, spiritual, time, geographical, economic, political, and other boundaries, multiple disciplines are required.

The author has an acquaintance who lives in a hilly, wooded area near St. Joseph, Missouri. He built his house in an octagonal shape with windows facing eight directions. Every view outside differs and to know what is in the house one would have to look in from each of the windows. Each window provides a different perspective to the interior of the house, but no single window provides a full view. However, every view is complementary and consistent with the other views. In a similar way, different disciplines allow one to peek into the complex realities of the *missio Dei*. When conducting research with rigorously reliable and valid methods, each discipline will provide a complementary and consistent view. As the author's friend's family may change the furniture or add new furniture, thus changing the interior design in their house, human situations are always dynamic. One may need new combinations of views to explain both what is happening and what to do about it. Human contexts are always dynamic and often require fresh combinations of methods both to explain what is occurring and to provide a base for missional action in that context. Differences in worldview lead to differences in exegetical and hermeneutical methods undergirding theological perspectives which aim at trustworthiness and truth.

Dressel and Marcus in their book, *On Teaching and Learning in College* (1982), present a useful description of the components of a disciplinary structure. Their perspective, while not specifically targeting missiology, presents the range of issues that one would expect to find in an academic discipline. The following sections are based in part on their outline.

Conceptual Components

A range of conceptual issues serve to provide the substance of missiology. These issues all fall within the broad concerns of the mission of God, or as they are referred to in this text, the *missio Dei*. Van Engen in his helpful chapter, "What is Mission Theology" (1996, pp. 11-36), presents missiology as an academic discipline from a mission theology perspective. In this chapter he points to five key component parts of missiology which require multidisciplinary research with a theological core:

- *missio Dei* (the mission of God),
- *missio hominum* (the mission of humans),
- *missiones eccesiarum* (the mission of the church),

- *missio politica oecumenica* (mission as it draws from and impacts global human civilization),
- *missio futurum* (mission as it relates to the "predictable issues of God's mission as they work out in human history), and
- *missio adventus* ("the in-breaking [the advent] of God, of Jesus Christ in the Incarnation, of the Holy Spirit at Pentecost, of the Holy Spirit in and through the Church" [pp. 29-32]).

Others have written from different disciplinary perspectives including: Tippett (1973) of Fuller Theological Seminary and Whiteman (1987) of Asbury Theological Seminary from a social science perspective, Forman (1987) of Yale University from a history perspective, and Zahnheiser (1987) of Asbury Theological Seminary from a religions perspective. Van Rheenen (1996, 2006) formerly of Abilene Christian University has written a wide range of missiological books and articles.

Arenas of Interest

The central concern for missiology is the *missio Dei,* mission of God. As a subject area, it spans human history from the time of the creation of Adam and Eve because they were initial players in the mission of God. The main concern focuses on God's desire to reconcile humankind to Himself. The revelation of *this plan,* the initiatives taken in *this plan,* the players in *this plan,* and the opponents to *this plan* all come within the scope of the concerns of missiological concern. Missiology, while primarily focused on God's mission for humankind, ranges across three major arenas: the physical environment in which people live, their socio-cultural environment, and their spiritual environment. As each of these concerns relates to God's central mission for humankind, it comes under the concerns of missiology.

In 1982 the author used a Venn diagram that served to explain some missiological research he was doing among the Samburu people in north central Kenya. From this diagram he raised seven questions about relationships and the integration of the standards of the biblical text with both the context and the mission community. This diagram illustrates the need for an integrated multidisciplinary approach to missiology.

Each of the numbers in Figure 2 relates to a question that needed to be addressed. The same kinds of issues arise in many kinds of missiological research.

FIGURE 2
Contextual Frame for Samburu Study

1.   What is the biblical standard? What does the biblical text say?
2.   What are the characteristics of the people and situation being served? In this case it was the Samburu people who were being studied.
3.   What are the missionary/missional perspectives and values? What do they bring to the situation?
4.   What is the relationship between the missionary values and perspectives and the biblical text? One must evaluate personal and cultural perspectives from the biblical text just as other culture's views must be judged by the same standard.
5.   What is the relationship between the values and perspectives of the people being served and the biblical values? An interesting finding in my study was that, in terms of leadership values, the traditional Samburu were in many ways closer to biblical values than the missionaries who were going to work with them.
6.   What is the relationship between the values and perspectives of the missionaries and the people being served?
7.   How should the values from the two human contexts be integrated under the biblical standard?

This simple diagram illustrates how at least theology, history, anthropology, sociology, political science, economics, comparative religion, geography, linguistics, and education can all provide useful disciplinary perspectives for investigating the complexities involved. Van Engen, writing in 1996, used essentially the same Venn diagram to illustrate the "Tripartite Nature of Theology of Mission" (1996, p. 21).

Key Assumptions of Missiological Research

Assumptions of people from other theological persuasions will differ from what is expressed in this section. However, some key assumptions that undergird evangelical missiology include the following: The mission to be studied is a *divinely appointed mission*. Human aspirations of power, colonialism, cultural imperialism, political aspirations, or economic conquest did not inspire this task. Human resources alone do not carry out this task, but rather it has an undergirding spiritual power dimension that is always present. While it is concerned about human sociocultural systems and structures, these systems and structures are not in themselves the primary focus, but serve as instruments to help or hinder the fulfillment of the *missio Dei*.

While a range of academic disciplines may serve to inform and provide methodological techniques to gather and interpret information about the *missio Dei,* these disciplinary approaches in and of themselves do not address God's mission except for theology. Theology is the outworking of people's thinking about how to interpret God's revelation and His action among them as God is working to accomplish His mission. Theology and missiology are then inextricably linked with the missiologist considering theology to be a subset of missiology. And, the theologian often considers missiology as a subset of theology. Throughout the interplay of the social science and theological methods, concerns, and assumptions the researcher must continue to engage critical thinking at every juncture. The social science contributions must focus on valid and reliable data even as the theological concerns demand trustworthiness and truth.

Scope and Types of Missiological Research

In present-day missiology, missiological research may be typically divided into two broad related, but differing arenas: academic missiology and applied missiology. Academic missiology typically seeks to broaden the theoretical bases of missiological research. Various forms of historical and theological research typically come into focus in this kind of missiological research. Broad encyclopedic studies often form major goals of this kind of research. Some outstanding examples of this kind of research would include such diverse works as Barrett's *World Christian Encyclopedia* (1982) and the annual updates to statistical estimates of the world Christian population published in the *Bulletin of Missionary Research* or Johnstone's *Operation World* (2001), in which current reasonable descriptions are given of individual countries, their Christian populations, and prayer needs.

Latourette's monumental *History of Christian Expansion* (1937-1945) or Orr's many works about the history of awakenings and revivals all serve this genre well. Bosch's *Transforming Mission: Paradigm Shifts in Theology of Mission* (1991) serves this genre from a theological perspective. All of these works have required an enormous amount of research leading to the development of missiological theory.

On the other hand, applied missiology is another genre of missiological research that takes on a much more immediate and practical sense. One could cite many outstanding examples of applied missiology as well. Some researchers keep this kind of research in-house for specific applications. Linguistic research done by Wycliffe Bible Translators or developmental research done by World Vision fit well into this genre. Applied missiological research has focused on such diverse issues as church planting, curriculum improvement for leadership training, contextualizing theology, Bible translation, leadership emergence patterns, cross-cultural communication, business as mission, and power ministries.

Both academic- and application-oriented research has contributed to the other arena. However, a given researcher may choose to focus on one, the other, or in some cases both. Each has an important role to play in missiology. Each broad approach has developed a set of risks. A risk that commonly accompanies academic missiology is its occasional overemphasis on the theory with little thought to the application or relevance of the theory to real-life missiological situations. A parallel risk from the more applied side of missiological research has often experienced a focus on immediate action without a firm rooting in what could have been learned from other precedent research (theory). For example, the author participated in a mission conference in which the pastor of a large congregation went to visit a South Asian country. He had never traveled there before. He did some observational "research." He was present in the country for about two weeks. What he saw, experienced, reported, and recommended while all true to what he saw and believed, did not take into account what has been learned in any precedent research (missiological theory) or ethnographic studies. The recommendations from his "research" would likely lead to long-term dependencies and strained relations (based again on the recorded experience of others—theory). If, on the other hand, he had only read the mission history of the area, read books about church planting and integrated development without the personal observation and relationship building, he probably would not have had the same passion or commitment to move ahead as he desired.

Previously Established Theory

Missiological research has established a significant body of theory. Beginning with biblical data theory about what or why, to what extent, and predictions of the outcomes of the *missio Dei* has received centuries and libraries of research. Currently, a vast repository of theory (theology and social science-based mission studies) is available as a theoretical base for missiology. Especially since World War II, thousands of articles and books have been written around missiological topics focusing on theology of mission, training in mission, descriptions of missional contexts, mission strategies, and historical accounts of mission.

Research from historical perspectives has formed another wealth of missiological theory. In his writing of more than thirty-five books including two earned doctorates, Orr built a strong historical theory of revivals and awakenings. From this theory one may discern ways to act and lead in the development of receptivity of new areas and renewal in established churches. Pierson (2000) has discerned nine historical principles that serve to explain how church movements have grown. These principles may be applied in planning missional activities to improve their effectiveness. Bosch (1991) provided a theological base recognized worldwide.

Significant bodies of missiological theory serve the church community in what may be broadly called "church growth." Beginning in the modern era with Venn and Anderson, others such as Tippett, McGavran, and Wagner have led in the formation of a large body of theory that treats comprehensive concerns, such as the effect of environment and demographics on church growth, social structures, and spiritual factors in church growth. Others have extended the theory by expanding the definitions and range of applications as they have looked at new situations, (e.g., Costas, Hunter, Van Rheenen and Bakke). Other specialized areas in mission strategy continue to emerge such as "Business as Mission" (Johnson and Rundle, 2010).

Missiology is concerned about crossing barriers with the gospel. Many of these barriers are cultural. Since anthropology addresses the breadth of cultural issues, a vast amount of missiological theory has been developed working from anthropology along with other disciplines (e.g., with theology resulting in a theoretical base in ethnotheology and contextualization, with history resulting in a theoretical base in ethnohistory, with communications resulting in based in cross-cultural communications). A wide range of missiological principles have emerged ranging from the much-debated "homogenous unit" principle to theories of worldview change on to strategic theories of implementing business as mission.

As missiological thinking interacted with studies in religion and comparative religion, missiological strategies emerged for communicating the gospel to Muslims,

Buddhists, postmodern secularists, as well as the more traditional animists (Wolf, 2010). Theory development in missiology has gone well beyond simple comparisons among equal, but different religions to developing theories about "points of contact" (Kraemer, 1947) or "redemptive analogies" (Richardson, 1976) so the gospel may be communicated effectively. Current theories treating contextualization have generated a significant amount of research and publications across widely diverse areas such as leadership and leadership development to Bible translation and its use.

One could select a topic in missiology such as "women in mission" to illustrate both the breadth of research that has already been done and significant frontiers for future research. As I have looked in such diverse libraries as the David Allan Hubbard Library at Fuller Theological Seminary, Farrel Library at Kansas State University, a midwestern Land Grant university, and Boston University, I found significant collections.

It is impossible in a paragraph or two to outline the body of organized missiological knowledge or even an encyclopedic work (Moreau, Netland, and Van Engen (eds.), 2000); Barrett, Kurian, and Johnson (eds.), 2001). It is possible, however, to point to both its breadth across disciplines and depth in terms of the number of sources on a given topic. Missiology as a subject area is taught in growing numbers of graduate seminaries and Christian universities across the globe. However, Christian faculty members in many other universities supervise missiological research in education, anthropology, sociology, development studies, psychology, history, geography, political science, business and management, comparative religion, and economics only to mention a few.

Numerous journals serve the discipline including: *Missiology, International Review of Mission, Missionalia, Evangelical Missions Quarterly, International Bulletin of Missionary Research, Urban Mission, Frontier Missions* as well as many others that are published by individual mission and development agencies. Online journals and databases provide a wealth of additional information. Missiological journals are published not only in North America, but in Europe, Africa, Asia, and Latin America. In addition to the many journals that serve missiology several publishers have mission-related books as their primary market. William Carey Library was established to help publish missiological theses and dissertations (Winter, 1995). Many other publishers publish a wide range of missiological materials including Regal, MARC, Orbis, Word/Thomas Nelson, Bethany House, William B. Eerdmans, Zondervan, Broadman Press, and Baker Books to mention only a few.

In addition to a range of publishers who serve the publishing needs of missiology, several professional organizations serve to keep vibrancy and diversity, pushing the boundaries of both theory and practice. The Association of Professors of Mission, American Society of Missiology, and the Evangelical Missiological Society are only three of many such American associations.

A quick look online will reveal broad categories and thousands of documents that have been collected under missions/missiological topics. A brief scanning of library holdings in such diverse American institutional libraries as Fuller Theological Seminary, Yale University, Columbia International University, University of South Africa, Dallas Theological Seminary, Boston University, Wheaton College, Harvard University, Kansas State University, the University of California at Los Angeles, the Library of Congress, and Abilene Christian University will illustrate the vast amount of missiological information that has been and is being collected and indexed. Missions and development agencies also have collected repositories of missiological information. The MARC library of World Vision in Monrovia, California is but one example of this kind of specialized collection. Specialized library collections further illustrate the vast amount of missiological information available. One such specialized collection is found at the Bresee Institute for Urban Studies in Los Angeles.

Most contemporary researchers will also have access to the vast range of online resources. Hundreds of thousands of full-text articles are available online through both higher education libraries and many public libraries. One may download the full text of dissertations through onsite library services. Bonk (2010) of the Overseas Missions Study Center (OMSC) notes that the *International Bulletin of Missionary Research* (IMBR) as of January 2010 has become the first missiological scholarly journal that is freely available to anyone worldwide with internet access (Bonk, 2010). In addition to being an online journal the IBMR has compiled a database of more than 6,000 dissertations about mission written since 1900 in cooperation with Yale Divinity School Library Additional missiological dissertations exist whose titles and/or abstracts appear as more disciplinary focused (e.g., education or anthropology).

Another way of looking at the breadth of missiological studies is to observe the range of institutions granting doctoral degrees related to missiology. In 1992 Smalley produced a ten-year summary of doctoral dissertations on mission. In this summary he identified 114 degree-granting institutions including seminaries, Christian universities, private universities, and state universities. He identified 512 doctoral dissertations written about mission topics. These topics range across entire discipline from world religions, history, specific people groups, training and individual biographies. In 2000 I noted 130 institutions which had granted 550 doctorial degrees between 1992 and 1999. Two-thirds of these degrees came from ten institutions (pp. 288-289). If one were to add master's degrees to the list it would grow significantly. Dissertation abstracts as produced by Proquest are indexed in a way which facilitates the discovery of dissertations and theses on almost every conceivable topic beginning with the obvious ones, such as: theology of mission, missions, contextualization, the church and mission to other broad topics that include nonmissiological studies such as leadership development, anthropology, worldview, sociology, urban mission, area studies and studies of individual peoples.[4] However, the range of missiological research is difficult to assess because countless persons engaged in mission have done or are doing research in universities, seminaries, and missions about topics that do not appear to be directly missiological. Christian seminaries and Christian universities direct much of this research. However, while the author was a doctoral student at Michigan State University, more than 300 other missionaries were contemporary students. While their research projects may well have related to missional applications, they may not be indexed as "missiological." One could point to disciplinary or interdisciplinary studies in state-supported universities across the USA, India, South Africa, the Philippines, Korea, Scotland, England, Canada, and many other countries where the intended significance of studies is currently and has been missiological.

Technical Language Components

As with any discipline, missiology has accumulated a range of technical terms related both to its core concerns and each of its complementary disciplines. Such terms as "mission," "missions," "missiology," "church growth," "leadership emergence patterns," "contextualization," "transculturation," "scripture use," "receptor orientation," "postmodernism," "emergent church," and "receptivity" all illustrate a range of technical terms used across missiology. Other technical theological terms serve to illustrate the development of the discipline from a mission theology perspective: *missio Dei, missio hominum, missiones ecclesiarum, missio politica oecumenica, missio futurum, missio adventus,* and "theology from above/below."

Like studies in statistics, biology, history, sociology, political science or education, missiology has its own range of technical language. And, as a younger discipline, the language is continuing to expand.[5] These new elements of missiological language are

---

4   See the *International Bulletin of Missionary Research Resource Center* for a broad listing of dissertations: http://www.internationalbulletin.org/resources.

5   New "missiological" terms such as "consilience" and "oikoscode" challenge theological, historical, and missiological theory and practice (Wolf, 2010).

"part of the search for an identification of key theories, ideas, concepts, or processes leading to further exploration of possible relations and explanations" (Dressel and Marcus, 1982).

Organizing Components

Mission theology serves as the integrating and essential core of missiology around which all of the other parts cluster. Without the theological core, one would simply be doing studies in comparative religion, anthropology, sociology, history, or one of the other academic disciplines. Theology at its heart is borne out of a missiological enterprise. One only has to look at the writing of scripture to see how God's initiative catalyzed the reflections about God and His mission in both the Old Testament and the New Testament. The gospels describe how God sent his Son to accomplish His mission. The epistles were all missionary letters. The book of Revelation describes the *missio adventus*. Van Engen clearly shows this interaction and integration of many around a theological core of the person of Christ (1996, p.14). He has countless "disciplines" or subject areas linked into the center. Pictured as a sunflower, each "petal" is an individual "discipline" or subject area while the integrating center of the "flower" is Jesus Christ.

The central set of assumptions in missiology focus around the *missio Dei* and God's revelation of Himself in Jesus Christ, in and through the power of the Holy Spirit. The central core serves then to constrain the extent one can proceed in cognate disciplines as they support missiology. It constrains the disciplines' assumptions, fields of inquiry, methods, and interpretations of the data. It also provides guidelines for the inquiries in each of these disciplines. As these cognate disciplines are constrained and guided by this central theological core, the discipline of missiology is increasingly well served. The theological core of missiology serves then as a dynamic integrative center. The center continues to expand as more research is done about God's revelation in scripture as well as what He has done and is doing in the world today.

Other missiologists have proposed other kinds of core elements in the past. Tippett placed the social sciences much closer to the center while still advocating a strong theological center (1973). Others writing or lecturing from their own disciplinary perspective have seen their own discipline as closer to the center. Researchers recognizing the interdisciplinary nature of missiology often write from an interdisciplinary perspective. Shaw and Van Engen combine theological and anthropological assumptions in a communicational framework in their book,

Communicating God's Word in a Complex World: God's Truth or Hocus Pocus? (2003). Van Engen, Woodberry and Whiteman address similar interdisciplinary issues in *Paradigm Shifts in Christian Witness: Insights from Anthropology, Communication and Spiritual Power* (2008).

Value Components

Values in missiology emerge from and orbit the *missio Dei* and what God has revealed in Jesus Christ. God has taken the initiative to reconcile all humankind to Himself. "He is patient with you, not wanting anyone to perish, but everyone to come to repentance" (2 Pet 3:9). As we see that "For God so loved the world that he gave his one and only Son, that whoever believes in him shall not perish but have eternal life" (John 3:16), several values immediately spring to our attention. God values people. He has taken the initiative to reconcile all people to Himself.

Respect for culture and cultural differences clearly began to emerge in the church in Jerusalem with the concern for the Greek-speaking widows (Acts 6:1) and later expanded out of the Jerusalem Conference (Acts 15). One could point to the Jerusalem leaders sending Barnabas to Antioch as an exercise in cultural sensitivity (Acts 11:22). Missiologists have clearly expounded these values related to culture in many different ways and in countless books and articles. One only has to look at the index of one of the missiological journals mentioned above or to look in a database such as WorldCat to find more than 316,000 catalog entries for "missions" or more than 2,000 entries for "missiology!"[6]

In his 2010 dissertation, Wolf explored the question about the message and values that served to transform the Mediterranean Basin in the first century. He demonstrated how faith, love, and hope led to the incredible growth in the first century and how these three themes come together to continue to provide openings into the Muslim, Buddhist, and Hindu worlds of today.

Relationships to Other Disciplines

The relationship between missiology and other disciplines is seen throughout the above discussion. In missiology the core integrating dynamic is the person of Jesus Christ and the working out of the *missio Dei*. Many academic disciplines serve as ways to discover truth and carry out the human part of God's agenda through mission.

---

6   Retrieved from http://www.worldcat.org/search?q=missiology&qt=results_page.

In 1995 Burrows identified five arenas for continuing missiological research. These issues arise out of the current missiological context and discussions. These issues provided a theme for the recent Lausanne Conference in South Africa.

1. Problems that arise from social and historical studies indicating that Christianity has been syncretistic from its origins have not been resolved.

2. Insight into the syncretic nature of every instance of . . . historical Christianity leads to insights into its particularity. This makes claims to universality problematic . . . How can that universality be made clear in the light of critiques—for example from the poor, women, Asians, Africans . . . that powerful groups within Christianity monopolize what counts as orthodox?

3. Although Majority World Christianity—in its concreteness . . . is not taken seriously in the north, it is the living center of the Christian tradition.

4. Clarifying the meaning of mission in a contemporary situation with its hostility to the notion of conversion combined with respect for all religious and cultural traditions is a major task confronting Christian theology.

5. A major ecumenical, interdisciplinary, and intercontinental study and research effort is required today to help the secular academy and Christians take account of the emergence of world Christianity as a communion of local enculturation of Christianity. In particular, research is required to help Christians in the West, as well as Third World Christians, understand the historical, spiritual, ethical, anthropological, philosophical, and theological dimensions that form their respective syncretistic forms of Christianity.

The identification of these areas for further missiological research suggests the vitality of missiology as a discipline. Many questions remain to be answered. New questions are arising. Faithfulness in the *missio Dei* demands further research in missiology—hence, the justification for this text.

2

FOCUSING ON THE CENTRAL RESEARCH ISSUE

This chapter introduces the central research issue and its related issues. This issue serves as the primary guiding and constraining perspective throughout the whole study.

The first task facing a researcher is to identify the central research issue for the study and the context in which it is to be addressed. This central research issue may be a problem to be explored or a thesis to be tested. It not only is the first thing to do; it is the most important issue to resolve for the whole study. This issue, once defined, will guide and constrain every other part of the design, research process, reporting, conclusions, and application(s).

Identifying and focusing the central research issue is often the most difficult part of a research project. The process of bringing the central issue into clear focus normally requires several iterations as each the following issues is addressed: topic selection, stating the purpose, stating the goals, stating the problem or thesis statement, stating the research questions or hypotheses, setting the delimitations or scope, reviewing the precedent research, and choosing a methodology. One's personal research skills, experience, resources, and worldview also bear on the formation of the central research issue. Bringing focus to this issue as it relates to these other parts of the study will help a solid basis to ensure the research is both valid and reliable. Furthermore, constant focus on this central issue will help insure the issues of continuity (a focus on the same issue), sequence (a logical progression) and integration (unity or coherence) of the whole study and research report.

The researcher who does not carefully consider the focus of the central research issue will find many unmanageable and disruptive problems arising all the way through the process. Some of these problems include: ambiguity in every part of the study, an inability to know why, what, where, how much, when or whom to ask, and uncertainty about when the research has been completed. Whether the study is a theological study, an anthropological study, a historical study or a combination of these disciplines or others, defining the central research issue is the primary initial task of the researcher.

Research Topic Selection

The goal of selecting a research topic is to have a topic that is narrow enough to be done well by the researcher but broad enough to be significant to the researcher, the constituencies with whom the researcher is affiliated, and to the related academic disciplines. It is important to decide as early as possible about the research issue to address. In an academic program the earlier one decides, the better. In an academic program, every paper in every course should focus in some way around the topic or projected central research issue so by the time one is ready to begin designing the proposal for the primary research, the foundation will have been laid from a variety of perspectives. One should ask the following question in every course, from every book and research study read: "What can I learn from this set of perspectives about my major concern?" When a person views the central issue from a variety of disciplinary and research perspectives, a wider range of new and creative problem-solving approaches may be generated.

The topic should be narrow enough that the researcher can do it given the research skills and resources available. The research should be narrow enough to be done within the time constraints of the researcher. On the other hand, it should be broad enough to be significant both for the researcher and the community being served. The topic should be researchable. One might ask, "Can I, in fact, discover valid and useful information about this topic?" The question about what kinds of information can be discovered is significant. If the researcher is working only with secondary sources, the study will probably have significance largely for the researcher. It will not have significance for the academic discipline or for others who are acquainted with the subject area. It may have some significance for one's ministry or agency. The topic should be fresh. The person who comes with a box full of old data will be soon discouraged and bored. The old data will likely prove to be less useful when the central issue is defined and the research questions or hypotheses established.

Old data will likely only serve as part of one's precedent research. Often, because of the ways the data were collected, they only provide a set of suggestions for the researcher. The topic should be fresh enough to be a challenge to one's ministry of crossing barriers with the good news of the gospel, regardless of its academic level. The topic should be related to the person's life experience and goals. Bradley and Muller (1995) wisely observe that the choice of the topic can be expected to influence a person over the coming decades. One should then take a long-range view of approaching the research topic, rather than just the meeting of an assignment or the counsel of a single professor. To do research well requires a significant commitment of time, attention, resources, and energy.

One should recognize, however, that selecting the topic and maybe the preliminary title of the research project does not mean that the central research issue has been finalized. By the time that the problem statement or thesis statement is in its final form, it will likely have been significantly narrowed and will certainly be in much sharper focus even though the general topic may be the same. The author frequently advises doctoral students to expect to revise the central issue at least fifteen times through the iterations with precedent research and the formation of the methodology.

One should ask, "Is what I am about to research just new to me or is it a new contribution to my academic or work arena?" A major purpose of evaluating precedent research is to answer this question (Bradley and Muller, 1995, p. 67).

When selecting the topic, the researcher often risks the selection of a topic that is too broad to be adequately treated. To focus or narrow the topic may require attention to some or all of the following concerns:

- subject matter
- geography
- time period
- number of potential research subjects (i.e., population and sample size)
- available resources (e.g., finances, logistical support)
- personal research skills
- prerequisite knowledge of the subject
- time required for the study
- access to primary and secondary sources (e.g., archives, people)

One may answer the question, "Where does one start?" in a variety of ways. Creswell (2009) argues the most reasonable starting point in the development of a "purpose" statement. He writes, the *purpose statement* "conveys the overall intent of a proposed study in a sentence or several sentences" (p. 111). The purpose statement answers the question of "Why?" for a given research project. Certainly, answering "why" must come very early in the research design process, but a person or agency may face a set of circumstances that need answers. The genesis of a research project may emerge from one of the other journalistic question that lead back to "why" such as "what," "who," "where," "when," "how" or "how much?" Whatever the original source of the original topic, it needs to go beyond the meeting of a course of degree requirement. The question of significance for the researcher, the immediate community to be served and the broader discipline of missiology or the accomplishing the *missio Dei* must come into focus.

A researcher may state the topic initially as a proposed title for the study. However, the topic will inevitably change as the other elements of critical thinking bear down on the focus whether considering the worldview/assumptions, precedent research, feasibility (e.g., time, competence, research-ability, resources) or significance (applicability of the research beyond the research exercise) the topic purpose, problem, and/or the central research issue will be sharpened. The focus of the topic will then allow the researcher to judge among the options from a wide range of qualitative, quantitative, or mixed methods involving appropriate academic disciplines.

Often a researcher finds himself or herself in an academic department committed to a given discipline or because of a given set of circumstances (e.g., funding a grant, a department with competency, a given method, employment expectations, personal experience or desires), the research topic-purpose is almost predetermined to be shaped in a certain way. Critical thinking remains no less critical. Again, Creswell's analogy (2008) of a human body's interconnected systems requires the researcher to critically examine the dynamic interplay of the systems as with the circulatory, nervous, digestive, and subfile hormonal systems of the body. Beginning with a given discipline to do missiological research does not excuse one from critical thinking.

A researcher can expect as many as fifteen to twenty iterations of the purpose statement as well as the various come into play and replay before an integrated whole study emerges. The original issue will, through these interactions, experience a sharpening of focus that contributes to the issue of significance and feasibility.

Background

A description of the context of the study provides a justification for the study and a perspective for understanding the research. In many cases some research is required to describe the context in which the study is set. This description should not be seen as part of the research questions, but rather as setting the context for the study. The setting of the context allows the reader to understand why the central research issue is in fact an issue needing attention. It also provides the reader with a perspective of the researcher's perspective both for doing the research, interpreting the findings and then applying the interpretations.

Background issues set the stage for addressing the central issue. An understanding of the cultural, historical, political, economic, geographical, theological, demographic, and/or some other dimension of the background may be required in order to understand the setting for the present study. A common thread running through the background bases for significant studies is the researcher's own worldview, personal history, experience, and passion.

Writing the background section generally requires the researcher to draw on both personal experience as well as secondary sources (precedent research) to set the stage for the study. One's personal experience always shapes perceptions and the approach toward an issue. While the background section does not necessarily have to be autobiographical, the researcher should note any personal perspective in that context to provide an understanding of the assumptions and perspectives used in the design, methodologies, and interpretative approaches to be used. These two bases should not be reported as findings or serve as a base for either conclusions or recommendations. Primary sources are generally reserved for the central focus of the study. While personal experience may provide first-hand or primary information about a situation, personal recollection, perspective or opinion generally lacks the required rigor for the study without additional research into the topic at hand. Personal experience and/or recollection generally falls outside of the established methodology for the study and may pose a threat to the reliability and validity of the study.

If specific issues or events prompted the choice of the central research issue and these issues or events are beyond the scope of the study, they should be treated in the description of the background. In some cases the background section of a final report or dissertation may be one or more chapters.

Purpose: The Intentions for the Research

The intentions for a research study should be stated both for the study itself and for its uses. Internal intentions are normally stated on at least two levels. The purpose statement is the broadest of the several levels of statements of intent. It answers the primary question of "why?" Goals and objectives move to more specific issues to be reported in the study.[7] Significance statements provide a means of stating the external intentions to apply the study after it has been completed.

The purpose of a research study addresses the chief aim or intention of the study. After reading the purpose, the mission or reason for the study should be clear. The purpose sets the direction of the research. The purpose should be closely linked with the central research issue (either stated as a problem statement or a thesis statement). The difference between the purpose statement and the problem statement emerges as the problem statement identifies the key variables and relationships that are to be addressed whereas the purpose statement shows the broader direction of the study. The purpose statement addresses the question, "Why should this study be done?" One should be able to identify the problem statement and the purpose statement as related to the same issue: one looking at the general outcome, the other looking at the issue to be studied. For example, in one proposed study, the researcher's stated purpose was to provide a basis for resolving conflict in a certain group of Chinese churches in the Los Angeles area. The problem, however, was defined as a description of the relationship between the cultural, theological, and leadership characteristics of these churches and the conflict they were experiencing.

The purpose statement will show the direction one wants to go in the study of a set of related particular issues. However, the purpose and central research issue will be closely related. One cannot write the one, probably, without the other. And, one could start with either one and move in either direction. One could start with the purpose and move to the problem statement. Or, a researcher could develop the problem statement and move to a clear statement of purpose. In the same way one might begin with a series of goal statements. The purpose statement may well go beyond the study into your ministry and the broader impact. However, the goal statements will relate specifically to the study and will be reported in terms of conclusions and recommendations in the last chapter. These specific outcomes relate

---

7   In American education as an academic discipline goals are considered as broader statements of intent than objectives. However, from the American business community and the British education perspectives, these two concepts would be reversed with objectives as the broader concept. In this text the order of specificity is as follows: purpose, goal, objective with purpose being the broadest statement, and objective as the most specific and narrow.

to the variables identified in the problem and purpose statements. These outcomes are often specifically related to the research questions/hypotheses.

As one states the intention for a research study, only one purpose should be stated. Multiple faceted purpose statements lead to confusion and ambiguities. They invariably lead away from a focused study.

Goals

The goals for a research study include the expected outcomes of the study that will be reported in the conclusions and recommendations. The goals should be stated in ways which are consistent with what can be reasonably expected as outcomes of the study. Goals should not be stated which cannot be reported as outcomes of the study. If intentions for one's ministry or application are noted, they should be moved to the "significance" section of a proposal. The goals should be stated as products of the research, not processes. If multiple goals are stated, they must all closely relate to the singular purpose of the research. The research should have a singular direction as defined in both the purpose and central research issue. The expected outcome(s) must clearly focus on this central singular issue. The projection of multiple studies through having multiple unrelated outcomes will not only complicate, but may well invalidate the study.

Significance

Significance statements are "goal" statements for the application of the study after it has been completed. The significance should be reported in at least three ways: personally, for one's ministry and for the building of theory. They may also relate to a related agency, academic department or some broader initiative.

The research should be significant personally to the researcher. If it is not significant personally, one should not do it. One should not waste his or her time, because the commitment to the project may not see it through.

One's ministry, work or profession should benefit from the study. The research should then relate to one's ministry situation (e.g., to the agency, to the church with which one works).

The research should contribute to the testing or development of theory. If the research is not done in connection with an academic program, it should provide at least one or more of the following theoretical functions: an explanation of the situation, a prediction of what will likely occur in the context, a basis for acting in the context or a means for control.

In the case of a master's thesis or professional doctorate (e.g., DMin, DMiss, EdD, DBA, JD, PsyD or the like), the significance should bear out on the application of theory in a given ministry arena. In the case of a PhD, the significance should include the contribution of new theory, or a new understanding of theory, of the building of theory even while it should have practical applications as well.

Stating the Central Research Issue

The central research issue, however stated, provides the key focal point for the whole study. This central research issue should be stated in one statement or question—in a *simple* statement or question. A thesis statement is stated as a proposition to be tested. One should state the central research issue as either a problem or a thesis statement, but not both. The way that one states the central research issue will set the direction for the research methods to be used. However, a well-conceived central research issue may often be stated in a variety of ways. Once stated, the researcher will need to choose which way best suits the issue, the researcher, resources, and the context to be researched. The remainder of the design depends on how the central issue is stated.

The central research issue should define, clarify, and set the limits of the research intent. It should provide that unifying issue around which everything else is built. It should be simply stated to the point. It should be stated in a way that will advance eld that the research is being done and not duplicate research one. It should fit the skills, the interests, and the resources of the researcher. And, it should have adequate external applicability (significance) to justify it. A researcher should have determined before finalizing the problem from precedent research and the other contributing components whether the proposed research will contribute to the general advancement of knowledge or just to one's personal edification. The central research issue should show the relationship between the variables to be studied. One should be able to identify the dependent and independent variables in the problem. The relationship between or among variables to be examined should be clear. This statement/question should suggest the kinds of questions that are to be raised in the research questions or the hypotheses.

The central research issue should be stated in a way that gives explicit direction for the research questions or hypotheses. The significance of the study, for the goal(s), objectives, the undergirding assumptions, the delimitations or the scope of the study, should all be implicit in the statement of this central issue. This set of conditions explains why it is difficult in a single simple sentence of twenty-five words to put it all together. It is the most difficult sentence, by far, of the whole thesis or dissertation.

Again the central research issue and the purpose statement, while related, contrast in at least one significant way. The purpose statement will point to the "*why*" of the study, whereas the problem statement will point to the "*what*" of the study.

The central research issue will be expanded and addressed by either a set of research questions or a set of hypotheses. Hypotheses *should not* be considered unless a thesis statement is presented. Hypotheses are used to support the examination of a thesis statement. A thesis statement should not be used if the central research issue is stated as a question or a "problem." These two approaches of stating a central research issue normally require different research methods to address them. The one set of methods typically leads primarily into qualitative research, whereas the other leads into quantitative approach.

Problem Statement

A "problem statement" differs from other kinds of problems. It is not like family problems. It is not like mission problems. It is not like church problems. It is a technical term used to identify the central research issue—the central question that is to be addressed. It may arise out of conflict. It may arise out of need. It may arise out the common use of the word "problem." "Problem" as it is used in this text is a technical research term.

The central research issue may be stated in either way across a whole range of missiological disciplines. Whether using history, sociology, anthropology, leadership, economics, comparative religion, geography, political science, communications, Bible translation, leadership emergence theory, or theology, one may state the central issue either as a problem statement or a thesis statement.

Research Questions

If stated as a "problem" statement, the central research issue should suggest the issues to be addressed in the research questions. These questions should be comprehensive, that is, they should cover all the issues raised in the central research issue. The research questions should also be mutually exclusive and should not duplicate each other. Each research question should address a single issue or relationship. A researcher will often find it helpful to state the research questions as parallel questions with the same kind of structure. Frequently, a clearly focused research issue will suggest only three to five research questions. When more than five research questions are raised, questions about the central issue and the research questions arise: Is the scope too broad? Do the questions overlap? Are some of the questions related to background or goal issues? Occasionally, a central research issue will suggest only two research questions. When more than five questions are raised, the researcher should review the scope of the study and the criteria for research questions noted above.

Research questions will suggest both categories for reviewing precedent research and for methods of collecting and analyzing data. These questions may suggest multiple methods or a multidisciplinary approach if the topic is complex. For example, some work requires research in history, theology, and maybe case studies—three different methods. The research questions often suggest the categories for the findings chapters in the final research report.

The research questions most logically immediately follow the statement of the central research issue. Having read the central research issue one is ready to address the primary set of questions which will treat that issue.

Several common errors frequently occur in the early drafts of research questions. For example, often background issues that serve to describe the context of the research issue, the need for the research or assumptions for addressing the problem appear in the research questions. Frequently, as one thinks through the whole proposed research sequence, the goals for the research will appear as the last question or two. If the central research issue is not clear, often one of the research questions will emerge as a restatement of the issue or even a better statement of the central research issue.

Thesis Statement

In some research studies it is better to state the central research issue as thesis statement—a proposition to be demonstrated or tested—rather than as a statement or question to be explored. Again, it is *inappropriate* to include both in a single study because each requires a different approach to the subsequent methodology. If one chooses to use a thesis statement or a proposition to be tested, then the subissues are identified as hypotheses to be tested.

A thesis statement generally sets the stage for a quantitative study aimed at testing theory. It should raise the issues between the key independent and dependent variables. As with a problem statement it should, in a very succinct way, identify the context in which the research will occur and provide the base for both the supporting hypotheses and goals for the research. Clearly, it must unequivocally align with the purpose again showing the "what" of the research as the purpose states the "why."

With a mixed method approach and/or an interdisciplinary approach, the complexities of the proposed methodologies must be stated in a clear simple proposition. Complex propositions often lead to difficulties with either the design of one's methodology or the interpretation of the findings.

As with the setting for the topic or purpose, one should expect the development of a thesis statement and supporting hypothesis to require several iterations to assure a comprehensive integrated treatment of the central research issue.

Hypotheses

Hypotheses are propositional statements that may be tested. A hypothesis states or predicts a specific expected outcome. Normally, only two variables will be stated. Often hypotheses are stated as "if-then" statements. The "if" introduces the "independent" (causal) variable and the "then" introduces the "dependent" (result or outcome) variable. Because it is impossible to conclusively "prove" a positive statement, when hypotheses are tested, the negative of the hypothesis (the null hypothesis) is actually tested. If one can disprove the null hypothesis, the hypothesis will be stated as being supported (but not proven). In a research study using a thesis as the central research issue and hypotheses to be tested, two sets of hypotheses then need to be developed—the alternative hypotheses and the null hypotheses.

If the hypothesis specifies a single direction or outcome, it may be termed a "one-tail hypothesis." One might hypothesize an increase with one variable in which case it would be a "one-tailed hypothesis." If the outcome may occur in two directions (e.g., more or less/increase or decrease), the hypothesis may be called a "two-tailed hypothesis." A researcher should remember to formulate the hypotheses with the same constraints as research questions. They should be mutually exclusive and comprehensive. The hypotheses should account for all of the possible outcomes. The hypotheses should be stated in a way that allows for a choice between them. If the proposition or prediction is correct, then the null hypothesis would be rejected. If the original projection is not supported, then the null hypothesis would be accepted. (A description of the statistics related to this process is beyond the scope of this text.)

The reasoning supporting hypothesis testing rests on two basic principles:

- the formulation of two mutually exclusive hypothesis statements that, together, exhaust all possible outcomes
- the testing of these so that one is necessarily accepted and the other rejected (Trochim, 2009)

Again, as with research questions, one should examine hypotheses to assure parallelism and to clear focus on the thesis statement. Whenever the number of hypotheses exceeds five, one should look for issues treating the background or context, a restatement of the thesis, redundancies or expected goals or outcomes of the study. Another risk with an excessive number of hypotheses is an unfocused thesis statement. Sometimes, one of the hypotheses turns out to be a better statement of the thesis statement than the one it is designed to support.

As one approaches a set of hypotheses, the impossible issue of trying to approve a positive statement will emerge. For example one cannot "prove" all crows are black without examining the whole universe of crows. The issue of a *null hypothesis* arises whereby one seeks to disprove or demonstrate the opposite of the hypothesis. Research then testing the theory does not "prove" in a conclusive way the truth of the hypothesis, but may disprove its opposite. The result is support for the hypothesis at an acceptable statistical level. The issues of statistics and their use are beyond the scope of this text.

One may write directional or nondirectional hypotheses in which an outcome in a certain direction (e.g., more/less, greater/smaller, higher/lower) is anticipated. Nondirectional hypotheses only anticipate a difference as being correlated or not.

As Creswell notes (2009, p. 136), unless demographic variables serve predictive functions, nondemographic variables such as values or cultural patterns should serve as the dependent or independent variables. Demographic variables (e.g., age, gender, residence, or marital status) more typically serve as intervening, moderating or even confounding variables.

As with research questions, hypotheses provide both constraints and guidance for what is ultimately addressed in the review of precedent research, how the methodology is designed, how the findings will be reported and how the conclusions or recommendations will be constructed or expressed. The required interactive process of the design will repeatedly involve the research questions or hypotheses.

Delimitations/Scope

The delimitations consist of the boundaries one establishes around the research. They define the scope of what will be studied and what will be excluded from the study. Typically, in the delimitations the researcher will recognize the importance of issues which are outside the scope of the present study, but will, with the statement of delimitations, exclude these issues because of their irrelevance to the immediate topic. These issues may be excluded because it is not possible to address them for some other legitimate reason such as logistics. The delimitations may be set in any number of ways. Scope may be defined by time, place, number, or many other ways. In one preliminary draft of a proposal the researcher suggested she would study the emergence of Christian women leaders. Without some delimitations the draft suggested that all Christian women who have become leaders would be researched—all Christian women beginning from the first century in every country would simply be impossible. Later, the scope was delimited to be in the twentieth century, in three churches, in the Los Angeles area.

Researchers normally set delimitations as they become more familiar with their research topic. If they are experienced in doing research in the area of the present research, extensive research into secondary sources or precedent research may not be needed. However, for a person who is initiating research in a new area, careful research into secondary sources or precedent research is essential.

Occasionally, novice researchers will confuse delimitations and limitations. Used in this context, delimitations are set by the researcher while limitations are the inherent weaknesses of the design threatening the validity, reliability or the trustworthiness/truth of the research.

Assumptions

A researcher should specifically clarify foundational assumptions for the reader to assure an appropriate interpretation or evaluation of what is being presented. The researcher should identify his or her cultural background. One's culture reflects the person's worldview. A person's worldview sets the assumed base for classifying, person-group relations, time/event relations, and space. When the researcher's cultural and experiential origins are known, the expected worldview and general perspective may be known.

One's assumptions may be simply stated or documented and used from other sources. A researcher must, however, remain consistent in the employment of these assumptions or explicitly note when diverging from them. Inconsistency from one's assumptions will result in confusion through the research negatively affecting every part.

Assumptions serve as the foundational perspectives for the study. They are not debated in the study. They are not the issues to be addressed in the research. They provide the readers of the research with the essential perspectives that they would not otherwise know and without which they would not be able to interpret the study appropriately. One's assumptions may be based on personal beliefs/perspectives or on established precedent research.

A reader may well question one's assumptions if they are outside the realm of what would be commonly accepted. If a researcher suspects that the assumptions may not be shared or may be questioned, the assumptions should be supported by precedent research.

Definitions

Definitions are a kind of assumption. Often, one needs to define a set of key terms to be used throughout the study. These definitions should be provided early in the study. If terms are used in a unique way even though they are common words, they should be defined. In order to aid the reader, one should consider the inclusion of definitions immediately after the description of the central research issue and related research questions or hypothesis. Only the key definitions should be included in the text. Others may be reserved for a glossary.

One should avoid coining new terms or using terms outside their normal usage without definitions. Then, the defined terms should be used consistently throughout the text with the context supporting the definition. As would be the practice with introducing new terms to new leaders, the newly defined terms should be used at least three times within the next page or two to reinforce its meaning and expected usage.

Overview

Finally, an overview section clarifies the central research issue and its related components, a brief overview of the whole study is often useful for the reader. This brief overview should include an overview of the review of the purpose, central issue, precedent research or literature, a brief overview of the kind of methods and the categories of anticipated findings. This overview in a proposal should not be more than two or three paragraphs. It may contain visuals to help portray either or both the theoretical base of the study and/or the research flow of the study. These visuals may show the relationship between the problem, the review of the literature, methodology, findings and conclusions to give the reader a sense of direction through the whole study.

Target Audience

The target audience for the final report should be clearly identified as the proposal is being designed. The style of writing, the detail of the design and the focus of the study will all be influenced by the ones who will be reading or using the study. The target audience will also influence what is appropriate for the background, assumptions and definitions sections.

Summary

The central research issue is the governing issue for the whole study. A frequent suggestion for students is to work hard on this statement and then paste an enlarged copy of it over their computers to remind them of it as they work through every section of their design, data collection and analysis, presenting their findings and finally in the application of their findings. Table 1 presents a summary of concerns between the central research issue whether it is stated as a problem statement or a thesis statement to the other major parts of the research design.

TABLE 1
Relating the Central Research Issue Section to the Overall Research Design

Section of Design	Contributions to the Central Research Issue	Contributions from the Central Research Issue
Background	Sets the context for the central research issue	Defines what context should be described
Purpose	Sets the overall direction for the central research issue and defines the "why" of the research	Defines the variables to be researched or the "what" of the research
Goal(s)	Set the expected outcomes of researching of the central research issue to be reported in the conclusions and recommendations	Define the scope of the goal(s) for conclusions and recommendations
Research Questions/ Hypotheses	Define how variables identified in the central research issue will be addressed	Set the scope and relationships among the variables to be addressed
Delimitations/Scope	Defines the specific scope—what will be included and what will be excluded from the central research issue	Identifies the broad boundaries of what will be done in the present study

Section of Design	Contributions to the Central Research Issue	Contributions from the Central Research Issue
Assumptions	Set the general perspectives for approaching and interpreting the central research issue	Identify broad issues to clarify in assumptions
Definitions	Set the specific perspectives for addressing key concepts	Help identify issues needing definition
Review of Precedent Research	Defines values, variables, significance, potential methods to approach and theoretical perspectives to interpret and apply	States the relationships of the variables to be evaluated from precedent research
Data Collection	Will raise questions of validity, reliability, and feasibility along with the basic questions of how, when, why, where, who, what, how much data to collect about the central research issue	Defines the arena(s) for data collection methods by answering the basic questions of how, when, why, where, who, what, how much data to collect
Data Analysis	Will raise questions of validity, reliability, and feasibility along with the basic questions of how, when, why, where, who, what, how much data to analyze about the central research issue	Defines subject arena for data analysis; may suggest analytical direction or procedures
Limitations	Will raise questions of potential threats to validity and reliability to researching the central research issue that may require revising it	
Findings		Define the subject arena(s) for reporting the findings
Conclusions		Define the subject arena(s) for reporting the conclusions
Recommendations		Define the subject arena(s) for reporting the recommendations

3

EVALUATION OF PRECEDENT RESEARCH/ REVIEW OF LITERATURE

This chapter introduces the evaluation of precedent research to support a research project.[8]

Every researcher designs investigations based on research foundations established by others. Some may have researched the chosen topic or related topics. Other researchers will have laid the perspective (theory) bases for approaching, interpreting, and applying research about the chosen topic. A wise researcher will carefully evaluate the bases upon which to design any new research. Often, useful precedent research will be present in divergent disciplinary approaches. For example, history, anthropology, theology, economics, comparative religion, political science, and geographical/ecological studies may all contribute in addressing a single missiological research issue. Different disciplines provide different windows into the issue. This chapter introduces what is often called a "review of the literature."

A researcher should review or evaluate two kinds of literature: secondary sources and primary sources. Secondary sources are sources written *about* the subject at hand. Primary sources *are* the subject or are *participants with or eyewitnesses to* the subject. Historians using diaries, letters, and interviews with eyewitnesses (all primary sources) write historical accounts (secondary sources) about the subject. A theologian would use Luke-Acts (a primary source) to describe the work of the Holy Spirit in the church at the time of the apostles. The same theologian would use the writings of the second century historians (secondary sources) to supplement the study. The same theologian might use the writings of other twentieth century

---

8   In this chapter, the phrases "review of precedent research" or "evaluation of precedent" research will be used as a synonym for review of the literature.

theologians' writings about the same subject who had gone back to study the original text (secondary sources) to determine the extent of what had been written about the subject, to determine what new contributions the present research might offer or whether the study was simply for personal enrichment. If, on the other hand, the theologian had as the central focus of the study what second century historians thought, then their writings would be the *primary sources.*

An anthropologist would read all of the ethnographies and worldview studies (secondary sources) available about a people in preparation to examine primary sources such as personal observations and interviews with the people.

Several key questions in this chapter focus around the issue of precedent research, including the following:

- Why consider others' research?
- Relating research logic to precedent research;
- Basic issues in reviewing precedent research;
- Where to look;
- Selection of appropriate precedent research or literature;
- Documentation, and
- An overview of the review process.

"Library" research and "precedent" research are distinguished in this chapter. "Library" research simply refers to the broad use of library resources for research purposes. Libraries provide repositories of books, dissertations, theses, journals, microforms, digitized information, online databases, and many other kinds of other archived materials. Moreover, libraries provide important links to vast information networks and incomprehensible stores of data and information beyond their geographic locations. One may do either primary or original research with original documents (primary sources) in libraries. Or, one may use the resources of a library to establish the foundations for additional research (secondary sources). The latter is the main focus of this chapter. Both original research and research in precedent studies may be done in a library. Simply to refer to one's research as "library research" reflects a naive view of research. Researchers must be careful not to confuse the more general term "library research" with the more specific term "precedent research." This chapter seeks to describe the foundations for doing original research by an evaluation of research that has already been done.

Why Consider Others' Research?

Before engaging in any research, one should consider what research has been done previously about the topic. What has been done previously provides the means to:

- Validate the significance and scope of the central research issue
- Establish the boundaries of what has been previously researched so appropriate research questions may be raised
- Provide the perspective(s) or theory to investigate and interpret what is found
- Establish values or criteria for an evaluative study
- Set the research in the broader context of what has already been researched about the topic

Central Research Issue Significance Validation

The evaluation of precedent research should establish the significance of the existing research. As one begins to explore what research others have done about the topic and topics related to the project at hand, the significance of one's own research soon becomes apparent. The degree to which others have examined the issue in the past or have expressed the need for research in the area provides a basis on which one may judge the significance of the present project and the appropriate scope of the project. While a specific topic may lack much focus or attention in precedent research, a broader reading may reveal its importance to the community. One may find statements in articles, books, online, or research studies calling for or recommending research in new areas or for the proposed research topic. For example, research is currently limited to missiological principles for evangelizing and nurturing the second- and third-generation Korean Americans. However, other research provides much insight about second and third generation converts, not only among immigrant communities in the United States, but other Asians and peoples from the Pacific Rim, as well as Africans and Europeans. Each immigrant community will differ significantly because of its own culture and reasons for immigration. Communities who were displaced because of slavery, economic pressures, religious persecution or natural disasters all face both unique and common challenges. The cultural distance between the immigrant community and the receptor community including the religious divergence emerges as one evaluates the precedent research. One may also benefit from studies about culture and worldview change with other immigrant populations.

One can seldom say, "Nothing has been researched or written that is relevant for my project." As Solomon wrote more than 3,000 years ago, "What has been will be again, what has been done will be done again; there is nothing new under the sun" (Eccl 1:9). Often the technical language or philosophical assumptions of other precedent research may differ, but invaluable information is likely to be available. Parallel studies about related ethnic groups or parallel situations may prove helpful. What is true in one city may be true in another city with similar demographic, political, religious, and economic characteristics. A broader search with a trained research librarian may uncover multiple leads. For example, a researcher can find a plethora of materials about the missiological approach of the Apostle Paul. However, a creative PhD dissertation was completed at the beginning of 2010 that brought new light to the message and methods of Paul through a fresh study of both secondary and the primary sources of the New Testament (Wolf, 2010).

Establishing Boundaries

One may establish the boundaries of what has already been researched by a review of precedent research. By identifying the frontiers one can better determine what still needs to be done. One can answer the questions about the appropriate scope of the present research. If definitive research about the topic one has selected has already been concluded, one need not proceed. However, by identifying what has already been established, one may use those bases as a foundation for further research. Again to cite the above example, if one were to research the principles for evangelizing and nurturing the second- and third-generation Korean Americans, a strong theory base exists from numerous other immigrant communities and from communities who have now gone beyond the second and third generations of being Christian from both similar and dissimilar cultures. A review of what has already been researched then provides a base for knowing where to begin one's research and the existing bases upon which one may build.

Setting Theory Perspectives

By looking into what has been previously researched around one's topic, the researcher may set perspectives both for collecting data and interpreting the data. The theories one uses will determine both the means of data collection and analysis. The theoretical bases will also serve as the interpretative base for drawing conclusions and recommendations. By looking at what has already been done, one may evaluate both the validity and reliability of the methods used. Some methods simply will not produce appropriate (valid) results while other methods will not produce consistent (reliable) results. One may have a set of findings from a research project, but not know how to interpret the results. For example, the author was asked to evaluate the receptivity of the Turkana people in northwest Kenya to the gospel in order to inform a mission's decision-making process about mission strategy and placement (Elliston, 1987). At the time the author did the research, the Turkana were not obviously responsive to the gospel. Several missions had been working in the Turkana District for as much as twenty years with few results in the towns and almost no response among the traditional Turkana. Virtually no research had been done to assess their receptivity (Elliston, 1987, 2000, pp. 809-810) to the gospel. Only a handful of books, articles, and academic studies were available about the Turkana people. These studies, while not addressing the issue of receptivity, were invaluable to understand the environmental, cultural, political, and economic context. Such an understanding was crucial to add to other information. However, much other precedent research had been done about receptivity, worldview, worldview change, and pastoral peoples living in arid regions. Some ethnographical studies, economic studies, and government development reports were available as precedent research. Ecological studies from other regions provided insight into the local context. From this "precedent research," a theory base was established for doing research among the Turkana. This theory base provided clues about what questions to ask and what to observe while doing research among these people. After collecting the data suggested by the theories that were used, he was able to predict "that based on their present rate of worldview change and on the missiological strategies of previous missions that these people would likely be receptive to gospel" (Elliston, 1987). Responsiveness would depend (as based on theories derived from precedent research) on some significant shifts in mission methods and of course the working of the Spirit. Twenty-five years and more than sixty new congregations later, these theoretical positions have been validated.

Precedent research should identify the whole range of theoretical explanations for the present study project, regardless of the complexity of the multidisciplinary approach(es) that may be used. The review of precedent research should provide the perspectives needed to interpret the findings of the study.

Research Questions

The kinds of needed questions are often identified from the precedent research. People who have done research in the past may have identified significant variable issues that remain to be treated. Frequently, as one is working through a research project, many new questions arise that fall beyond the scope of the present study. These questions, when reported in a section entitled "Recommendations for Further Research," often provide a jump-start for the next researcher.

Hypotheses

As one reviews precedent research and identifies the key variables and theories which undergird the topic, the final hypotheses may be brought into an appropriate focus. Even as the central research issue, when stated as a thesis, is brought into focus from precedent research so the subtopics are also addressed. Hypotheses are typically employed to test theory in a given context. The precedent research provides the theory or theories.

Since a theory is typically employed to explain, predict, and provide means to control phenomena, as well as provide bases for action and means to test the theory, hypotheses typically address one or more of these functions. A review of the precedent research then provides both the bases for the breadth of the hypotheses and delimits them. This kind of review helps establish what is valid (addressing the right issue) and what is reliable (what will produce consistent results).

For a given research, one may have to choose from among competing theories. The theories chosen must fit with one's assumptions and be justified in the evaluation or review of the literature before the theories may be used to support one's thesis and hypotheses.

Setting Values or Criteria

Often research studies aim at evaluating a situation, a set of actions, or a program. The evaluation requires not only the collection of information about the situation or the actions in question, but also the establishment of a set of criteria or values against which one may make judgments. These judgments may relate to the worth, merit, adequacy, quality, theological orthodoxy or some other value. Evaluation is never possible without values. Values provide a critical ingredient for all evaluation studies.

One may do original research to establish values or one may turn to what has already been researched to identify and set the values to be used. Often, a researcher will decide only to collect data about the situation, actions or program in question while relying on other research to set the values to be used in the evaluation.

Precedent research providing the values may come from studies from a wide range of disciplines including theology, anthropology, economics, comparative religion, geography, political science, sociology or others. By establishing one's values from precedent research one links his or her research to precedent research and the broader research community.

One's values also provide constraints to what may be considered as valid research. Values will aid the researcher in knowing not only what questions to ask, but then to make judgments about the information that emerges from the range of data collected.

Values not only provide the bases for judging what valid data are in social science-based research, they provide the bases for setting the hermeneutical or exegetical approach in theological research. One's values provide bases to determine what a person perceives to be true or trustworthy. While one's review of precedent research may serve to identify values, the worldview one brings to the evaluation of precedent research or the existing literature will certainly affect how one identifies or extracts values from precedent research. For example, an evangelical Christian, a Sikh, and a Sunni Muslim will each approach each others' "holy" writings with a very different set of worldviews, values, and related hermeneutics.

Contextualize the Present Research

A review of the precedent research allows researchers to place their study in the context of the broader research community, so that the researcher knows how the current research fits with other research in the same field. One may be doing studies, for example, about leadership in the Baltics and find that the application of this research fits with others who are in oppressed areas, or in former communist areas in other parts of the world, maybe in Asia, maybe in some places in Latin America, or even some places in Africa. And so, they find where the study contextually fits in the broader world of research. The study of women, for example. It is not just what happens in Kenya, but what happens in Nigeria, and maybe what happens in the Ukraine, Thailand, and Indonesia. One will see where the current research fits in terms of relevance or significance to contemporary missional and societal issues.

As one reads about completed research, it will become apparent how the present research fits in the broader context. Too often church and/or mission related research is done in isolation and not set in the broader context. By understanding how the research fits in the broader context one may interpret the findings much more appropriately. For example, recently the author read a research study conducted among the Seventh-Day Adventists (SDA) in Southern California. The study focused in part on the history of the growth/decline of that denomination in a recent period. While confident that the author's findings were accurate and valid for the SDA Church, it would have been helpful for him to have placed the growth/decline patterns in the context of other denominations in the same area over the same period. Parallel studies did exist. That perspective would have allowed him to interpret the findings to show both what was unique to the SDA Church and what issues were common across denominational lines. A broader reading of precedent research would have allowed him to compare the history of the SDA Church in that region with other regions.

The review of the literature then helps one make a judgment about the significance of the findings. How important are they? How significant are they not only to one's own ministry and agency or situation, but to one's own discipline? It is important for one to see what others have written to judge the importance of one's own work in the broader community and to apply what has been found.

For multidisciplinary studies the applicability or significance of the study should be explained in terms of each of the disciplines involved, not only missiology. A review of precedent research will allow one to see the significance of the present study in terms of each of the academic disciplines employed in the research. A review of the literature needs to be done in a way that treats each of these disciplines so that the whole can be brought together in a consistent, unified, integrated way.

An examination of precedent research then provides a critical base on which to build one's own original research. From the central issue and key questions to the design, methods for collecting and analyzing data, to the perspectives for interpreting the findings to draw conclusions and recommendations, a careful analysis of previously-done research stands as an essential component.

However, in the evaluation or review of precedent research, a researcher must make a judgment about the key research issues of reliability and validity, as well as trustworthiness and truth from a theological perspective. Was the precedent research conducted in a reliable or trustworthy and valid way? Was the set of conclusions and recommendations appropriately related to the research method? To base one's study on an invalid or unreliable base will only serve to discredit one's research. Just because a research study has been published does not mean that it was done with rigorous reliability or validity.

Relating Research Logic to Precedent Research

Whether one approaches research from a strict, deductive perspective or from a more cyclical or iterative inductive approach, an examination of precedent research serves each critical stage along the way. Beginning with a description of the context through the formation of conclusions and recommendations building on the foundation of precedent research is essential. Some issues based in previously done research that commonly occur in research studies include: background, purpose, goals, central research issue, research questions, precedent research, methodology, findings, conclusions, and recommendations. Any one or a combination of these resources may prove to be helpful in the design of a new study.

Identifying or Developing Research Methods

Reviewing what others have done provides an initial guide to know how to address all of the knotty methods' questions. How does one collect the data? Should questionnaires be used? Should people be interviewed? What kind(s) of observations are reliable and valid? How should the data collection be developed? How should one limit the population and select a sample? What are the information needs? How much information is needed? What complementary methods should be used? How should complementary methods be used? Should complementary methods come from a different academic discipline? An evaluation of research that has already been done in one's topic area typically will address most of these questions along with many others that will emerge. No researcher should embark on a project without knowing what others have done before to address the same kind of topic.

A careful evaluation of previously done research will inform 1) a researcher's choice of methods, 2) how to employ those methods both in data collection and analysis, and 3) the integration of methods from other academic disciplines. A review of the literature then provides a survey, generally, of the variety of methods being used, or have been used to address one's particular problem. One can identify in the review of the literature in what others have done, useful instruments and/or instruments which ought to be avoided. Some kinds of methods do not work well. A review of the literature will help one see those kinds of methods. For example, as one is working in a preliterate society, one will soon see that questionnaires are simply inappropriate. Similarly, researchers may find that if they are working in a society that is not highly individualistic such as their own, they may find that individual interviews are not appropriate. They may have to do group interviews. That insight will come out of the literature. One can see how the methods are validated in the literature. Both the failures and successes of others will provide useful insights in the development of valid and reliable instruments that one can use.

An evaluation of the literature often assists one to establish both the levels of validity and reliability for the methods that are chosen. If standardized instruments are used, previously established levels of validity and reliability may apply. If new instruments are developed, precedent researchers will assist in noting the pitfalls and risks to both validity and reliability.

Community Conversation

Part of what a researcher is doing is joining in a community that deals with a particular set of issues, and by joining, contributes to an informed and written conversation about those issues. The conversation is not face-to-face but in a written conversation in which the researcher is writing articles, reports, theses, dissertations, or books; someone else then responds in a similar manner. One is in a protracted kind of conversation and the review of the literature provides the orientation to become a part of it, to know what needs to be said, what does not need to be said and how to express the ideas in the conversation. A review of the literature acquaints one with the language and conventions of the conversation. The review of the literature will help provide an understanding of the boundaries of what has already been studied. The review of the literature will help one understand what has not been studied. A careful evaluation of precedent research will allow the researcher to know how to submit his or her research into the broader printed conversation about the topic and the advancement of knowledge.

Conducting and reporting research without this base in precedent research may very well lead to the generation of new technical language, thus unnecessarily complicating the field. Such studies also often result in blind spots. A recent set of student papers about the topic of "servant-leadership" clearly revealed a lack of knowledge of the biblical precedents and no knowledge of the person of Robert W. Greenleaf beyond the fact he had served as the CEO of AT&T and had written about the topic.[9]

Basic Issues in Evaluating Precedent Research

For the review of precedent research to serve the functions noted above, a researcher must address several issues ranging from selecting the literature to its interpretation and reporting. The "how" of the evaluation of precedent literature eludes some beginning researchers. One need not miss the rich store of information that typically awaits every researcher who is approaching a new research project.

---

9   http://www.greenleaf.org/whatissl/ retrieved 1/31/2010; Kirkpatrick, 1987; Bennett, 2002.

A valid evaluation of the precedent research requires completing several steps, including:

- Development of an accurate understanding the precedent research,
- Development of a clear set of values or criteria for judging its worth, and,
- An application of these values/criteria to the precedent research.

Selection of Appropriate Precedent Research/Literature

The selection of appropriate precedent research or literature is a critical task for the researcher in the beginning stages of a research project. Two objections frequently appear as emerging researchers begin to look into printed or digital resources for what relates to their proposed research project. Inexperienced researchers say, (1) "Nothing has been written about this topic so I do not know where to go for precedent research." Or they say (2) "I have found so much information I do not know where to begin or where to stop. I have found not just a few books, but hundreds or even thousands of books and articles about the topic." In both cases the question of selection of the appropriate precedent research comes into focus.

Start With Central Research Issue

The obvious beginning point from which to begin to select precedent research is the vantage point of one's own research issue. The issue will undoubtedly be reshaped as the precedent research is studied and evaluated, but the beginning point is one's own topic. If one can begin with a very clearly focused central research issue and an initial set of research questions/hypotheses, then the broad categories of the literature can be identified.

The following sequenced suggestions provide a base from which to begin investigating a given topic:

- Start with the key words related to the central research issue to search easily accessible databases—for example, the subject file in a local university or community library catalog, the subject file in a major library's computerized holdings file, the Library of Congress, specialized databases[10] such as ERIC, EBSCO Host, Proquest,

---

10   ERIC stands for Educational Resources Information Clearinghouse. ERIC contains educational related papers, theses, conference presentations and other documents many of which have not been published. Dissertation Abstracts available through Proquest provides a wealth of information with abstracts of both masters and doctoral level theses and dissertations. Missiological Abstracts published by Fuller Theological Seminary contains abstracts of theses and dissertations done in missiology at Fuller

Google Scholar, Dissertation Abstracts, Missiological Abstracts, Religion Index, Periodicals Index, Books in Print, published reviews of the literature or even encyclopedias. Even a review of current books available through a major bookseller such as Amazon.com may be helpful.

- Open online searches using either a popular or specialized search engine to find unpublished papers, blogs, newsletters, conference materials and other clues about precedent research.
- A research librarian is always a major resource in the research process.
- Start broadly with recent general texts and articles from different perspectives—theology, history, anthropology, sociology, leadership, psychology, political science, comparative religion, geography, and/or economics.
- Look at bibliographies to identify key and often cited authors.
- Study the outlines of recent books and articles to identify the key issues others are addressing about your topic.
- Read the reviews found in journals or even in online booksellers.
- Narrow the focus of the central research issue and principal questions.
- Decide on the theoretical and methodological perspective(s) from which to address the issue (theology, history, anthropology, sociology, leadership, church growth, political science, linguistics, communications or whichever theoretical perspectives fit).
- Delimit the review of precedent research to fit the specific research.

Evaluation of the Precedent Research

The researcher should review of the literature or precedent research with two key perspectives in mind:

- The original author's perspective and intentions.
- An evaluation from the perspective of its relevance to the central research issue of the present study.

As a matter of integrity, a researcher must interpret the writings of each other author from that person's intention while seeking to understand the original perspective. Basic exegetical principles apply regardless of the text being examined. One should be aware of the basic hermeneutical questions: Who wrote it? Why was

---

Theological Seminary. Religion Index provides an index of journals dealing with religious topics. Books in Print provides an index to titles, authors and publishers of current books in print. More general online databases provide access to hundreds of thousands of full text articles and books. Databases such as EBSCO, Emerald, and FirstSearch are but three of hundreds of online databases.

it written? When was it written? Where and to whom was it written? What is the point the author was seeking to communicate to the original audience? What were the author's credentials to address the subject? What was the context of the writing—cultural, missiological, historical, and economic to note only a few perspectives.

Second, after the precedent research has been understood, the question arises, "How is it relevant to the present central research issue." The question may be "So what?" How does the prior research provide a basis for understanding the present issue? How does it provide a means for examining the issue? Does it provide information about what has already been researched around the topic? A researcher looks at prior research to see what relevant "precedents" can be found for the present research. Again, the primary criterion for evaluation of the precedent research is its relevance to the present research issue. While it will not likely answer all of the specific issues, it should be expected to catalyze new ideas for further research.

As one is evaluating the precedent research, the usual critical issues must be raised. Did the author do both reliable and valid research? Was it based on original research or was it simply the author's opinions based on secondary sources? The quality of the precedent research must be examined. Just because an author has been able to have a research report published does not mean that it is either reliable or valid. Similarly, one may find serious design flaws in many studies including theses and dissertations that have been accepted for degrees. A careful evaluation of the literature used to support a study is essential for the credibility of one's own work. If the theoretical foundation upon which a research project is designed is faulty or one's assumptions about what has been researched about a topic are incorrect, the whole project may collapse!

When Is Enough Enough?

How much review of precedent research is enough? When does one know that enough review of the literature has been done? If one is working on a PhD, the answer is when one has evaluated *all* the relevant books and articles. That means that the problem needs to be well defined and narrow. The master's level student should be able, again, to identify all of those issues that relate to that particular research issue and have read all of the *significant* references. In some cases where the researcher is well acquainted with the precedent research, he or she may choose to deliberately delimit the sources and provide reasons why a limited number of sources has been selected.

Disciplinary Differences

For research based primarily in written sources (e.g., theology, history) researchers must take care in distinguishing between their own research and the research they are seeking to evaluate as a base for their own work. For the evaluation of the literature in these disciplines one should be careful to ask, "What is this author able to contribute to my study?" "What is this author's perspective?" Again, "is what is written produced from a valid and reliable research method for that discipline?"

Questions that often lead the researcher into confusing an evaluation of the *precedent* research and the *present* research include such questions as the following: What information does this author present that I may use? How can I use this text as a basis to support or report my own research?

Disciplinary approaches that depend much more on questionnaires, interviews, and/or observations do not present these kinds of problems. Similar questions may be asked, but the confusion is less likely.

When treating precedent research, a researcher should critique recognizing his or her value base including theological and missiological values. This kind of evaluation should be explicit rather than implicit. The researcher should be prepared to critique the worldview assumptions from a theological and biblical perspective. And, after having done that, one should move ahead always testing to be sure that it fits the data and the spiritual dimensions of the present research.

Common Errors in Addressing Precedent Research

Researchers often commit two common and serious errors: misusing precedent research or misunderstanding its potential functions. With either error, a valid theoretical framework of the study is unlikely to emerge. If the theoretical foundation upon which a research project is designed is faulty, again the whole project may fail!

Listing Sources

Researchers should avoid simply a listing the sources. A listing of sources is not a review or evaluation. To list authors, books, articles or email addresses is simply not appropriate as a review of precedent research.

Simply Summarizing

Reviewing precedent research requires more than a presentation of a summary of the precedent research. While it is important to be able to state what was presented in the precedent research, the issue is not the summary, but an evaluation of the relevance of the research from the perspective of the researcher's central research issue and the contributions it may make to the present study.

Reviewing by Author

A third common error inexperienced researchers make is commenting on individuals' contributions rather than evaluating by topic. The result of this approach is a disjointed series of comments or evaluations which will fail to provide a coherent integrated theoretical or value base.

A summary of one's evaluations is very important, but just summaries of what various authors may have written about a subject will not serve the researcher's purpose. Each major subsection of a review of precedent research should present a summary of the evaluation so that the theoretical perspective, the boundaries of the research, and a validation of the methods to be used or similar summary.

"Proof-texting" Error

A frequent error occurs when the precedent research is not clearly understood. Some researchers, in an attempt to lead the reader to believe that they have considered what has been researched previously, will simply lift quotations out of the literature to say what the researcher wants to say without regard to the original author's context. This "proof-texting" error of quoting or paraphrasing a passage for one's own purpose without regard to the original author's intention shows a lack of integrity.

Misinterpretation Error

A theologian would call a reading into the text something that is not there "*eisogesis*." To draw conclusions about a text that the original author did not make and then attribute these conclusions to that author would be an example. A researcher might project what an author would say, thus misinterpreting that author. The goal of exegesis is one severely restricted outcome: "to arrive at the meaning of the passage intended by the original author, as that author meant the original readers to understand it" (Hagner, 1993, p. 29).

Plagiarism[11] Errors

Whenever a researcher begins to write after having read the work or seen the graphics of another person, the responsibility of using the other sources appropriately emerges. The work of another person is that person's property. One must be careful not to abuse it or to steal it.

Plagiarism constitutes a much more serious integrity issue when dealing with previously produced materials by another person. Any idea, text or graphic produced by another person cannot be used legitimately without giving appropriate credit to that person. Modifications of a text like a paraphrase or modifications of a figure or graphic must carry a citation to the original source. Copyright laws clearly apply. Even if a person has not had a copyright formally registered, any original text including poetry or artwork is protected by law as soon as it has been written, drawn or otherwise produced.

Researchers need not fear the threats that accompany plagiarism if they cite the other person's work. In fact, researchers will only improve their own credibility if they do cite others and not try to deceptively take credit for what others have done.

One might ask, "What is the minimal number of words that require a citation?" The answer may be one! Whenever an idea, statement, expression or artistic piece of work is attributable to a person, a reference should be made.

Markman, Markman, and Waddell describe three kinds of plagiarism: "word-for-word plagiarism," "patchwork plagiarism," and "lifting out the perfect phrases" plagiarism (1989). A word-for-word copy without a citation would be very simply described as plagiarism. However, some people will substitute or transpose words thinking that by the insertion of different words one is not plagiarizing. However, if one follows the sentence structure and the thought structure with only the substitution of words, the charge of plagiarism will stand. Changing a few words does not constitute a "paraphrase" which in itself must be referenced (1989, 120). The second kind of commonly found plagiarism is what Markman, Markman, and Waddell call "patchwork plagiarism." One plagiarizes "when whole phrases are lifted out and are put into a framework of your own wording" or into a "different arrangement of the original" (p. 122). With this kind of plagiarism one simply takes phrases out of another person's writing and intersperses them in one's own text without citation. The third kind of plagiarism noted by Markman, et. al. resembles "patchwork plagiarism." They write, "Though more subtle and clever, this kind of plagiarism is similar to . . .

---

11   *Webster's Ninth New Collegiate Dictionary.* Springfield, MA: Merriam-Webster, 1983, defines plagiarize as follows: "to steal and pass off (the ideas or words of another) as one's own; use (a created production) without crediting the source; to commit literary theft; present as new and original an idea or product derived from an existing source."

patchwork [plagiarism]" (p. 123). These "perfect phrases" are woven into the text in a way that they appear to be the author's own words. Of the three types of plagiarism noted here all would be considered as plagiarism without documentation or a citation! Plagiarism is a sure way to discredit one's work. It undermines the integrity of the whole project. Penalties are usually assessed. In academic programs failure, dismissal, or similar serious penalties may be expected. Universities have been known to withdraw degrees even after they have been granted because of plagiarism.

Paraphrase

A paraphrase, on the other hand, may be constructed and used instead of a quotation. One may follow a text and restate the ideas and words in one's own words. A paraphrase, however, may not change the intended meaning of the original author. The words may be one's own, but "the thoughts and opinions are not" (Markman, et. al. p. 126). A paraphrase requires acknowledgment of one's debt to the original author. A citation is required. An undocumented paraphrase, while more difficult to detect, nevertheless, presents a serious ethical violation.

One helpful way of illustrating the rigor expected of a paraphrase is to place a series of Bible translations side-by-side. One might look at a New International Version, an English Standard Version, The Message, and a New Living Bible. If asked, "which is a paraphrase?" the correct answer is every one because none is in the original language. Each one is paraphrased in a different way with a different purpose in mind. However, every one aims to accurately reflect the original text in Greek.

For multiple examples of paraphrases ranging across the continuum of a formal equivalence to dynamic equivalence read the following passage from the following translations of the Bible: (1) The passage: John 3:16, (2) The following versions of the Bible: the New Revised Standard Version, the New International Version, Today's Living Version, The Message. Each one translates the passage differently, but each one intends to convey the same message. These translations range across the continuum of formal equivalence to dynamic equivalence. However, each translation is functionally equivalent to the original language source. The intended audience for each one differs. The purpose for each translation differs. In each case care has been taken to keep the outcome functionally equivalent and faithful to the original intention of communication.

A paraphrase must accurately reflect the original author's intention for the intended audience. A paraphrase does not involve just the substitution of a few words using a thesaurus. Rather, a paraphrase is a restatement "in other words." It may be more "literal" or "formally equivalent" or more "dynamically equivalent" depending on the intended audience. A paraphrase must also be cited. While the form of the citation differ, from a direct quotation, a citation is nonetheless required.

A person who translates either spoken or written communication into another language is always engaged in "paraphrasing." Every translation is a paraphrase. Its accuracy may be judged on the basis of its functional equivalence to the original. Every paraphrase must account for two primary contexts: (a) the original context, and (b) the context of the receiver. To accurately paraphrase one must remain faithful to both in conveying the intended meaning.

Frequently, as one does research, it is more appropriate to paraphrase a section than to quote it. When constructing a paraphrase, one must keep several variables in mind, including: (a) the intended message of the original author; (b) the intended purpose for the present research; (c) the style of writing in the present research; and (d) the audience for whom the research is being written.

With these variables in mind, the researcher may choose the reiteration or translation of the original author's message along a continuum of functional equivalence for the present audience. At one end of the continuum is "formally equivalence" in which the original words or structure are followed in a literal translation intended to convey the same meaning. This approach is frequently used in language translation; however, a paraphrase will not be accurate if only a few synonyms are exchanged in a text from a thesaurus. Indeed, reiteration of the phrasing of the original author and only replacing selected words can result in charges of plagiarism in an academic environment, as the author has not been credited for the reuse of their phrasing.

On the other end of the paraphrase continuum, one may translate the message to have "dynamic equivalence." This approach to a paraphrase also intends to generate the same meaning and impact on the listeners or readers as to the original, but with the form and patterns of communication altered to meet the needs of the receiver. Dynamic equivalence frees the writer to present the original source material in the clearest way to the audience. Either form of a paraphrase may provide a trustworthy rendition of the original. However, in either case one must take care to avoid "adding to" or "detracting from" the intent of the original author. A paraphrase is indeed "a statement in other words."

The length of the paraphrase may vary. In some cases it will be shorter; in some cases it will be longer; and, in some cases, it will be about the same length. Whatever the case, it must convey the same meaning as the original.

Three terms need to be distinguished:

- A "quotation" accurately restates what the original statement.

- A "paraphrase" accurately restates the original statement "in other words."
- A "summary" presents the principal ideas of the passage concerned.

Every case requires a citation. The citation for a paraphrase and the summary should be the same. Depending on the format style being used, a paraphrase citation will differ from a quotation. However, citations for quotations, paraphrases, and summaries always must be included.

"Lazy" Research

Often in the course of one's reading through precedent research a person will find references to another researcher. That other researcher may be quoted in a way that is relevant and useful for the topic at hand. "Lazy" researchers will simply lift the quote of a quote and cite it as their own resulting in plagiarism. The careful researcher who has integrity will find the original source and review it to see if it is indeed relevant to the topic at hand. Even in published text books with multiple citations, a researcher would be well advised to look at the original source(s). The textbook author will have had a different purpose in writing and may well interpret the original from a different perspective than what fits the present research.

Confusing Precedent Research with Findings

Historical and theological research often depends on printed resources both for precedent research and as sources for one's primary or original research. A related error is the confusing of an evaluation of precedent research with one's original research or one's own findings. This error may be avoided if one has a clear research issue statement and systematically approaches precedent research as described in this text.

Documentation

While the taking of notes is not a difficult issue, some basic issues should be addressed that will serve the researcher in the preparation both of the precedent research and as one is doing the original research as well. At least the following basic rules will serve to help:

- Keep a complete and accurate bibliographic record.
- Take notes only around topics suggested by your research questions and needed in your outline.

- Keep a careful distinction between direct (word-for-word) quotations and paraphrases. In either case the citation should be correct. For example, a direct quotation might be cited as follows: (Pfannenstiel, 1988, p. 238). On the other hand, if the reference is simply an interpretation or paraphrase of the author the citation would be as follows: (Pfannenstiel, 1988). Again, if one is using a computerized database or spreadsheet the same kinds of categories should be kept.
- Unmarked quotations result in plagiarism, which may result in a failure for a paper, course, expulsion from a degree program, termination from a teaching position, or legal action.

It is not difficult using a standard word processor or database program to devise a simple note system. Notes should be taken in the same format as the final product whether in APA, MLA, or some other format so that when they are carried into the final document, they will be correct and the citations will be correct. Given the number of notes normally required for a project, thesis or dissertation, a systematic way of tracking which notes have been used is essential.

Several note-taking software programs are available. One popular program is called "Endnote." It facilitates the taking of notes, keeping track of citations, assisting with references cited, and then generating the appropriate citations in the correct format. The current edition, for example, is fully updated with APA 6th edition. It will also work with Portable Document Format (.pdf) files and track DOI information from online documents. It is widely available for purchase.

Organizing an Approach to Evaluate Precedent Research

The review of the literature should demonstrate that the author is "conversant" with all of the significant authors and issues as they have written about the central research issue being addressed in the study. The review of the literature may comprise a single chapter or several chapters in a research study.

Major Categories

The evaluation should be divided into the categories which support the major concerns of the study including the background, major issue, research questions or hypotheses, theoretical framework, values, methodology, and significance of the study. The evaluation of the precedent research should broadly address the categories of the research questions or hypotheses. The others mentioned categories may be needed to address the background or context of the study and the specific method(s) to be used. If the study will serve as an evaluation, the establishment of the values may be a significant section as well. The categories of the evaluation should allow one to validate the problem and methodology easily.

Summaries of Evaluations

The evaluation of literature related to each category should conclude with a summary. The summaries should provide the perspectives upon which the study will be made not just what different authors may have written. As one has considered all of the perspectives, a summary will give direction to the whole study will serve both the researcher and the reader.

Value(s) Identification

If the study is an evaluative one, the review of the literature should identify the values which are to be used. Again, the evaluation of the issues at hand should be relevant to the central research issue. If the identification of values constitutes a stage in the original or primary research, a section supporting that section should still be included in the precedent research section.

Location of the Evaluation

The location of the review of the literature may logically precede the statement of the central research issue or may follow it. It will normally precede a description of the methodology unless the methodology is simple and included with the central research issue in an introductory chapter.

Constraints to the Evaluation of Precedent Research

The review of the literature is to be tightly constrained in both the proposal and final dissertation to reviewing only what is germane to the central research issue. Several questions may serve as constraints to guide the selection of the literature: 1) Does it help one understand the context and background of the study? 2) Does it follow the categories suggested by the research questions or hypotheses? 3) Does it serve to establish the values or criteria for making judgments about the data that are to be collected? 4) Does it serve to guide in the selection and validation of appropriate methods? 5) Does it provide a theoretical base for the interpretation and application of the findings? The only literature that should be reviewed then is literature that serves to assist one in addressing the central research issue. For missiological research this precedent research may come from a variety of disciplinary perspectives, unless the study has been delimited to a single discipline. However, regardless of the discipline, the evaluation of precedent research must be constrained by the scope of the central research issue.

Summary

A review of the precedent research serves as a critical foundation for a research project. Only the naive and foolish researcher would be so bold as to launch into a study with the audacity to assume that his or her research is the original and only relevant research about a given topic. Wise researchers will always turn to what has been done previously for counsel and insight about every stage of the research design. Table 2 suggests some of the ways a review of precedent research relates to the other parts of a research design.

TABLE 2
Relationship of the Review of Precedent Research to Research Design

Stage of the Design	Contributions to a Review of Precedent Research	Contributions from a Review of Precedent Research
Background	Selection of categories	Information about the context
Purpose	Initial narrowing of scope	Justification of the purpose
Goals	Further narrowing of scope	Justification of the goals
Central Research Issue	Identification of key variables	Identification of key variables, justification of central issue; provision of the theoretical perspective(s) to understand and address the issue
Research Questions	Provide categories for literature to review	Identification of what questions have been answered, what questions need to be asked, and how to ask the questions
Significance	Provides questions about how the study will relate to ministry, application, and the academic disciplines involved	Provides insights for applications personally, to agencies or churches, and to the academic disciplines involved

Stage of the Design	Contributions to a Review of Precedent Research	Contributions from a Review of Precedent Research
Values	Provide a set of criteria for evaluating the precedent research	May provide the values for an evaluation study
Assumptions	Provide perspective(s) for interpreting the precedent research	Provide the foundations for describing one's assumptions.
Definitions	Provide perspective(s) for interpreting the precedent research	May provide standard or precedent research-based definitions
Delimitations/Scope	Defines the arena for both primary and secondary research	Helps one identify what has been researched previously and what still needs to be researched
Data Collection	May require a return to the literature to provide valid and reliable ways to analyze what is found	Provides information about valid and reliable ways to collect, analyze, and interpret data
Data Analysis	A review of precedent research is not to be a part of the data to be analyzed	Provides information about valid and reliable ways to analyze the data as well as the values for evaluative studies
Findings	What is discovered in precedent research may not be considered as findings because this information and/or theory has already been reported as found!	Provides perspective(s) the values and theoretical bases for reporting the findings
Conclusions	No conclusions may be drawn from precedent research because the research "belongs" to the original researcher	Provides perspectives, criteria, and values for drawing conclusions
Recommendations	Recommendations may not be drawn from precedent research	Provides perspectives for making recommendations both in terms of the application of the present research and what may be recommended for further research

4

RESEARCH METHODS

This chapter introduces the principal issues of selecting an appropriate research method or methods for a missiological research project.

Research methods address two fundamental issues: the collection and analysis of data. The proposed methods in a research *proposal* should describe in adequate detail what methods will be used so the research design could be done by another competent researcher. The data collection and analysis procedures along with any expected limitations should be clear to the reader. The naive researcher who simply passes off the proposed methodology as doing "library research" or "field research" has simply not done the essential work. The methods section in a *completed report* should describe the methods used well enough for another competent researcher to evaluate the methods for reliability and validity or to replicate them. If the study contains a theological component the author should clearly address the issues of trustworthiness and truth.

Methodological Foundational Issues

Two foundational issues require attention from every research method used to support missiological research. Different social science discipline-related methods address these issues somewhat differently, but *validity* and *reliability* require consistent serious attention. Validity refers to asking the right questions, securing the right information and making the appropriate applications. Reliability, on the other hand, relates to consistency or the stability of the results. Because of the multiplicity of methods available and the number of occasions where multidisciplinary approaches are used to address missiological research, a researcher must evaluate the potential methods to be used. While a given topic may be approached from more than one methodological direction, the questions about reliability and validity must be asked. Methodological approaches from differing disciplinary perspectives will produce different findings. The researcher must decide which is the most valid approach for the given central research issue. One should not select a research methodology because it is the favorite of one's mentor or because it may produce the results one assumes to be true. One should begin with the central issue and ask, "What is the most valid and reliable way to approach this issue?"

In a parallel way theological research requires attention to the parallel issues of trustworthiness and truth. (For a more comprehensive consideration of these two characteristics see the chapter by Van Engen.)

Validity

Validity is the central issue of a research methodology. One must ask, "Does the study indeed address the issues it claims to address?" The issue may relate to the design of the study or research or it may relate to the way it is applied. If the design is faulty, then one may not draw trustworthy conclusions or make reasonable recommendations based on the research.

The issue of validity carries an ethical dimension as well. After research has been done, the researcher often claims and is perceived to be an authority or expert about the subject at hand. However, if the research design was not valid or if the application of the results extends beyond what is justified by the design, the person will be guilty of deceit. For example, if a person does research about the equipping of Christian leaders in a Western cultural context and then seeks to apply the findings of the study in a non-Western setting, the validity of the study may be called into question because of generalizing beyond the scope of the research.

The issue of validity arises in every kind of disciplinary research in the social sciences. However, because methods and subject matter differ from one discipline to another, the issue is treated somewhat differently. However, a researcher must ask, "Is this study indeed addressing the issue it is claiming to address?" The following table lists some of the commonly noted kinds of validity addressed in research-related literature.

TABLE 3
Types of Validity

Type	Major Issue	Method to Test Validity	Application	Example
Face validity	Does the instrument appear to measure what it claims to measure from a popular perspective?	Opinion by people observing the research method	Simple non-technical check of a research instrument	Pastors asked if a questionnaire would indeed measure the attitudes of parishioners about a different ethnic group in their community
Content validity	Does the instrument indeed test or measure the issues about which conclusions will be drawn? (Isaac and Michael, 1985, p. 119)	"Logically conclude whether or not the test [or instrument] comprises an adequate definition of what it claims to measure" (Isaac and Michael, 1985, p. 119). Does the measure test the full range of meanings in the subject to be examined?	Achievement test, questionnaire treating cultural issues	An examination in a class used to assess whether students have mastered the content of the class. Or, does a given questionnaire measure intergenerational worldview differences?
Criterion-related, concurrent or predictive validity	How well does an instrument relate to an external criterion?	Administer the instrument and see if it measures what it claims to measure	Tests are often given to predict behavior	The TOEFL exam is commonly given to test English proficiency to determine one's ability to succeed where English is required. If one's test results match the expected results the test is considered valid
Construct validity	Do the variables being tested logically and theoretically relate to the ones in the instrument?	"Based on the theory underlying the test, set up hypotheses regarding the behavior of persons with high or low scores. Test the hypothesis" (Isaac and Michael, 1985, p. 119)	Testing whether concepts or theories apply	One might ask, "Does Clinton's 'Leadership Emergence Theory' apply to Chinese Christian women?"

Type	Major Issue	Method to Test Validity	Application	Example
Internal validity	With experimental research has one controlled for all of the variables which may confuse or confound the experiment? The question is whether the independent variable really did bring a change in the dependent variable	All of the variables must be controlled in a way that extraneous variables cannot influence the outcome of the experiment*	Whenever an experiment is conducted, these issues must be addressed	One might question whether one teaching method produces better results than another method. To test the question an experiment could be conducted
External validity	To what extent are the findings generalizable or applicable?	How was the sample selected? Did all members of the population have an equal opportunity to be chosen? Was the selection selective or random?	The conclusions and recommendations of a study are applied. The applications can only apply to the extent the sample design permits	Having drawn a sample from a group of missionaries and studied these missionaries, recommendations are made to all of the missionaries from the "population" from which the sample was drawn

The question of external validity, generalizability, or applicability of the findings of a study often generates errors with emerging researchers. They invest a significant amount of time, effort, and expense in a research project and then genuinely believe that the results of the study can be applied much more widely than can be justified. Often, researchers doing missiological research will produce findings that would not necessarily be discovered by another person. The person has personal experience and

---

* Campbell and Stanley (1966, p. 5) describe eight extraneous variables that may threaten internal validity. These variables include the following: History, that is, have other events happened during the course of the study other than the experimental treatment that may influence the outcomes? Maturation, that is, are there normal processes in the group that may produce results that could be mistakenly confused with the experimental variable? Pretesting, that is, the administration of a pre-test may influence the final outcome. Measuring instruments, that is, changes in the measuring instruments or the observers may change the outcomes. Statistical regression, that is, if a group is selected on the basis of an extreme score, regression toward a more normal situation may appear to be the result of the experimental variable. Differential selection of subjects, that is, the control group and the experimental group may be different from the beginning and not different due to the experimental variable. Experimental mortality, that is, some respondents may be lost from either the control group or the experimental group thus biasing the results of the study. Selection-maturation interaction, that is, an interaction may occur between the experimental variable and certain preexisting differences in the subjects. This interaction rather than the independent variable may cause the change or lack of change.

insight in a situation and interprets the findings out of the perspective of personal experience. When one seeks to apply these insights to another situation, care must be taken because the perspective is certainly less of a proof or absolute truth than personal insight. In missiological research, researchers may often use small samples or case studies in order to gain a deeper view of the issue at hand or to build theory.

Neely (1995, pp. xvii-xix) notes how case studies may be useful for bringing together more comprehensive views of a given context. This comprehensive view may include descriptions of a wide range of contextual variables, personal variables, history and the inclusion of other related studies. The study of cases may prove extremely valuable for the missiologist in planning strategy after looking at a complex situation. He writes,

> case studies utilize all these approaches by selecting incidents in the lives of one or more persons, focusing on their experiences in their historical contexts, identifying the issues involved, and coming to individual an collective conclusions as to what should or what did in fact transpire. Careful analysis—reaching a conclusion and defending it—is the goal of doing a case study, not consensus within the group. (1995, p. xvii)

This kind of in-depth study may produce very valuable new insights and open the way for the development of new theory. Babbie warns, however, "By its very comprehensiveness . . . this understanding is less generalizable than results based on rigorous sampling and standardized measurements" (1995, p. 302). A third common risk to external validity or generalizability relates to biases in the sampling. If the research has been done in a nonrandomized way, the selection of the respondents always presents a potential problem. Are they in fact "typical" of the whole? Do they represent the characteristics of others in the population for whom the study is intended? A biased sample will invalidate the applicability to the larger group.

The author once had a student who made this kind of error. The student was studying leadership in a denomination of about 1.5 million members. This denomination represented about 30 different ethnic groups in a single country. The student held a responsible position in the church leadership structure and so was personally acquainted with all of the senior leadership of the denomination. He designed a questionnaire and seeking to have a high return rate on the questionnaire, he sent it to all of his friends who were leaders in the denomination. These leaders while spread across the country were largely from one ethnic group which happened to be the same as the student's. He collected the results, drew conclusions, and prepared recommendations. These conclusions and recommendations were then applied across the whole denomination and across the whole spectrum of ethnic groups in that church. This kind of error in external validity or generalizability will discredit the research and mislead the people who seek to follow the recommendations.

Worldview and Validity

Issues of validity become much more complex when one crosses a cultural barrier because of differences in worldview. One's worldview provides the deep level assumptions about issues of cause, classification or categorization, the relationship between the spiritual, social, and physical worlds, the relationship between an individual and the group, the relationship between a person and the material universe, and issues of time and events (Kraft, 1996). People in a given culture or subculture, will share assumptions about which they do not need to speak or debate. However, people in another culture or subculture will not share these same assumptions. The implications for research are obvious. When one crosses into another culture or subculture, the assumptions will differ. Perceptions or assigned meanings of any given event or of a set of phenomena will differ. Also, all researchers go with their own worldviews and "perceptual grids." These differences can be expected to generate misunderstandings as well as new insights in the research. The differences in worldview are not just differences in language, but are major differences in the ways the world and experience are understood and acted upon.

The author was acquainted with a family in Kenya who all came to faith in Christ. The head of the family had been an influential diviner and was from a large family of diviners. When he was converted along with his family, he and his immediate family burned all of their fetishes and amulets on the day they were baptized. Their conversion prompted his relatives who were also diviners to pronounce a death curse upon him and his family. A short time later, he became seriously ill with tuberculosis. He spent several months living in a house alongside a missionary doctor who prayed with him daily and treated him daily with streptomycin and isoniazid (INH). He fully recovered. One might ask, "Why did he get sick? Why did he get well?" An American researcher from the World Health Organization might say, "His diet was poor. He was in a weakened condition because of a drought. TB is common in the area. He contracted TB because he was exposed to the TB bacteria and his body was unable to resist it. He recovered because he had improved food and medical care for several months."

The Turkana people among whom this man is a leader "knew" that the reason he became ill and nearly died was because of the curses the other diviners had placed on him. They knew the doctor was a Christian and that his prayers were often answered not only for people who are ill, but when he prayed for rain, it would often rain. They "knew" he recovered because of the prayers of the Christian doctor. The worldview (theological position) of a researcher studying this situation would influence at least the following issues:

- How the research issue would be framed and what research questions would be asked to address the issue.
- What precedent research in the area would be relevant (e.g., health surveys, local beliefs and practices about cursing, what biblical texts might or might not be cited).
- What method(s) would be employed to collect data about the situation.
- What evidence would be considered as relevant to be recorded.
- Who would be questioned.
- What lessons, conclusions, recommendations would be made.
- To or for whom the recommendations would be made.

The above illustration also shows that a given missiological situation might require more than one research method in order to understand fully. Notice that the medical doctor did approach the situation from two different, but complementary ways. He used modern medical research methods to diagnose the person. He did the usual microscopic exam of sputum after taking a case history. He treated the patient according to contemporary medical practice. He also, in taking the case history, looked for issues of cursing and believed that healing comes from God. He took the opportunity to pray daily with this patient and to use the three months of care for discipling and encouraging his recovering patient to talk to the broader community about his recovery and why he was recovering from his perspective. He combined medical research, anthropological research and theology to address this problem. Questions of validity arose within each of these disciplinary approaches as the case was being examined and actions were taken. In this case the theological issues of trustworthiness and truth were central for the medical doctor and the converted diviner. Incidentally, the "healing" of this former diviner was catalytic in the establishment of more than sixty churches among the Turkana (Elliston, 1987).

Validity in Multidisciplinary Research

In a multidisciplinary approach the research methods may differ, but the conclusions and recommendations to be valid should be complementary. Truth, even as seen from different perspectives, will not be contradictory, but complementary as the example given. Often when valid research has been conducted from a set of multidisciplinary perspectives, the results will challenge or enlarge the worldview of the researcher and the commonly held assumptions in each of the disciplines employed. Whenever multidisciplinary research is done, each method used needs to be rigorously evaluated in terms of how validity and reliability are addressed. The same constraints apply for a multimethod approach within a given discipline.

Reliability

Reliability is the degree of consistency of a research instrument or method. The question of reliability is "whether a particular technique, applied repeatedly to the same object, would yield the same result each time" (Babbie, 1995, p. 124). Reliability serves as a major "subset" of validity. If a research study is not reliable, it will not be valid. A thermometer is expected to be reliable, that is, it is expected to produce consistent results every time it is used. A reliable thermometer would be expected to always produce the same results as another reliable thermometer that is designed to measure the same range of temperature. However, a thermometer designed to measure the temperature of a human would not provide either reliable or valid results to measure either the outdoors temperature or Kelvin temperatures that measure light or color.

Reliability does not guarantee validity. One can consistently measure the wrong thing and obtain consistent results! When I was learning to speak the Maasai language, the goal was to learn to speak correctly so to be understood and understand all that others would say. Along the way, I was encouraged to take a written exam to measure my progress. I refused because the test would not be valid, even though it might provide reliable or consistent results.

Reliability does not ensure accuracy. One may adjust a scale to weigh either heavy or light. The scale would reliably or consistently weigh with whatever adjustment would be made and not be accurate. A consistent error from a research instrument relates to the validity of the measuring instrument. "A measuring instrument cannot be valid if it is not also reliable. Reliability is an essential component in validity" (Ary, Jacobs and Razavieh, 1972, p. 201).

Two kinds of errors occur when considering reliability: random errors and constant errors. Random error could be illustrated by the ancient measure of a cubit (i.e., the length of a forearm). If a long distance were to be measured, random error could be expected because different people have different length forearms. If a person were to use translations of a questionnaire with different language groups, random errors could be expected because the instruments differ. Constant errors could be expected from an inappropriate research instrument as with the proposed written exam to test oral and aural competency.

Random error is a principal threat to reliability. One can assume that even with the best instrument to measure social or spiritual issues some errors will occur. While it is beyond the scope of this text to probe the depths of theory of reliability, these issues should be treated as one selects and develops the method or methods for a given research project. The errors of measurement need to be addressed whether one is using a questionnaire, an interview guide, or observation in a community or experiment.

To improve reliability one may use at least three different common methods: test-retest, equivalent forms, and split-half (all of which are based on correctional procedures). Other statistical methods may be employed, but they are beyond the scope of this text.

Test-Retest

One may administer the same instrument to a group on two occasions and correlate the results. For example, a typing test could be given on successive days and the scores correlated to provide a reliability coefficient known as *the coefficient of stability*. This kind of procedure is limited in application because human qualities, characteristics, skills, and attitudes change over time. The instrument itself may initiate some change. These changes would probably result in an underestimation of the reliability of the instrument being used (Ary, et al. 1971, p. 205). This kind of procedure is inappropriate where memory may be a factor. It is largely applicable for skill applications.

Equivalent Forms

The procedure of administering equivalent forms (sometimes referred to as alternate or parallel forms) is used when the group might recall their responses to a previous test. An example, commonly used in institutions of higher education to test English competency for international students is the TOEFL© test. Five alternate forms of this test are commonly used in the USA (Ary, et al.). If two forms of a test are administered at the about the same time the measure of reliability (reliability coefficient) is called the *coefficient of equivalence* (p. 205). This measurement of reliability is "the most rigorous measure available for determining the reliability of a test" (p. 205).

Split-Half Reliability

Reliability may be measured from a single administration of an instrument by using "split-half" procedures. A single instrument is administered one time to a group. The items on the instrument or test are then divided into two comparable halves. Scores for each set of items or questions are then correlated. This procedure presents problems of securing equivalent or comparable halves. Obviously, longer tests would be more reliable than shorter ones using this kind of procedure. When using the Spearman-Brown prophecy formula[12] this approach to checking reliability tends to overestimate the reliability.

Interpreting Reliability

If reliability coefficients range between 0.70 and 0.90, Ary, et al. (1971) suggest most researchers will be satisfied. However, as one looks at the interpretation of the measures of reliability several variables ought to be considered, such as the length of the test or instrument, the heterogeneity of the group, the readability of the test or instrument for the research subjects and technique for interpreting the reliability (p. 210).

The standard error of measurement estimates "the range of variation in a set of repeated measurements of the same thing" (p. 210). If one were to measure the same thing repeatedly, differences in the measurements could be expected. The standard deviation of these variations is the *standard error of measurement*. This standard deviation may be interpreted as any other standard deviation. This measure may provide a useful alternative for measuring reliability.

Applying Reliability to Other Methods

Reliability issues apply to every kind of research including research done in church or mission contexts. One may reliably measure some dimensions of "spirituality" by counting the number of times and the amount of time one spends in prayer, Bible study, and worship. However, while this set of measurements may be reliable, they may not produce valid results. These issues are not all of the variables and so

---

12   http://www.economicexpert.com/a/Spearman:Brown:prediction:formula.html retrieved on 1/31/2010.

would not be valid even though one could obtain consistent results by applying the same research instrument repeatedly.

One may enhance reliability in social related research by asking respondents questions that they can be expected to answer knowledgeably. For example, while many pastors would understand some basic issues in missiology, to ask technical questions or theoretical questions about missiology of a group of pastors would likely result in less than reliable responses. Similarly, if a researcher uses technical language in other contexts in questionnaires or questionnaires, reliability decreases.

Reliability increases by asking the questions in the same way. Reliability often becomes a problem when one is interviewing because the questions may be asked in slightly different or subtly different ways. A different facial gesture, a difference in tone, rhythm or stress or a difference in word order can generate significantly different responses. Even when questionnaires are administered, reliability can be seriously threatened if the explanations are not given in precisely the same way. Some researchers prefer to record the instructions rather than risk lowering the reliability of the findings. The context where the questionnaire or interviews is administered may also alter the reliability.

Crossing cultural boundaries poses numerous threats to reliability. When one crosses a cultural boundary, one can expect that the worldview will differ and the respondents' assumptions will differ. The ways that the questions will be perceived and answers will differ. A questionnaire or interview guide that is valid and reliable in one culture cannot be expected to be reliable in a second culture. An unreliable measure is always invalid.

Accuracy of information from questionnaires and interviews is an essential component to reliable statistics. When accuracy is lacking, reliability obviously will be low. A researcher may use a statistical expression of reliability called a "Coefficient of Reliability" as an expression of the level of reliability of a given instrument.

If one is depending on the use of precedent research, then the researcher must give attention to the validity and assumptions of the original design. One may have impressive statistics, prose descriptions or graphics, but if the original design was faulty, the results will not be reliable and hence not valid. The results can only mislead a researcher in new research.

The following figures are adapted from Babbie (1995) and show the relationship between reliability and validity. If the measurements are unreliable, they are either measuring the wrong thing (if they are constant) or inappropriately designed (if they produce random errors).

FIGURE 3
Valid and Reliable (1995, p. 128)

Reliable & Valid

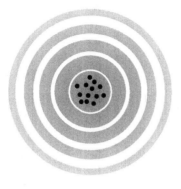

FIGURE 4
Not Reliable, Not Valid (1995, p. 128)

Not Reliable & Not Valid

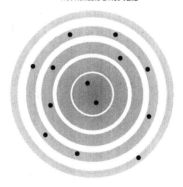

FIGURE 5
Not Valid, But Reliable (1995, p. 128)

Reliable, Not Valid

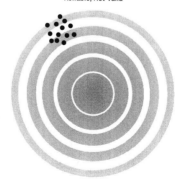

Methods Selection

As soon as one has the problem statement clearly written and the research questions clearly written, two or three different methods may work. Until the issue is clearly stated, only one method may appear as possible. However, not every method is as rigorous as another as it would be applied to a specific research issue. And, not every method fits one's skills, logistics, cultural context, resources, time, or other constraints. One has to balance what would best fit the immediate situation in terms of these variables to be as rigorous as possible. Some questions immediately emerge: What would in fact eliminate threats to validity? What would eliminate threats to reliability? What would eliminate alternative explanations? What would provide the largest possible sample? And, what method would allow the most powerful and most appropriate statistical tests? Or, what combinations of methods or disciplinary approaches could reliably and validly address the issue?

Initially, the researcher must ask several questions such as the following:

- Does the study aim to develop theory as a typical qualitative study?
- Does the study aim to test theory as a typical quantitative study?
- Does the study seek to provide useful information for decision making? If so, are the values established?
- What kinds of information are needed?
- Are values or criteria for making judgments needed?
- Is the research to be done in one or multiple cultural settings?
- What resources are available for the research—sponsorships, research assistance, and/or consulting?
- Does the researcher have the commitment, time, energy, skills, and requisite knowledge to address the proposed issue with the proposed method(s)?
- What alternative methods or combination of methods appears to be valid and reliable?
- Would an approach from another discipline shed new light in the resolution of the central research issue?
- Given the topic and propose context for the research, what precedent research is available?

Categorizing Research

For the purpose of this text, I divided research methods into three broad categories: descriptive, experimental, and evaluative research. The first and third categories are used extensively in missiological research; the second category is used less often. Research is often divided into quantitative or qualitative approaches. Clearly, both of these approaches may characterize the complexities of missiological research.

Descriptive Research

Descriptive research generally serves to *develop* theory. As one has described what has been or is true in a situation and then provides an explanation of the phenomena, theory is developed. Often one continues in the development of the related theory to show from the patterns of what has been described how to predict what is likely to occur in the future and to suggest basis for action based on the description of the phenomena. Presumably, since the description of the phenomena was done in a responsible way, the means for authenticating or validating the theory will also be done. The purpose then of descriptive research generally serves in theory development. Descriptive research may also provide the essential information for evaluative research. However, description by itself, of course, is not evaluation.

Descriptive research takes several significantly different forms and is supported by a wide range of research methods. Some commonly used forms of descriptive research used to support church-related research include: historical research, survey research with questionnaires and interviews, participant observation, ethnographic descriptions, applications of grounded theory, exegetical studies, case studies and theological research. In each of these approaches to the research, a description of what is or has been comes into focus. No manipulation or control of the variables is expected. Judgments are not made on the basis of outside values or criteria.

Any given research method has related limitations. For example, case studies are often used in missiological research (Neeley, 1995). However, the selection of the cases including the number of cases, range of variables to be addressed and the methods used to address the cases such as interviews, questionnaires, observation, documentary research, or other common methods all leave the generalizability at risk. Case studies may be useful for initial descriptive research to identify variables or develop a preliminary theory for testing, but one must be careful not to press the implications of the findings of case studies too far.

Descriptive research allows the combination of multiple methods in order to describe better a given situation. For example, participant observation may be combined with interviewing to provide a base for understanding a local situation.

Exegetical and theological research is also descriptive. Exegetical research provides a means for understanding what the text says. Theological research seeks to explain both God's Word and his works. In both cases the outcome is the development of theory which aims to be both trustworthy and truthful.

Descriptive research may be used to describe a wide range of variables from observable phenomena to other theories or values. The description of both values and a set of phenomena may serve as a base for "evaluative research" that will be described later.

Descriptive research is typically qualitatively applied in missiological research. The theoretical outcomes should serve to explain the phenomena being researched, provide bases for action, and provide bases for testing the theory.

Some descriptive research will involve quantitative methods. Many survey instruments provide vast amounts of numerical data requiring statistical analyses. The outcome of the analyses, however, serves to describe a context or situation. The surveys may aim at whole populations or a variety of kinds of samples (e.g., random, stratified). Even within a single discipline descriptive research may require highly complex statistical planning and analysis.

Experimental Research

Experimental research differs from descriptive research in its purpose and in key parts of the methods used. Experimental research falls into the category of quantitative research. Statistical analyses are commonly expected to address the numbers in the data generated. The purpose typically is to *test theory* in a controlled situation. A researcher will propose a tentative explanation of what is expected to occur (a theory as expressed in thesis or hypothesis) and will set up conditions in which the variables can be controlled, manipulated, and observed to test this proposed explanation. These three characteristics of experimental research set it apart from descriptive and evaluative research. To the extent that all of the variables can be controlled, manipulated and accurately observed one can test and refine the theory.

A researcher will seek to control all of the variables that may occur except the *dependent variable,* that is, the outcome or resulting variable. The researcher will manipulate the *independent* or causal variable or variables. With a multivariant analysis one would manipulate more than one independent or causal variable.

Observation follows the manipulation of variables. One must measure the outcomes of the treatment done by the researcher. The idea of the experiment is that one has controlled all of the variables including all of the extraneous variables that may have interfered with the possible outcomes. One then introduces the independent variable, or the causal variable. One can then say, "That variable caused the change." In some church and mission situations, it would be virtually impossible to do an experiment because one does not have the potential for maintaining control of the setting. And, in many cases it is not possible to manipulate the variables. One simply describes what is present and that is one of the reasons experimental research is not used as often in missiological research.

The assumptions about control are clear. If two situations are equal in every respect except for a factor that is added to or deleted from one of the situations, any difference appearing between the two situations can be attributed to that variable. That statement is called the "Law of the Single Variable." Now the second assumption: If two situations are not equal, but it can be demonstrated that none of the variables is significant in producing the phenomena under investigation, or if the significant variables are made equal, any difference occurring between the two situations after the introduction of the new variable to one of the systems can be attributed to the new variable (i.e., the "Law of the Only Significant Variable"). That is probably the more significant one that we have as we look at many kinds of social experiments. Experimental research in missiology is often inappropriate because of the sovereignty of God in His mission. One cannot control God's sovereign actions whether seen as prevenient grace or predestination. His spirit moves and acts as He wills without human control. While as believers we may expect God to act, we cannot predict His methods. Who would or could have predicted any of His actions recorded in the Scriptures?

Some situations allow for control and thus for experimentation, but many circumstances simply do not allow the conditions required for experimental research.

Controls must be effective for extraneous variables. And, one has to be careful that these controls do not affect the dependent variable. Controls need not be designed for variables which have no effect on the dependent variable (outcome). If one has an "if-then statement" he would say, If: independent variable, Then: dependent variable. Without control, confounding may occur, allowing extraneous variables to affect the dependent variable in such a way that effects of independent variable cannot be separated. For example, if one does not control for the normal extraneous variables, the reliability of the study will likely be seriously threatened. For example, if one does not control for history, that is, what happens over time, then the normal maturation will confound the experiment—let us say one is doing a study over time, an experiment of development of leaders over time. Look at the question of training. Did the training make a difference? It may be that simply the training that people are having makes the difference, and the experience they are having outside the training makes no difference. It may be that the experience occurring outside of the training is more significant. It may be that the people who are getting the training are getting one kind of experience and the people who are not getting the training are getting another kind of experience. These kinds of variables must be controlled. It may be that the testing—the very testing that the researcher is using—is affecting the outcomes. All of these kinds of variables must be controlled.

One can assure control in a variety of ways. Probably, the most commonly used and easiest one to think about is simple randomization. Theoretically, randomization is the only method of controlling all possible extraneous variables. Several methods are available to randomize to initiate control.

The second characteristic of experimental design is manipulation. Manipulation is the treatment or the operation that researcher does. Either a single variable or multiple variables may be manipulated. For example, in a class one might at some point design an experiment to test whether a lecture is more effective or whether a seminar group is more effective. One would randomly select students from the population of students, and then set up control groups out of the sample. Then the researcher would be careful to measure the difference between the control group who was not treated and the experimental group that was to examine any variance in their scores.

The following table adapted from Isaac and Michael (1985) suggests eight different experimental designs. These designs vary in terms of control and reliability. The designs address different kinds of reliability issues.

TABLE 4
A Comparison of Eight Experimental Designs

Design Number	Description	Design
1	One-Group Pretest-Posttest	$T_1 \ X \ T_2$
2	Control-Group Pretest-Posttest	$E_R \ T_1 \ X \ T_2$ $C_R \ T_1 \ . \ T_2$
3	Randomized Solomon Four-Group Design	$E_{R1} \ T_1 \ X \ T_2$ $C_{R1} \ T_1 \ . \ T_2$ $C_{R2} \quad X \ T_2$ $C_{R2} \quad . \ T_2$

Design Number	Description	Design
4	Randomized Control-Group Posttest Only	E_R X T_2 C_R . T_2
5	Nonrandomized Control-Group Pretest-Posttest	$E\,T_1$ X T_2 $C\,T_1$. T_2
6	Counterbalanced Treatments	$X_a\ X_b\ X_c\ X_d$ 1 A* B C D 2 B D A C 3 C A D B 4 D C B A *A, B, C, and D represent each of four groups of subjects, respectively.
7	One-Group Time-Series	$T_1 T_2 T_3 T_4$ X $T_5 T_6 T_7 T_8$
8	Control Group Time Series	$T_1 T_2 T_3 T_4$ X $T_5 T_6 T_7 T_8$ $T_1 T_2 T_3 T_4$. $T_5 T_6 T_7 T_8$

(Adapted from Isaac and Michael, 1985, p. 74)

Legend:

X—Experimental treatment (independent variable)
$T_5 T_6 T_7 T_8$ —Post testing (Designs 7-8)
X_2, X_3, X_4, X_5 (Design 6) —Treatment variations
E—Experimental group
. —No treatment

C—Control group
T_1 —Pretest (Designs 1-5)
$_R$—Random selection
T_2 —Posttest (Designs 1-5)
$T_1 T_2 T_3 T_4$ —Pretesting (Designs 7-8)

When one examines this series of eight experimental designs, the issue of differential control becomes immediately obvious. Some of these designs obviously control for various threats to validity. Depending on one's situation one or another of these experimental designs will serve better. The issues one would have to consider would be the potential threats to validity and reliability, the ethics of the situation, and one's resources. Any of these three sets of concerns could either encourage or discourage the use of one or another experimental design.

TABLE 5
Relative Validity of Experimental Designs

Sources of Invalidity	Little Control		Rigorous Control			Partial Control		
	1	2	3	4	5	6	7	8
Internal Validity								
Contemporary history	No	Yes	Yes	Yes	Yes	Yes	No	Yes
Maturation processes	No	Yes	Yes	Yes	Yes	Yes	Yes	Yes
Pretesting procedures	No	Yes	Yes	Yes	Yes	Yes	Yes	Yes
Measuring instruments	No	Yes	Yes	Yes	Yes	Yes	?	Yes
Statistical regression	?	Yes	Yes	Yes	?	Yes	Yes	Yes
Differential selection of subjects	Yes	Yes	Yes	Yes	Yes	Yes	Yes	Yes
Experimental mortality	Yes	Yes	Yes	Yes	Yes	Yes	Yes	Yes
Interaction of selection and maturation	?	Yes	Yes	Yes	No	?	?	Yes
External Validity								
Interaction of selection and X	No	?	?	?	?	?	?	No
Interaction of pretesting and X	No	No	Yes	Yes	No	?	No	No
Reactive experimental procedures	?	?	?	?	?	?	?	?

(Isaac and Michael, 1985, p. 76)

Qualitative research rests at the heart of much missiological research. The issues of "qualities" or the most important dimensions of social, cultural, and/or spiritual life often characterize missiological research. Worldview issues, values, attitudes, and spirituality are only a few of the kinds of issues addressed in qualitative research. This perspective of research may fit into the categories of "descriptive" or "evaluative" research, but generally not into experimental research where the findings are often reported in numerical or statistical form.

Cresswell (2003, pp. 181-183) suggests a list of qualitative research characteristics. "Qualitative research," he writes,

- "takes place in the natural setting. The qualitative researcher often goes to the site . . . to conduct the research . . .
- uses multiple methods that are interactive and humanistic . . .
- is emergent rather than tightly prefigured . . .
- is fundamentally interpretative . . .
- views social phenomena holistically . . . Qualitative research tends to be broad, panoramic views rather than micro-analyses. The more complex, interactive and encompassing the narrative, the better the qualitative study . . .
- The qualitative researcher systematically reflects on who he or she is in the inquiry and is sensitive to his or her personal biography an how it shapes the study . . .
- uses complex reasoning that is multi-faceted, iterative and simultaneous. Although reasoning is largely inductive, both inductive and deductive processes are at work . . .
- adopts and used one or more strategies of inquiry as a guide for the procedures in the qualitative study."

Missiological research very often fits into this set of characteristics. Researchers frequently engage in the ministry context to discover information related to their missiological concerns and, as has been noted above, engage in multidisciplinary or multimethodological research. Whether doing participative observation as an anthropologist or Grounded Theory, the process is iterative: observe, hypothesize, observe using the emerging hypotheses and then correct with further observation. While details for a given method may vary, this broad outline will be followed. The following diagram illustrates how a qualitative research process typically functions.

FIGURE 6
Inductive Reasoning Process[13]

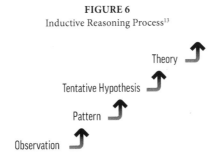

Many research methods depend on numbers and the interpretation of numerical data with the use of statistics. Descriptive, experimental and evaluative research may depend on quantitative methods. Whether a person uses questionnaires, demographic data, psychometric data or other countable measures, the research may be described as quantitative. Countless texts have been written about tests, measurements and statistics. In missiological research quantitative research continues to provide a crucial base along with quantitative research to provide useful information for building theory, testing theory and decision making. Quantitative research may follow inductive or deductive reasoning patterns. The data may fall into nominal, interval or ratio scales for counting and processing. Since this book is not focused on methods, but on research design, the details of neither qualitative nor quantitative statistical methods will be described.

Validity and reliability are issues for every kind of research, that is, for descriptive, experimental, and evaluative methods whether they are qualitative or quantitative. The questions of validity come out very strongly in experimental research. These issues may be more subtle in descriptive and evaluative research.

Validity in data collection has been described as collecting the right or appropriate information. An example cited earlier, the tests from the author's language learning, was giving consistent results—was reliable—but were not valid. It did not test the specific goals for learning of the language.

Several kinds of *internal validity* relate to experimental design. Each of these issues needs to be treated in the design and implementation stages to prevent serious threats to one's study.

Contemporary History – Sometimes the subjects experience an event in or out of the experimental setting, besides the treatment. That experience may affect their scores, that is, the history, whatever else is going on in their context.

---

13   http://www.socialresearchmethods.net/kb/dedind.php retrieved on 1/31/2010.

And something may be present or happen to one of the groups, either the experimental group or the other group that would affect that whole group, thus affecting both the reliability and validity of the research.

Maturation – When doing developmental studies over time, the normal maturation process may be expected to bring change. This maturation process may influence the dependent variables. One should account for the issue of maturation when doing longitudinal studies or studies over time whether of an individual, a group, or a community.

Interaction with Researcher – Interaction with the researcher may influence the process. The pre-testing may bring change, or may bring a bias, and may not help one in terms of understanding the effects of the independent variables. The measuring instruments can affect the outcomes. Sometimes one test is more difficult than another; sometimes they are not equivalent. Sometimes respondents react to the instruments. They do not like the instruments. They may not like the questions. They may have "survey" or "instrument fatigue." They may not like the kinds of scales that are used, and so they give very biased information. Learning styles differ among the same group of people. The interaction with and relationship with the researcher may be expected to influence the outcomes. Even if the respondents do not know the researcher in person, the perceptions of the researcher and the research being done may be expected to have an influence on the responses.

Statistical Regression – In some research, groups are selected on the basis of extreme scores. Whenever people or other variables are selected on the basis of extremes, as they are studied over time, they become more normally distributed and it may not have anything to do at all with the independent variable. It is simply a statistical regression. For example, the students do exceptionally poorly or exceptionally well on one test. And then, a researcher selects them to do an experiment. The mean or the average score of either of these groups will move toward the mean of the parent population on a second test. For example, out of a class of fifty, ten receive "A"s. If a researcher gives them a second test, the mean of that ten will move toward the mean of the whole group, that is, toward the average of the whole group. Again, that is an example of statistical regression. In the selection of people or subject, one needs to be careful about that risk of statistical regression. This risk not only influences experiments, but descriptive research as well.

Differential Selection of Subjects – If the experimental and control groups are exposed to the independent variable, a method of teaching spelling, for example, and afterward a test is given, the test results may reflect a pre-treatment difference in the two groups rather than the effect of X, or the effects of the treatment. Perhaps, the experimental group could spell better than the control group to start with. If one selects the subjects in some way other than randomly, the difference in terms of selection, the bias in terms of selection may generate the results rather than whatever the researcher does.

Differential Experimental Mortality – If a subject drops out of one group after the experiment is under way, the differential loss may affect the findings of the investigation. And, if the group changes over time, that change may seriously affect the outcomes.

Summary – While descriptive research may provide highly accurate and reliable information about relationships among variables, experimental research moves a step further to allow the researcher to address the issue of cause in relationships.

Experimental research is virtually impossible in social and spiritual contexts because it is not feasible to control all of the causes (independent variables) that may be affecting an outcome (dependent variable). Neither research in social contexts nor research about spiritual phenomena can ever be fully replicated in the way that experiments may be replicated in the "hard" or "physical" sciences such as chemistry, biology, or physics. Experiments related to church- or mission-related subjects are often limited because of ethical limitations.

Evaluative Research

Evaluative research does not require a different methodology, but rather depends upon either a descriptive or experimental approach or combination of approaches to collect the required data. However, it differs from the other two basic methods because it requires the establishment of values and the application of these values to what has been discovered from either the descriptive or experimental research methods. The purpose of evaluative research is to provide useful information based on values for decision making. Much church- and mission-related research is evaluative research.

Evaluative research will generally consist of the steps depicted in the following diagram. This diagram is modified from one developed by Ted Ward and John Dettoni (1974, p. 208).

FIGURE 7
Evaluation Research Process

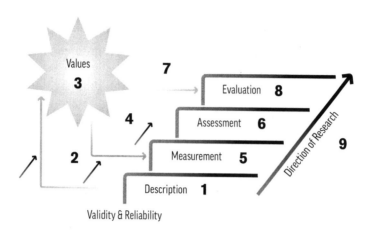

1. The following numbers correspond as an explanation of Figure 7.
2. One begins with a description—that is a description of the problem, a description of the issue, or a description of the decision to be made. This description provides the categories for establishing the structure or process of the evaluation.
3. One uses the central issue or description of the problem to move toward a description of the values.
4. The values or criteria are established outside of the sequence of the principal study. The identification of these values may be a separate, but related study. They may come from any domain that can provide value-based information such as exegetical studies or cultural studies. They provide the criteria for assessing, validity for social science research, or truthfulness and trustworthiness for theological research.
5. Once the values have been established, the next step in the evaluative process is the identification of valid and reliable means to collect measurements of the significant variables. The collection of measurements or data collection must be done so that the methods validly and reliably relate to the values. For theological research the researcher collects the relevant biblical or other information with the truth constraints defined in the values statements.

6. After the appropriate measurements have been taken, a summary of these measurements or an assessment will be made. This assessment needs to be done in a way which meets the standards of validity and reliability that relate to the established values.

7. The values or criteria are then applied to the assessment to provide the evaluation.

8. Without the application of the values or criteria, the summary of measurements or assessment would not be useful information. With the application of values to the assessment it becomes useful for making decisions relative to the original issue around which the values were described.

9. The direction of the research in terms of sequence may be seen by this arrow.

Whether using this model for evaluation or another, the process of evaluation should be seen as a cyclical process that provides useful (value-based) information for decision making (Stufflebeam, 1973, pp. 128-142).

Whether one uses descriptive or experimental research to provide the data collection and analysis parts of evaluative studies, the validity concerns with those methods apply. However, with evaluative studies an additional set of concerns arises. The research must be related to a set of values or criteria. The central issue will provide the focal point for the values, but will in itself seldom provide the values. The values must be obtained from precedent research or perhaps from original research into the relevant values.

Once the central issue has been established along with the relevant values, these values then become important to the guiding of the collection of the data, the processes for summarizing and analyzing the data, as well as interpreting the findings and making applications. They will serve as a set of constraints for checking validity.

Methods—Principal Concerns

For any research project two primary methodological issues must be addressed along with one secondary issue. Regardless of the research method the first issue is data collection. Each academic discipline has its own ways of data collection. After data have been collected, each research method used must provide a way for analysis and reporting. Given any research method or combination of methods, one runs the risk of limitations to the study. These limitations are risks of *validity* and *reliability*. Any limitations or weaknesses of the research method(s) will affect the *generalizability* or *external validity* of the research. While a combination of methods from a given discipline or a multidisciplinary approach will address some potential threats, simply having multiple methods whether in the same discipline or in multiple disciplines, threats should be expected and addressed.

Data Collection

Whatever the research method, a key issue is data collection. Whether it is done by observation, testing, questionnaires, interviews, reading archived documents or experiments, the researcher is expecting to collect data about a given subject. A valid study rests upon the reliable collection of data. If the data collection method is not reliable, then the resulting study cannot be considered valid. Collecting the "right" data is essential for a study to be considered valid.

The selection of a research method is a critical part of the decision-making part of research design. Different methods obviously produce very different results and so one must give attention to the selection of the method(s) that should be used.

Another way to look at research methods is in terms of the interaction with the research subjects. Obviously, for some kinds of research interaction is not possible. However, when dealing with human subjects, often interaction is desirable or essential. One should look from two perspectives: reactive and nonreactive.

Reactive measures include all of these circumstances where the people being studied react to the researcher through questionnaires, interviews or even in participant observation. One key issue the researcher must take into account is the reaction of the respondent. Is it a reliable response? Is it a "typical" response or is the respondent shaping the response to please the researcher or to help the researcher reach the research goals? Would the respondent react in the same way(s) to another person? Reactive measures are essential in social research, but they carry reliability risks with them.

Nonreactive measures, on the other hand, do not influence the measuring. For example, we can go to the library and we can count the number of times a book has been checked out. That does not affect the book; it does not affect the number of times it is going to be checked out. In many kinds of studies, no reaction occurs at all. They are nonreactive. One can look at archives and records. One can do unobtrusive observation.

A given missiological research design may require both reactive and nonreactive measures. Reactive measures may allow one to get into the measures more directly, some of the things that we want to see. However, to validate the findings, one may want to use nonreactive measures as well. If complementary measures are used to affirm reliability or validity, they should be described along with the implications. As one thinks about the methods, one should consider employing both of these kinds of complementary methodologies.

Data Analysis

Analyzing the findings' data comprises an essential part in any research method. Whether one is reviewing the archives of the KGB in Latvia to discover what was done to Christian leaders or whether one is compiling the results of questionnaires from pastors in Los Angeles about small groups, the analysis of the data remains a critical part of the process. If one is doing exegetical work on the role of the Holy Spirit in Luke-Acts, or evaluating the missiology of the Baptist Convention in Myanmar, one may expect the generation of data and the need for valid and reliable analytical procedures.

As with the procedures for the collection of data, data analysis requires rigor to present reliable and valid findings without an ethical offense. The interpretative procedures must obviously fit the data and the collection procedures. One must consider the issue of interpretation before the data are collected to be sure that one has the financial, time, analytical, and other needed resources. A person who has limited skills in statistics should be very careful about embarking on a study which leads to the generation of numerical data.

It is beyond the scope of this text to describe the specific analytical procedures of any specific method. The purpose here is simply point to the fact that a researcher must give attention to the issue of data analysis at the time when the research is being designed. At that time the researcher needs to assess personal skills and resources that will be needed for whatever method(s) may be chosen. If multiple methods are planned, then the integration of both the analysis and outcomes of each method needs to be planned.

Limitations

Regardless of the method or combination of methods used, one may expect risks to validity and reliability along the way. These risks in the research method may limit the study in terms of its reliability and validity. Given any method or combination of methods, the researcher will be expected to seriously consider the potential limitations before initiating the study. These *potential* limitations or weaknesses should be described in the proposal along with the measures that are expected to be taken to ameliorate them. In the final report the *actual* threats to reliability and validity should be described as limitations. Researchers are expected to note these limitations as a matter of integrity at both stages of the research process. The conclusions and recommendations should be restricted with these limitations in mind. Addressing these ethical concerns will either build credibility or serve to discredit the research.

Limitations must be distinguished from delimitations both in the methodology and in the description of the central research issue. "Limitations" at the proposal stage are expected threats or weaknesses in the study that may weaken any of the dimensions of reliability or validity. Limitations arise not only from the nature of the research methods, they may arise externally from the context. One will not be able to anticipate all of the threats that may arise, but will be able to predict many possible issues, having reviewed precedent research to see what others have faced. The researcher should address these anticipated threats to data collection or analysis in the proposal. For example, if one were to use questionnaires in a form of survey research, one will find discussion in the literature what to do about the serious problem of people not returning their questionnaires. The nonreturn of the questionnaires places a limit on the reliability and ultimately on validity of the research. One may anticipate this kind of problem and take steps to facilitate the return of questionnaires and treat the nonrespondents.

Relationship of Methods Section to Other Parts of the Research Design

The relationship of the methods section in both the proposal and the final research report to other parts of the research design requires careful attention. The relationships should be clear through the design of the methodology both in the collection of data and analysis of the data. The following table outlines the key relationships between the methods section and the other parts of the design.

TABLE 6
Relating the Methods to the Overall Research Design

Section of Design	Contributions to the Methods Section	Contributions from the Methods Section
Background	Sets the context for the methods and may provide useful information about anticipated limitations or threats to the research	May provide useful information to describe the context of the study
Purpose	Sets the overall direction and justification for the methods	Helps determine feasibility
Goals	Sets the expected outcomes of the methods	Helps determine feasibility
Central Research Issue	Sets the scope and variables to be addressed; will likely determine whether the research will be qualitative, quantitative or evaluative	Helps determine feasibility
Research Questions/ Hypotheses	Defines how the relationships among the variables will be addressed in both the data collection and analysis stages	Helps determine feasibility
Delimitations	Defines the scope—what will be included and what will be excluded from the methods	Helps determine feasibility
Assumptions	Sets the general perspectives and ground rules for both data collection and analysis	May help identify issues to clarify in assumptions
Definitions	Sets the specific perspectives for addressing key concepts	May help identify issues needing definition
Review of Precedent Research	Validates both the data collection and analytical methods; suggests limitations to avoid and means to address them; suggests ways to report the findings for the specific target audience	Will raise questions of validity, reliability, and feasibility along with the basic questions of how, when, where, who, what, how much data to collect and analyze

Section of Design	Contributions to the Methods Section	Contributions from the Methods Section
Findings	If arenas of findings do not fulfill what was expected, may require additional means of data collection or analysis; may provide alternate ways of reporting the information derived from the findings to assure accurate and ethical communication with the target audience	Provides the only means for supplying the information for the findings
Conclusions	If the findings do not provide adequate, reliable or valid information for the conclusions, then the methods may need to be revised and redone	Provides the only information upon which conclusions may be based
Recommendations	If the findings or conclusions do not provide adequate, reliable, or valid information for the recommendations as called for by the goals, then the methods may need to be revised and redone	Provides the only information upon which recommendations may be based

5

FINDINGS

This chapter describes what should be reported as "findings" from the research methodology. The chapter will describe how only what is discovered from the applied methods and what relates to the central research issue is to be reported. Other information, whether from personal experience or precedent research, is to be excluded.

The "findings" chapter(s) comprises the substantive part of the research report. These chapters consist of what has been discovered about the central research issue through the employment of the designated methodology. The findings should be reported from the theoretical perspectives developed from the critical review of precedent research.

This section of the final research report makes up a very significant portion of the research report. It often emerges as the longest part of the report (thesis or dissertation). The findings may result in several chapters.

Organizing the Findings

The most obvious way to organize this section both in the proposal and in the final report is to follow the order and categories of the research questions or hypotheses. In most cases each research question or hypothesis will be subdivided for more detailed analysis of the central research issue. These subcategories will serve well as subheadings in the findings chapters. Depending on the length of the report and the extent of the findings, each research question or hypothesis may serve as the principal issue for a single chapter. Both the findings chapter in the proposal and the corresponding chapters in the final report should have a predictable relationship to each of the other sections in the proposal.

Findings and the Central Research Issue

The central research issue provides the primary controlling constraint for what should be reported in the findings regardless of what may be uncovered in the research. In most research studies much peripheral or incidental information will be discovered. This information may be interesting and useful for the researcher or others around outside the scope of the study. All of this information should be saved for reporting in another report. However, the only information that should be reported in the findings chapter(s) should be what relates to the central research issue. Moreover, *all* of the information that relates to this issue should be included. No relevant information should be hidden or withheld even if it does not support one's assumptions, hopes or hypotheses. Such ethical lapses discredit the research.

Findings and the Research Questions or Hypotheses

Answering the research questions or the testing of hypotheses drives the methodology. The methodology emerges out of the means to collect and analyze the issues raised in the research questions or hypotheses. The findings then should be organized in response to the research questions or hypotheses. At the proposal stage the research questions will suggest the *categories* for the findings section. In a proposal it is highly inappropriate to report "anticipated" findings beyond the categories suggested by the research questions or hypotheses. Reporting "anticipated" findings serves to bias the study significantly so that the researcher will be less likely to see anything beyond his or her own presuppositions, thus invalidating the study. Such a reporting of "anticipated findings" may also constitute an ethical lapse. However, in the final report, integrity demands a full reporting of all that one has discovered from primary research in response to the research questions or hypotheses.

Findings and Precedent Research

The theory perspective developed through a critical review of the precedent research provides the framework for presenting the findings. If, for example, one is seeking to explain how a Christian leader has emerged, one might review the research done by J. Robert Clinton. His "Leadership Emergence Theory" (1997, pp.

149-182) provides a useful theoretical structure to explain how a person becomes a leader and how the patterns of the person's life may be expected to progress into the future.

One must be careful, however, not to present as findings what has been reported in previously done research. This kind of confusion often occurs among researchers who do their research in published materials. A person might do original research, for example, about the development of the homogenous unit principle in the writings of Donald A. McGavran. The documents that would provide the primary data would be McGavran's writings. As a part of the research one would also critically review what others have said from their own research about the development of this idea, with McGavran. From the research that others have done, one might characterize periods of McGavran's writing, influences which led him to develop this idea and so on. These perspectives might be used to help categorize one's own reading or findings about this research issue as secondary research. However, a researcher simply cannot report what others have discovered or deduced as their own findings. Such reporting is considered plagiarism.

Research in theology or biblical studies should be reported in a similar way. One may ask, "What does the Bible teach about . . . ?" The primary source is the Bible and the findings should report what is discovered in what is written in the Bible. What commentators have said should be considered, but their writings will be secondary sources and not to be reported as findings. They may provide perspectives and constraints for interpretation, but what they have written does not constitute the primary source and should not then be reported as findings. "Writings about" the topic may provide the perspective to report the findings, but they are not the findings to report.

Findings and the Methodology

Clearly, the findings should report what has been discovered from the employment of the methods used in the research. In missiological research, multiple approaches are regularly used for the collection and analysis of the data. One may use a combination of approaches based on theology, sociology, anthropology, education, history, political science, comparative religion, geography, economics or some other academic discipline to both collect and analyze the data needed to address the central research issue. The findings section of the report should report all of the relevant data from these various data collection and analytical approaches. Relevance is judged by the data's relationship to the central research issue.

The integration of these findings should be reported. The integration of the multiple perspectives often generates significant new insights.

Obviously, the findings should not include any information that has not emerged from employing the methods of the study. The reporting of unsubstantiated opinions or feelings as findings is inappropriate as is the reporting of any "finding" from other research.

Results of statistics, analyses, and any statistical tests should be reported in the findings. The researcher should include the results of all of the analytical procedures that produce significant findings. One should not just report the summaries of interview or impressions from questionnaires. The details should be reported. However, in many cases where the research has been complex, the reader may be overwhelmed with minute details from statistical tests. In such cases the less significant charts and statistical tables should be placed in an appendix and simply referenced in the findings' chapter(s).

Findings and Conclusions or Recommendations

The findings provide the information bases for the conclusions and recommendations. After stating the findings, one should be able to write, "Therefore. . . . " The findings' sections or chapters themselves, however, *should not* contain any conclusions or recommendations. The conclusions and recommendations should be reserved for the sections or chapters devoted to conclusions and recommendations. When a reader looks at a research study, two things are often scanned first: the research issue and the conclusions or recommendations. If the researcher has written conclusions or recommendations in the midst of the findings, they will simply be lost to many readers. If the conclusions and recommendations are scattered in an undisciplined and unsystematic way through the findings, it probably indicates that the researcher has not reflected systematically about all of the findings and how they should be integrated. It means that the work was left incomplete.

General Principles

The researcher must report negative and positive results. Researchers are often tempted to report only what supports their bias. He or she may see other information as irrelevant or undesirable. However, whatever is discovered that relates to the central research issue should be reported. Often information that differs from the researcher's expectations contributes to the most significant findings of a study. Often, information that differs from the researcher's assumptions complicates the study. Whatever the case, a researcher is ethically bound to present all of the relevant information for the benefit of the reader(s).

The findings should be reported so they communicate accurately what was found. They should be reported so they can be easily understood. Researchers must keep their reading audience in mind. While most researchers do not deliberately set out to mislead, the reader may be mislead in a number of ways. One may mislead by misplacing emphasis in the order of the structure, by not bringing significant findings into focus, or by misusing graphics.

Typically, a researcher will discover many interesting facts that fall outside the focus of the central research issue, research questions and delimitations. While one may be tempted to report these findings, they should not be reported unless one goes back and revises all of the preceding sections of the proposal or final report (i.e., purpose, goals, central research issue, research questions, delimitations and so on). These discoveries should be kept for related research articles or books, but not included in the present research report.

Applying basic principles will help the readability and application of the research. If the research reporting cannot be understood, it will benefit no one except the researchers. And, if the researcher cannot express what was found clearly, he or she probably did not understand the outcomes well either.

Focus Writing to the Readers

The first principle in writing one's findings is to write for the people who are expected to read the report. The text and graphics should be presented in a way that they will understand and that will meet their needs. The information should be given in a way that is relevant to what they should know about the present research. In writing with the audience in mind, one should take note of their perspectives, viewpoints, worldview, values, and knowledge level to present the findings so the readers can understand. The researcher should consider the subgroups in the audience such as decision makers or opinion leaders. One should ask the question, "What does the intended audience need to know to understand this research?" The findings should be presented in terms of the action that the intended audience needs to take. One should take care to recognize the amount and kinds of information that the intended audience can understand. They should not be overwhelmed with statistical tables, obscure graphs, or irrelevant information. Rather, write using a standard journalistic practice by starting with the most important information first.

Focus on Readability

The researcher's task is to focus on readability with the reader in mind. One may ask, "What will help the reader understand what I am trying to communicate better?"

- Variety in the text helps.
- White space helps.
- Short simple sentences help.
- Large simple graphics help. One can often improve graphics by dividing them into multiple graphics and then combining them into a whole.
- Parenthetical statements often do not help (e.g., This statement does not help the explanation in this point, but only adds unnecessary words which could all be deleted.)
- Avoid technical language as much as possible. When technical language is used, be sure that the context provides information for understanding what is written.
- Use personal illustrations.
- Use frequent headings so the reader may easily follow the thought progression.

Clear, Direct Writing

Write clear, easy-to-understand sentences and paragraphs. Keep as much of the text in active voice as possible. When writing, begin paragraphs with a topic sentence. Topic sentences clearly state the subject for the whole paragraph. Keep the sentences as short and simple as possible. Each sentence in the paragraph should support the topic sentence as an explanation, argument, or illustration. Long sentences with multiple subordinate clauses present more difficulty in reading and remembering. A rule of thumb is to keep the sentences less than two lines long.

Avoid smothered derivatives. For example: Write, "He explained the situation." Do not write, "He provided an explanation of the situation." Use action verbs rather than the nouns or adjectives that are derived from them. Avoid the over use of the word "there," with forms of the verb "to be." Do not write, "*There were* three missiologists *who* wrote about Oromo history." Rather, write, "Three missiologists wrote about Oromo history."

Redundancy makes a report boring to read. Most research reports could be trimmed by 20-40 percent with no loss of information. Eliminate phrases like the following: "The one who came to see us was named John." Rather, write, "John came to see us." Concise writing does not mean shallow thinking; it rather suggests clear thinking.

The following phrases illustrate weak redundancy. Any of the following phrases should be replaced with *one* word:

- in the amount of
- for the purpose of
- in the nature of
- subsequent to
- with regard to
- on the occasion of
- in view of the fact that
- give encouragement to
- despite the fact that

- give instructions to
- make an adjustment
- on the order of
- along the lines of
- in connection with
- on the basis of
- give consideration to
- is of the opinion
- with reference to

Clear, direct writing allows one to not only express what has been found in less words, it facilitates the organization of the report. Having the report clearly organized will help the reader both read with comprehension and remember the written document.

Organization

The effective writer connects each part of the text to every part of the document, beginning within the sentence structure, through paragraphs, sections, chapters and finally to the whole. Three concepts serve to assist one's thinking about organizing the text: continuity, sequence, and integration (Tyler, 1949). *Continuity* refers to the reiteration, repetition or redundancy that is built into a text. The same concepts and ideas should be used consistently throughout. If a definition has been given in the beginning of the text, that definition should be followed through the whole text. *Sequence* refers to the orderly progression through the text. The order of the presentation should follow a sequence that makes sense from the findings and to the reader. The order may be clarified by the frequent use of headings and connecting phrases that link the parts together. *Integration* serves as the third key to organizing one's text. All of the parts should fit together as one unified whole. Having a single purpose supported by a single related central research issue assists the researcher in keeping the whole study organized as a meaningful whole.

Keep It Simple

One can always complicate the text. Rather, use simple, direct language. In academic writing technical words may occasionally be needed, but they should be used in ways that clearly assist the reader to understand. Writing simply does not detract from the quality or rigor of the writing. It simply makes it easy to understand. Communicating one's findings remains the clear goal of the researcher.

Authors may avoid the stilted language that formerly was expected in research reports. An author may refer to himself or herself as "I." The plural "we" is no longer acceptable, unless one is writing to include the reader or a specific group where the term "we" would be appropriate. Similarly, use of the second person should be avoided unless the reader is being specifically addressed as may be seen in much of this text.

Some kinds of constructions should be edited out! Avoid the use of contractions (e.g., can't, you've). Colloquialisms, puns, and other "cute" expressions are simply inappropriate in academic writing.

Avoid coining new words. Some people like to make up new words or technical terms. More often if one is aware of the literature in the field the terms for the concepts will already be available. Often, the same concept or construct will have multiple terms in precedent research. The introduction of new terms always makes a text more difficult to read unless the new terms are used with enough frequency for the reader to become familiar with them. If one needs new terms or many technical terms, a glossary will serve the reader. One should include key terms in the "definitions" section.

One may greatly aid the simplicity of reading the text with format devices including boldfacing, italicizing, using bullet lists, increasing the number of headings in the text and increasing the number of graphics. The old saying, "A picture is worth a thousand words," is true in research reports as well!

Charts, Graphs, Figures

The general principle to remember is "to construct tables and graphs first" (Morris and Fitz-Gibbon, 1978, p. 48). By starting with the visuals one can specifically address the questions that are to be answered. The preparation of visuals often helps the researcher gain new insight about interpretation of the data and potential applications. As the visuals are prepared, the text should flow to explain them. The readers' attention will be drawn to the visuals and they often present the first impressions of the interpretation of the data. The text should be organized around the visuals as the data are presented. If one has any doubt whether to use a graph or a table to aid the reader, choose a graph (p. 49), but choose the appropriate kind of graph. Tables may then be included in an appropriate appendix. Many readers initially scan a text by looking at the graphics. Since that approach is true, one should present the graphics in ways that clearly communicate. They should be self-contained with all of the essential information about a given set of data. One should be careful about including all of the relevant labels and keys to understand what is in the graphic. Information that is not addressed in the text should not be included in the graphic. One should not rely on graphics to carry all of the information to the reader.

Visuals often assist the reader to gain an understanding more quickly and comprehensively than tables or numbers. Visuals often serve to clarify the conceptual basis of the study and its sequential process. One should design visuals with the readers in mind. Readers should not be overwhelmed with information. Tables with figures are better than numbers in the text. However, if many tables are required, graphs and charts may communicate better. Graphs and charts may appear to be less precise. If that is the case, then the tables may be presented in the appendices.

Give attention to the appropriate choice of graphics. Bar graphs, histograms, and frequency polygons all show frequency distributions. Pie charts are useful for reporting percentages. Pie charts are useful to present percentages even when the numbers are small. Typically, numbers less than 100 should not be reported in terms of percentages because the percentages may inflate the significance of the findings. Pie charts avoid this risk. Scatter plots usefully display the frequencies of cases based on two variables when showing correlation studies. Semi-log graphs show comparative rates and may show multiple variables in the same graph. Flow charts help the reader see the sequence or progress of events such as the progress of a given study. Venn diagrams and other diagrams may be very useful for presenting holistic pictures of a concept. Maps, photographs, pictographs, line drawings, and other visuals may add significantly to the information and the comprehension of the readers. As a reader is reading through the text, the best place for the graphics is in the text in the sequence of thinking. The selection and design of graphics in the reporting of one's whole project deserves careful attention. It should consistently and validly present what is being presented in the text in a different format. Appropriate graphics can dramatically increase the reader's comprehension of the text. However, inappropriate graphics, while technically correct, may serve to confuse or misinform the reader.

Typically, as one presents graphic summaries of the findings, a significant risk emerges. While the information presented in graphical form may all be technically accurate, the ways it is perceived may differ widely. A typical simple graph and a semi-log graph may present the same data, but their shapes will likely differ, significantly generating very different visual impressions. For example, Figures 8, 9, and 10 present the same information in different ways from the data found in Table 7. Table 7 presents some hypothetical statistics about the growth in attendance of a congregation from 1995 to 2010. From Table 7 an inexperienced researcher might suggest steady growth over this period. Both Figures 8 and 9 as a typical histogram or bar graph and line graph also suggest steady growth over the period. Figure 10, however, differs significantly. While based on the same data set, it depicts the rate of growth over the same period. Clearly, the rate of growth consistently slowed over the whole period. Naive church leaders or researchers would likely boast using the first two figures. However, discerning leaders or researchers would undoubtedly be aptly deeply concerned about the interpretation of the semi-log graph in Figure 10.

While a set of graphics may be technically accurate, the visual imagery may generate widely differing and misleading perceptions. The researcher needs to know the purpose for which the graphics are being prepared and who will be interpreting them. The mode of presentation may well raise ethical or integrity issues.

TABLE 7
Hypothetical Growth Pattern

Year	Total Members
1965	10
1970	100
1975	200
1980	300
1985	400
1990	500
1995	600
2000	700
2005	800
2010	900

FIGURE 8
Typical Histogram

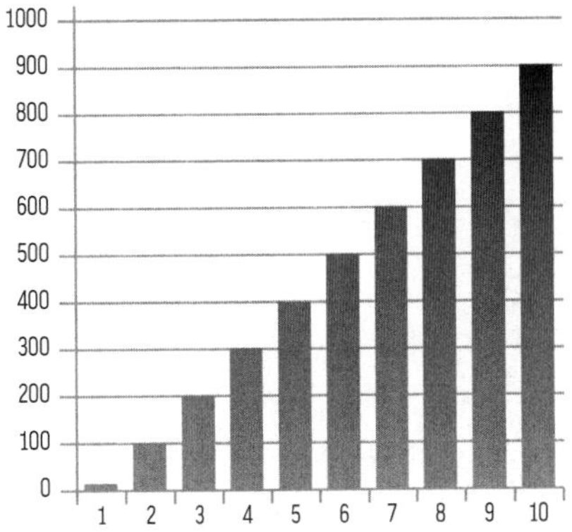

FIGURE 9
Typical Line Graph

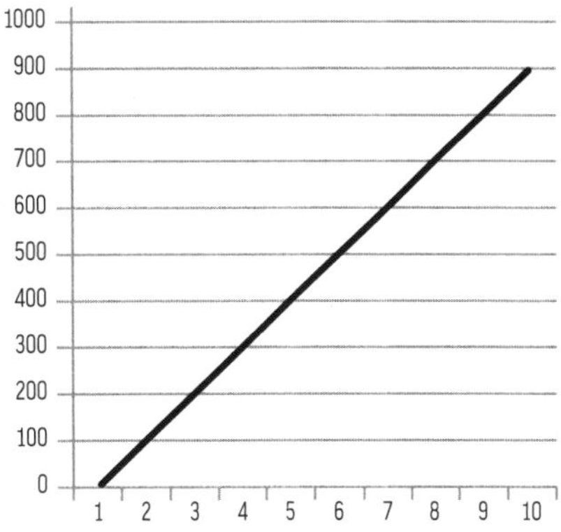

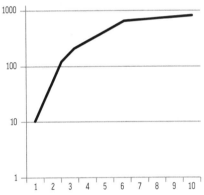

FIGURE 10
Typical Semi-log Graph

Be Specific

Avoid generalizations.[14] Use specific, definite or concrete terms. Do not say, "a seminary official" when the specific description would be the "Dean of the School of Intercultural Studies." Whenever possible to use names, use them instead of the generic "someone." Avoid undocumented research generalizations. Do not say, "Someone has written . . . " or "Research has shown . . ." If someone has reported research, that person will have a name. If research has shown something, that research can and should be documented!

---

14   This generalization is no exception! Generalizations may present overstatements, while others may be appropriate.

Use Inclusive Language

Typically in the past, one wrote in sexist noninclusive archaic English. Singular masculine pronouns commonly referred to an indefinite person. However, that practice effectively excluded women. Old style manuals used terms like "mankind" for all people. Language and writing style values have changed. In contemporary English such exclusive language is not acceptable. Many researchers have learned English composition using "he," "him," and "his" as the correct way to refer to any person. To correct this practice and to conform to contemporary values, some simple editing procedures may be employed. In a few cases, one might use both pronouns (e.g., he or she, him or her, his or hers), however, in many cases the subject may be changed to a plural or to the specific name of the person or role. Using plurals allows for the use of inclusive plural pronouns. In other cases the author can simply edit the sentence structure to avoid exclusive language. One must however keep the pronouns agreeing in number with the nouns to which they refer.

In the past many roles were defined in gender-specific terms (e.g., chairman). A more acceptable and contemporary practice is simply to refer to the person in nongender specific terms, (e.g., chair of the board). Many contemporary English style manuals provide many more suggestions about this change in writing style.

Summary

The findings should be presented as evidence to address the central research issue. They should answer the research questions and serve to either support or not support the hypotheses. They should establish what is true and trustworthy. The evidence of the findings must be relevant, that is, it must clearly relate to the central research issue. It must carry weight in the issue at hand. It must be competent, that is, derived from qualified and trustworthy sources. The findings should distinguish fact from opinion. They should emerge out of primary, not secondary, sources. They must fit together into a logical or reasonable pattern. The findings provide the only basis for the research conclusions and recommendations. They must be presented then as evidence leading to the conclusions and recommendations focused around the central research issue.

The findings, however, should not contain conclusions or recommendations. Many researchers are tempted to include words like, "should," "ought," or "therefore" in their findings sections. The conclusive or recommendation type of statements should be avoided and kept for the chapter of conclusions and recommendations.

If spread through the findings, other researchers may miss key ideas as they scan the conclusions and recommendations of a research project.

The following table suggests how the findings section relates to the overall research design. It may be used as a checklist for reviewing one's design.

TABLE 8
Relating the Findings Section to the Overall Research Design

Section of Design	Contributions to the Findings	Contributions from the Findings
Background	Sets the context for the findings	
Purpose	Sets the overall direction for the reporting the findings	
Goals	Set the expected boundaries and categories for reporting the findings	May provide additional information not anticipated in original goals that may allow a slight expansion of the goals
Central Research Issue	Sets the boundaries of what must and may be reported	
Research Questions/Hypotheses	Sets the primary categories for the reporting of the findings	
Delimitations/Scope	Defines the specific scope—what will be included and what will be excluded from the findings	
Assumptions	Set the general perspectives for approaching, interpreting, and reporting the findings	
Definitions	Set the specific perspectives for addressing key concepts	
Review of Precedent Research	Defines variables, significance, potential methods to approach, and theoretical perspectives to interpret and apply	May raise questions about interpretation of what has been found

Section of Design	Contributions to the Findings	Contributions from the Findings
Data Collection	Will provide the raw data to report	
Data Analysis	Will provide the analyzed or interpreted information to report	
Limitations	Will provide questions of potential threats to validity and reliability to report	
Conclusions		Provides the only information base upon which the conclusions may be drawn
Recommendations		Provides the only information base upon which the recommendations may be made

6

DESIGNING CONCLUSIONS AND RECOMMENDATIONS

This chapter describes what should be included and
excluded from the conclusions and recommendations
section of a research study.

The conclusions and recommendations sections of a research report emerge directly out of the findings. These sections generally present little difficulty to develop. If
one has produced what was suggested by the research questions and methodology
in the findings, then the first place to go for the development of the conclusions
and recommendations is to the goals. The goal statements should provide the outline of categories for the conclusions and recommendations. The findings provide
all of and the *only* information that is legitimately available for the conclusions.

Summary

As this section is written in a final report, the first section to write should be a summary overview of the study. A brief review of the central issue, research questions,
methods used, and principal findings will help the reader to better understand the
conclusions and recommendations. This overview section should not exceed a
page or two.

A summary of the findings should then follow. The summary should contain
only findings that have been previously reported in the findings section. It *should not*
contain information from the review of precedent research, because the summary
should be of one's own original research. It should not contain any new information or findings that were previously unreported. If each major subsection in the

findings chapter(s) has been appropriately summarized, then the findings which bear directly upon the conclusions to be drawn and the recommendations to be made should be noted in this final summary.

Conclusions/Recommendations

Conclusions and recommendations may *only* be drawn *from* the findings of the study *about* the central research issue. No conclusions or recommendations are acceptable from the precedent research or background statements. The relationship of precedent research to the findings section is to provide the theoretical perspectives to interpret the findings. No conclusions or recommendations are normally allowable anywhere else in the study except in the chapter which treats conclusions and recommendations.

The conclusions will be constrained by two major issues in the design of the study and the employment of the methods. While the conclusions may only be built upon the findings of the study as they relate to the central research issue, the issue of external validity or generalizability must be considered. To what extent does the design of the study allow the interpretations of the findings to be generalized? If the research design was built on a series of case studies, the conclusions and recommendations can only directly apply to these case studies. If any theory is developed for further testing, it must be noted that the theory is tentative because of the limits of generalizability.

If one has drawn a valid random sample from a population of 300 million as in the population of the US, it is only possible to generalize to the population from which the sample was drawn. One may not make applications to South Africa, Korea, or France. Generalizability in the making of conclusions and recommendations depends on the design of the study.

The other major constraint on the drawing of conclusions and recommendations is the set of limitations that may have developed while doing the research. One's original design may have been flawless, but if in the execution of the design some parts did not work, then these limitations will necessarily limit the extent to which one can apply the study in conclusions and recommendations. Any one of the following kinds of common problems would limit one's conclusions and recommendations:

- nonrespondents to questionnaires
- incomplete response to questionnaires

- nonresponse to some questions during interviewing
- people not being available for interviews
- original (primary source) documents not being available
- recognized researcher influence on the respondents

Several common errors plague emerging researchers as they are tempted to write conclusions before it is appropriate to do so. The author read a draft of a doctoral dissertation recently in which the student began to draw conclusions as he was describing the context in the first chapter. He continued to draw conclusions and make recommendations throughout the review of precedent research and all through the findings. He committed two different kinds of errors: He made conclusions from secondary source information (his precedent research) and second, he scattered his conclusions through his findings.

Often when a person picks up a research study to peruse, the whole study may not be read. Rather, the person will likely read the purpose and central research issue along with the research questions. Then the reader often will skip through the methodology to the summary and conclusions. Sometimes a person will simply go straight to the recommendations section. If the recommendations are strewn throughout the study, most readers will miss them and their significance. They will also miss the majority of the supporting evidence for these recommendations. Researchers should then seek to avoid this common error by going back through their chapters and looking for words like: "should," "ought to," "must," and the like. If these words are found and introduce conclusions or recommendations, they should be moved to the conclusions' chapter.

Virtually every research project generates information and/or questions beyond the central research issue. To avoid the loss of this information or question base, the researcher should include a section entitled, "Recommendations for Further Study." This section provides clues about the what, who, why, where and perhaps the how of addressing these concerns.

The following table summarizes the relationship between the conclusions and recommendations and the rest of the research design. The conclusions and recommendations do not provide feedback to the other parts of the study. Rather, they are built as the final part of the study and are derived solely from the outcomes of the study.

TABLE 9
Relating the Conclusions and Recommendations Section to the Overall Research Design

Section of Design	Contributions to the Conclusions and Recommendations
Background	Sets the context for applying the conclusions and recommendations
Purpose	Provides the reason for the conclusions and recommendations
Goals	Set the expected categories for what will be reported as conclusions and recommendations
Central Research Issue	Defines the boundaries of what may and must be addressed
Delimitations/Scope	Defines the specific scope—what will be included and what will be excluded from the conclusions and recommendations
Assumptions	Set the general perspectives for approaching, interpreting, and reporting the conclusions and recommendations
Definitions	Set the specific perspectives for addressing key concepts in the conclusions and recommendations
Review of Precedent Research	Defines the theoretical perspectives including values to make conclusions and recommendations Does not provide any information for drawing conclusions related to one's original research
Data Collection	Will provide the primary data base for conclusions and recommendations
Data Analysis	Will provide the analyzed or interpreted information on which conclusions and recommendations may be made
Limitations	Will limit the scope of the conclusions and recommendations that can be validly made
Findings	Provide *all* of the information base and the *only* information base for the conclusions and recommendations

7

ETHICS AND MISSIOLOGICAL RESEARCH

This chapter introduces the issue of ethics
in missiological research design.

The issue of ethics arises in the context of missiological research even as it does in other research. Ethical issues affect missiological research in a variety of ways:

- They reflect a researcher's credibility and integrity.
- They affect the subjects of the research.
- They affect the researchers who may come later to study the same subjects.
- They influence the quality of the outcomes.
- They reflect on the institutions and others associated with the research.
- They affect both believers who would serve the *missio Dei* and the people whom God through Jesus Christ seeks to save.
- They may affect people who are yet to believe.
- Church-related researchers face the same kinds of ethical issues as other researchers.
- The ways that researchers treat ethical issues reflect their values. Any research will reflect the values of the researchers at every stage including:
  - Design, evaluation of precedent research
  - Data collection and analysis
  - Reporting of the findings
  - Conclusions and recommendations
  - The ways that the research is published and used

Research is always a values-laden enterprise. Ethical concerns simply raise the issues of values to the surface for examination.

People who recognize the values involved in the decisions make good decisions that reflect the highest ethical and value standards. Christian researchers who are concerned about ethics will base their decisions on biblical standards of truth, love and justice. Or, in the "lifecode" of the primitive Church, "faith, love and hope" (Wolf, 2010). Christian researchers who act ethically will accept responsibility for all of the research including all of the categories mentioned above.

Knowing this set of responsibilities, the Christian researcher will take care at every stage of the research process and with every constituency involved to act in a "Christlike" way.

Often research will include subjects who are less powerful. Missiological research frequently includes concerns for the poor and minorities. Christian researchers should give special attention to their research not only to protect the "widow, the orphan and the alien," but to work toward their salvation, empowerment, and nurture.

Having completed research in a community or about a topic, a researcher will know that community or topic better than most other people. When opportunities arise to use that knowledge for good, the Christian researcher is ethically bound to do the right thing. The researcher should seek the salvation of the community, to seek its best interests and to use the information gained about the topic(s) of research to serve the broader community and the Kingdom of God. The researcher must remember the purpose of missiology is the *missio Dei*.

Trochim (2006) lists six foundational ethical protections which have been established in the social science and medical communities. These ethical concerns apply to missiological research as well:

1. Voluntary participation. Research subjects are not forced into participating in the research.
2. Informed consent. Research subjects are provided information about the procedures and any risks involved, and give their consent before the research is initiated.
3. Risk of harm. While Trochim names physical and psychological harm, one must also add the issue of spiritual harm for missiological research.
4. Confidentiality. Research participants should receive assurance their personal information will not be divulged to anyone outside of the study.

5. Anonymity. The guarantee of privacy even to the researchers themselves may be desirable, but may be difficult.

6. Right to service. When the research subjects are part of a control group as in an experiment, they may have nothing done to or with them. However, they should be provided equal rights to whatever beneficial effects that may result from the study.

When designing and conducting the research, one must take care not to cause offense in a way that would inhibit or preclude further research being done with the research subjects or the community at some future time. When conducting group interviews among the Samburu in north central Kenya, I encountered numerous individuals who had been offended by a previous researcher. He had not taken into account these ethical considerations and left a trail of angered and suspicious people. He missed the basic principle of respect for the respondents and failed in the promised follow-up.

Range of Research Ethical Concerns in the Research Process

Ethical issues arise at every juncture of a research project. Table 10 summarizes the principal concerns at each stage of the process. Not only are ethical concerns present across time in the research process, they are present in the relationships with each of the constituencies involved. Building and maintaining integrity in all of one's relationships in research should be a primary concern of the researcher.

The issue of plagiarism cuts across nearly every point in the research process to threaten the integrity of a study. One may plagiarize because of not knowing how to use the intellectual or artistic work of other people and provide appropriate citations to their work. Or, one may plagiarize more deliberately in an attempt to deceive and steal the work of others. In either case the ethical issues of honesty, integrity and responsible interaction with the work of others arise.[15] Plagiarized material may appear in any section of a research proposal or report ranging from the design through the final conclusions and recommendations.

The issue of plagiarism requires careful attention in missiology even as it does in other academic disciplines. Differences in cultural perspectives or ignorance of what constitutes plagiarism do not provide adequate or appropriate excuses. One risks not only discrediting of his or her work, but legal liability as well.

---

15   Please note that more has been written about plagiarism in the section dealing with the review of precedent research.

Plagiarism provides legal grounds for dismissal from academic programs, termination from a teaching or research position or legal action.

TABLE 10
Sequential Research Ethical Concerns

Stage of the Research Process	Principal Concerns
Design	That the design: • fits within the competencies and resources of the researcher • represents new work to be done • will "advance truth and not simply support a predetermined position" (Diener and Crandall, 1978, p. 216)
Review of the Precedent Research	That the precedent research will: • be interpreted fairly and honestly from the author's own perspective(s) and context • be evaluated from the perspective of the immediate central research issue • be appropriately cited • be examined widely to treat all relevant viewpoints and perspectives
Data Collection	That data collection will: • be done as proposed as much as possible • be done as rigorously as possible using research methods that will provide accurate, objective, or unbiased results (e.g., through appropriate sample selection, observation, and question design) • be done in ways that recognize and account for the researcher's bias(es) • be done with due regard to the research subjects including their emotional, social/cultural, physical, and spiritual environments • give consideration to the use of time of research subjects and respondents • give consideration to the appropriate fostering and maintaining of relationships with the research subjects/respondents • give due care to privacy and confidentiality both for the individuals, families, and the communities being researched • give due care to taboos, proscribed information, and subjects which may cause embarrassment to the people involved • take all necessary precautions to prevent any harm from befalling the individuals that may be physical, psychological, social, or spiritual • take care to avoid all forms of manipulation that might cause people to make any decisions they would otherwise not make • take care not to deceive the individuals, families, or communities in any way about the research that is being done

Stage of the Research Process	Principal Concerns
Data Collection Continued	• secure informed consent of the research subjects before doing the research (Diener and Crandall, 1978, p. 7) • take care not to generate negative effects outside of the study itself in the families, organization(s), or community involved
Data Analysis	That data analysis will: • be done as rigorously as possible • employ the most appropriate and rigorous analytical tools available that will not bias the results and not select and use analytical methods because of their "special capacity to yield a desired conclusion" (Babbie, 1995, p. 456) • take into account all of the data collected • not tamper with nor distort any of the data • "not knowingly make interpretations of research results, nor … tacitly permit interpretations, which are inconsistent with the data available"(Babbie, 1995, p. 456)
Findings Reporting	That the findings reporting will: • report honestly and accurately without distortion all that is found related to the research issue • not report anything that was not found from the reported methodology • take all of the relevant findings into account • present the findings in prose, tabular, and graphical forms that will communicate clearly and honestly with the intended readers • be the writing and findings of the author and not some other researcher • only be the findings emerging from the reported methodology and not be from some other source or altered to fit the researcher's bias
Conclusions	That the conclusions will: • only relate to the findings of the study • only relate to the central research issue of the study • relate to all of the findings that are relevant to the central research issue
Recommendations	That the recommendations will: • only relate to the findings of the study • only relate to the central research issue of the study • only be applied to the extent allowed by the research design/methodology
Applying the Research after the Study	That the researcher will apply the research: • only to the situations that validly apply • only in ways that benefit the individuals and communities involved (Diener and Crandall, 1978, pp. 215-217) • reporting the "findings and methods accurately and in appropriate detail in all research reports" (Babbie, 1995, p. 456)

Ethical Concerns with Research Constituencies

Table 11 summarizes the principal ethical issues in the relationships one has with the constituencies involved. Overall, the ethical aim of the researcher is to maintain integrity while seeking the good for every constituency. When apparent conflicts arise in what appears to be "good," the researcher should refer to biblical values as a means for resolution.

TABLE 11
Ethical Concerns with Research Constituencies (Babbie, 1995, pp. 456-457)

Relationship	Principal Concerns
Public	When dealing with the general public, the researcher will: • cooperate with legally authorized authorities • follow legally mandated constraints (e.g., government research permits, Institutional Review Board (IRB) requirements) • conduct the research in ways which will not generate cynicism, resentment, or otherwise alienate the community toward further research • maintain the right to approve the release of the findings • publicly disclose what may be needed for any misinterpretation of the findings, notwithstanding the obligations for confidentiality
Sponsors	When dealing with sponsors, the researcher will: • maintain confidentiality for the ones who sponsor the research except where dissemination of the research is expressly authorized • accept research assignments only for projects which fall within his or her time, competency, and logistics constraints
Colleagues/Other Researchers	When dealing with colleagues and other researchers, the researcher will: • disseminate as widely as possible the findings of the research • recognize the responsibility to contribute to the academic disciplines and profession(s) represented by the researcher

Relationship	Principal Concerns
Respondents	When dealing with respondents, the researcher will: • treat the respondents with respect in ways that would present a positive witness of the gospel of Christ to them • treat the respondents with respect avoiding anything that would lead to deceit, abuse, coercion, manipulation, or embarrassment • treat the respondents in ways that will build mutual trust, respect, and long-lasting relationships rather than using respondents simply as a means to collect information • allow the respondents to choose to participate based on being informed about the purpose, process, and expected outcomes of the research • conduct the research in ways which will not alienate the respondents for further research by other researchers • protect the anonymity of every respondent at least to the extent desired by the respondent • forgo researching subjects where confidentiality or anonymity cannot be assured through the process and the final published reports
The Church	When doing research, the Christian researcher will actively seek to continue to employ the research to: • fulfill the Great Commandment to love God and to love one's neighbor as oneself • fulfill the Great Commission to disciple all the nations

Cultural Concerns

When one raises the issue of values and ethics in missiological research, differences in culture will immediately confront the researcher. Crosscultural ethical dilemmas may arise with almost every matter or combination of issues raised in Tables 10 and 11. What may be expected and acceptable in one culture may be unacceptable, offensive, and illegal in another. For example, what people from some cultures would consider as public domain information, others consider restricted and support these restrictions with copyright laws. In these cultures it is considered appropriate to quote from published sources, because they are "publicly" published. Often, because of the veneration of the elders, one may gain credibility by quoting them. However, the standard set in this book expects researchers to cite all uses of ideas generated by someone else. While very few Christian researchers would deliberately seek to deceive the readers, some do not hesitate to use another person's words or ideas—because they have been published.

In research ethics the same basic principles apply as in other ethical issues. The undergirding principles include: love and integrity. Because of the sensitivities of ethical issues across cultural and subcultural boundaries, researchers must give all the more attention to these issues to build relationships to validate research and to obey God.

PART II

CONTRIBUTIONS FROM OTHER DISCIPLINES

One can point to virtually any academic discipline that examines human behavior to expand missiological theory and applications and to extend the *missio Dei*. This section presents four chapters to illustrate the possibilities of inter- or multidisciplinary approaches to missiology. While only brief essays about theology, anthropology, education, history, and communication are included in this text, parallel essays could be written from a score of other academic disciplines such as sociology, economics, political science, leadership, business, management, psychology, or law. Subdisciplines and the multidisciplinary approaches simply multiply the possibilities for missiological research in exponential ways as they combine with a theological base to inform the Church and its peoples to accomplish the *missio Dei* among *panta ta ethne*.

Theology undergirds all of missiology because missiology's focus is on the *missio Dei*. Theological research as a stand-alone research may serve missiological purposes. Or, theological research may be combined with methods from other disciplines to either establish value bases, perspectives or baselines for additional social science research.

Charles Van Engen has presented a brief essay about theological research and its essential range of contributions to missiology.

Educational research has supported missiology since the earliest days. Jesus commanded his disciples to "make disciples of all nations . . . teaching them to obey everything I have commanded you" (Matt 28:18-20). The earliest teaching in discipleship centered around the easily reproducible concepts of faith, love and hope (Wolf, 2010). Much current missiological research focuses on training and discipleship. This author has worked with more than 200 doctoral dissertations related to missiologically focused education with students from more than eighty countries. This body of research does not even scratch the surface of what has been done or what could or should be done.

The Book of Acts serves as the first historical research in missiology. It demonstrates a prime example of early historical research aimed at providing missiological instruction. Under the guidance of the Holy Spirit, Luke researched both what others did related to the *missio Dei* and recorded what he personally observed. His history of the primitive Church provides a record of an almost inexhaustible number of topics related to persons, places, missional outcomes, the work of the Holy Spirit, resistance and receptivity, cultural sensitivities and an occasional cultural *faux paus*. He documented records of the relations of political, economic, legal, leadership and communication systems. Both the miraculous and mundane events depict what has proven to be instructive for the Church in countless cultures now for twenty-one centuries.

Pablo Deiros shows the missiological significance of historical research in his chapter, "Historical Research." The study of history is virtually always related to missiological studies in one way or another. Deiros clarifies why.

Viggo Søgaard explains why communication serves as another foundational academic discipline for missiological research. He asserts the "task of the Church is primarily one of communication." This communication is at the heart of missiology and the *missio Dei*. God took the initiative to communicate and now expects us to communicate.

The section entitled "Qualitative Social Science Methods in Research Design" by R. Daniel Shaw presents one of the most foundational approaches to missiological research from the perspective of an anthropologist and linguist. Much of missiological research continues to focus on peoples who are yet to be reached with the gospel, hence qualitative research is the most appropriate social science approach to develop an understanding to evangelize and to educate.

8

BIBLICAL THEOLOGY OF MISSION'S RESEARCH METHOD

CHARLES VAN ENGEN[16]

This chapter presents the foundational contributions of
biblical theology to missiology complementary, but in
contrast, to social science methods.

The social sciences have heavily impacted missiology—and missiological research
during the past fifty years. In the social sciences and some other scholarly enter-
prises, one of the most important questions has to do with the basis on which one
can determine the *validity and reliability* of one's investigation. In the methodologies of the social sciences the matters of "validity" and "reliability" are held up
as two of the principle criteria of acceptable research. Normally, in social-science
research, the concept of validity has to do with the question, "How can we be sure
that we are collecting the right data in the right way?" And, the concept of reliability addresses the question, "How can we be sure that if the same approach were to
be taken again, the same data would be discovered?"

In biblical theology of mission these questions are not considered to be the right
ones. The mission theologian is not particularly concerned about the quality of the
empirical data nor the repeatability of the process so as to yield identical results. In
the estimation of the biblical theologian of mission, the empirical data gathered is of
secondary importance to the assumptions, ideas, goals, and conceptual framework
(paradigm) through which the "data" are being examined. One does not assume
that so-called objective facts exist (cf. Leslie Newbigin, *Foolishness to the Greeks*,

---

16   Most of the material in this chapter is taken from Charles Van Engen, *Mission on the Way*, pp. 29-31, with adaptation.

1986). Even the cultural lenses through which the "data" are collected will impact the effect that such data may have on the concepts being considered. In the eyes of a biblical theologian of mission, repeatability is also not a high value. Rather, the mission theologian typically takes the following matters very seriously:

- The researcher's approach to the Bible: their exegetical methods, their hermeneutical assumptions, their methods of interpretation of the biblical text;
- The researcher's unique faith pilgrimage and understanding of God;
- The researcher's worldview;
- The researcher's unique skills and abilities;
- The researcher's unique spiritual giftedness;
- The uniqueness of the Church in a specific time and place;
- The uniqueness of the context; and,
- The unique, creative and diversified ways in which the Holy Spirit works.

All these matters will mean that a particular theological understanding in a particular time and place, though holding many generalizable principal values, is in fact unrepeatable. This unique understanding does not erase the unity and finality of one revealed truth of the one gospel as found in the Bible. Interpretation is not to be equated with God's revelation. The canon is closed, but a multiplicity of interpretations (paradigms, if you will) occur constantly over time (Bevans and Schroeder, 2004; Bosch, 1991, p. 181-189; and Shaw and Van Engen, 2003).

The unrepeatability of theologizing in context is a major difference between most social-scientific methodologies and the methodologies of biblical mission theology. For example, people who have followed Karl Barth closely and borrowed from his thought are sometimes known as "Barthians." However, none of them would consider doing theology in the sense of being another Karl Barth—he was unique, there will never be another. There will never be another Augustine, Aquinas, Martin Luther, John Calvin, Charles Wesley, William Carey, J. Hudson Taylor, or Cameron Townsend. Each theologian is unique in his or her time, context, and worldview. Something is intrinsically unrepeatable in authentic contextual theologizing in mission. However, this fact does not relativize the truth-claims of biblically grounded mission theologians. Rather, it offers a multiplicity of understandings and interpretations of the same truth.

A very old fable serves to illustrate this point. In the ancient philosophy of India one finds the story of the five blind men who all want to know what it is that they are touching. So one says it is a rope, another says it is a tree trunk, another says a wall, a large fan-shaped leaf said another, and another a large snake. All five are interpreting reality as they perceive it. If one leaves the interpretation at this point (which is at times the case in Indian philosophy), one is left with five different perceptions of reality. All five are acceptable; all five are equally valid. This approach completely relativizes reality. In some popular forms of post-modernity this interpretative method would be referred to as "perception is reality." However, evangelical mission theologians would want to go one step further and add the assumption that truth is a unified whole to be found in God's final, unique, unrepeatable and unified revelation, written in the Bible. In the fable above, this would mean that it would be important to inform all five blind men that the object in question is an elephant. Their perception does not change what Kraft (1996) would call big "R" Reality. It is an elephant, no matter what each blind man says. However, each perception articulated by each blind man is also a significant, "accurate" (to a point) description of a particular perception of a small "r" reality expressed by each within their own contextual framework. Mission theology wrestles constantly with the question of the proximity or distance of the small "r" interpretation by the church of its participation in God's mission in relation to the big "R" Revelation of God's mission as found in the Bible. Evangelical theology, therefore, offers a particular way of recognizing acceptable research. The question of validity must be transformed into one of *truth,* and the matter of reliability must be seen as one of *trust.*

Before outlining the characteristics of *trust* and *truth,* a comment is necessary regarding "data," "literature review," and "primary/secondary research." First, for the biblical theologian of mission, the primary "data" to be investigated are not those normally chosen by social scientists. Rather, the primary data of the biblical theologian of mission are *ideas.* The concepts themselves are not ways of understanding or ordering the data (as social scientists might present the matter)—rather, they are the data itself. Secondly, this approach has implications with regard to something social scientists call "literature review," (meaning a review of what others have said about the social phenomenon, situation, or research issue being investigated). For the biblical theologian very little "literature review" exists in the social science sense expressed above. Rather, all ideas and concepts related to the central issue being investigated—all ideas, all reading, all conceptual articulations—become part of the data being investigated.

Thirdly, social scientists have a certain way of defining "primary research," involving an analysis, description, or study of the first-level research: that is, looking at the object or the persons or the culture itself. The secondary level is composed of literature written by others who studied a similar first level. The tertiary level is composed of those who reflect on what the secondary level writers or thinkers said about the first-level situation or context. Because biblical theologians of mission deal with ideas, the definition of "primary" and "secondary" literature changes dramatically.

Let me offer an illustration. I may study Karl Barth's concept of revelation. His concepts are primary data. I may in fact study how Karl Barth read and understood parts of scripture regarding revelation. If my focus is to understand Barth, then that too is "primary" data. However, if my doctoral study has to do with the relation of revelation to mission, then all those theologians and missiologists who speak about such things and offer ideas about revelation-and-mission (including their particular readings of scripture, church thought, and history of the question, even their reading of Barth on this particular subject) also constitute "primary data." However, if my focus is to study Barth's concept of revelation—and I read Cornelius Van Til, for example, in his critique of Barth's concept of revelation, then I am dealing in the case of Van Til with "secondary literature." However, if my focus is on the relation of revelation to mission, then both what Barth and what Van Til may say is in fact "primary research." My primary data are ideas. For the biblical mission theologian, the focus determines whether something is merely "literature review" or is in fact part of the primary data that should be included in the research questions.

Trust-based Questions for Research in a Biblical Theology of Mission

As one begins to evaluate the *trust* base for theological research in missiology, several questions may serve to assure a trustworthy basis for the research. These questions may serve as a checklist for the researcher doing theological research in missiology or for one who is evaluating theological research in missiology.

- Did the researcher read the right authors, the accepted sources?
- Did the researcher read widely enough to gain a breadth of perspectives on the issue?
- Did the researcher read other viewpoints correctly, fairly, and seriously?
- Did the researcher understand what was read—and demonstrate a basis for agreeing or disagreeing with what was read?
- Do internal contradictions exist either in the use (and understanding) of the authors or in their application to the issue at hand?

Truth-based Questions for Research in a Biblical Theology of Mission

In a similar way the following questions may be used to evaluate the *truth* base for theological research in missiology. Again, as one begins to design theological research, this set of questions may serve as checklist to assure the "truth" base is being addressed.

- Is there adequate biblical foundation for the statements being affirmed?
- Is there an appropriate continuity of the researcher's statements with theological affirmations made by other thinking, down through the history of the church?
- What contradictions or qualifications of thought arise? Does the mission theologian's work adequately support the particular theological directions being advocated in the study?
- Are the dialectical tensions and seeming contradictions allowed to stand, as they should, given what we know and do not know of the mystery of God's revealed unknown qualities as they impact our understanding of God's mission?

Evaluative Questions for a Biblical Theology of Mission

- Revelatory—Acceptable mission theology is grounded in Scripture.
- Coherent—It holds together and is built around an integrating idea.
- Consistent—It has no insurmountable glaring contradictions and is consistent with other truths known about God, God's mission, and God's revealed will.
- Simple—It has been reduced to the most basic components of God's mission in terms of the specific issue at hand.
- Supportable—It is logically, historically, experimentally, praxeologically affirmed and supported.
- Externally Confirmable—Other significant thinkers, theological communities, or traditions lend support to the thesis being offered.
- Contextual—It interfaces appropriately with the context.

- Doable—Its concepts can be translated into missional action that in turn is consistent with the motivations and goals of the mission theology being developed.
- Transformational—The carrying out of the proposed missional action would issue in appropriate changes in the status quo that reflect biblical elements of God's mission.
- Productive or Appropriate Consequences—The results of translating the concepts into missional action would be consistent with the thrust of the concepts themselves and with the nature and mission of God as revealed in Scripture.

One of the most profound differences in the way biblical theology of mission does its research as compared with social science-based research in missiology is that *biblical theology of mission is more intentionally and strongly prescriptive as well as descriptive.* It is synthetic (bringing about synthesis) and integrational (bringing about new conjunctions and interrelations of ideas). It searches for trustworthy and true perceptions concerning the church's mission that are based on biblical and theological reflection, seeks to interface with the appropriate missional action, and creates a new set of values and priorities that reflect as clearly as possible the ways in which the church in a particular context may participate in God's mission at a particular time.

When mission theology is abstracted from mission practice—and when missiological research is abstracted from mission encounter—it seems strange and far removed from the concrete places and specific people that are at the heart of God's mission. Such "objective" removal itself may lead the research astray from understanding the wisdom of the way God wants to work in mission. Mission theology is at its best when it is intimately involved in the being, knowing, doing, and serving of the Church's mission in a particular context. Persons who do not know Jesus Christ as their personal Savior and Lord may do some research in terms of "mission studies," but they will not be gaining true and trustworthy missiological insight related to the mission of God. Persons who research an issue or a mission question among people whose language and culture they do not understand may be involved in "research," but they are not gaining biblical "wisdom" with regard to what God wants to be doing through Christ's Church in that context. Biblical theology of mission is personal, relational, corporate, committed, and transformational. It constantly searches for new and more profound understanding and participation by the people of God in God's mission in God's world.

9

RESEARCH IN EDUCATION
EDGAR J. ELLISTON

This chapter introduces how research in education may
contribute to missiology.

Missiological curriculum and instructional concerns grow out of the *missio Dei*
as seen throughout scripture and made explicitly clear in the Great Commission.
The central command of the Great Commission as recorded in Matthew is to *make
disciples*. Jesus' concern for *instruction* was evident from the outset of his ministry
through the post-resurrection appearances. One can identify the *curricular* parts
of the Great Commission by looking at the "as you go" and the "teaching to obey
all things" participles as well as the central command to "make followers."

In the Old Testament the issue of instruction plays a prominent role in the
responsibilities of both the family and the Hebrew people. The instruction was not
only intended for the children, but for the nations around them.

The scriptures consistently focus on a holistic approach to the development of
the person in community to serve God's purpose. Modern secular education typically identifies three areas for instruction: knowledge (cognitive development), skills
(psycho-motor development) and attitudes (affective or formative development).
Often the first two of these instructional areas (cognitive and skill development)
become the focus of attention, but the third (affective development) differs significantly. Biblically, the issue of affective development is much better understood in
spiritual, character, and missional formation. Certainly, the focus is on relationships,
but the values of integrity and character development clearly appear through the
whole of God's revelation. The formation is not just for the individual's benefit,
but for the broader purpose to fulfill God's calling and broader plan. While this

chapter aims at the issue of methods, the foundational rationale for instruction is clear through scripture.

Contemporary missiological and church-related concerns for curriculum and instruction grow out of these clear biblical and theological roots. The planning of curriculum and the instruction of God's people continues as a great concern to the Church today. Christians everywhere are and must be concerned about these two related issues in order to:

- Instruct nonbelievers to lead them to Christ,
- To nurture believers,
- To teach maturing believers how to participate in the *missio Dei,* or
- To work with the Holy Spirit in the formation of the fruit of the Spirit as one employs the gifts of the Spirit.

To be effective in either the design or planning of curriculum or the actual instruction itself, one must know the local context. That information comes at least in part from local ongoing research. A well-designed curriculum and instructional program for any given situation will not fit optimally in another situation without some adjustment. Similarly, neither will the same curriculum or instructional methods be effective over time in the same context. Curricular variables are never the same from one situation to another. These differing variables always change the dynamics of the instruction and what is required for an optimally effective curriculum.[17]

When generational, worldview, and cultural differences emerge, subtle to major changes may be expected. What those changes should be can only be determined as one evaluates the local situation in the light of the revealed biblical values as applied in the local context. Research must continue both from a biblical and theological perspective in the changing local contexts.

Methodological Concerns

The research methodological concerns for the instruction, nurturing, and equipping of people to benefit from and participate in the *missio Dei* require attention in two major directions: values to be applied and the situation in which they are to be applied. Educators typically rely on other disciplines to provide the substance or

---

17   Some curricular variables include the following: purpose, content, control, costs, resources, selection of learners, selection of teachers, venue, timing, spiritual and community formation, community needs, evaluation and so on. Some further explanation of these variables can be found in Woodberry, Van Engen, and Elliston (eds.) (1996).

content to be taught, whether it is biblical knowledge, mathematics, history, biology, counseling, economics, or some other subject area. Educators are concerned with the value bases and delivery systems that will facilitate the holistic learning from a biblical perspective.

The range of methodological concerns facing the missiological educator then includes values both from a biblical perspective and the existing values in the local situation. When the values and local situation are known, one can identify what changes need to be made through an educational process. When one looks at a person in community two questions must be asked:

- Where is that person or community now?
- Where should that person or community be in terms of knowledge, skills, and spiritual formation?

The difference between the two answers provides the arena for the educator to work in instruction. The instructional questions include such concerns as "What can be done with the person to best facilitate the change from where he or she is now to match the value-based goals of knowing, doing and being?"

Common journalistic questions serve to raise curriculum and instruction concerns. Each of these questions must be answered in light of the responses to the others to have a balanced integrated educational program.

Why

Why should the content, skills, and formation be taught? Research into the local goals and purposes for the instruction is a recurring need.

Who

Who should teach? Who should learn? Who should make the decisions about the curriculum and instruction? Who is to be served by the learners? What are the characteristics, needs, interests, and perspectives of each of these constituencies? Answers to each of these questions will differ from one situation to another. Each difference will require research-based adjustment in the curriculum.

When

When should the different issues be taught? The timing issue includes both concerns about when in a person's relationship with the Lord, at what age of the person and when in relation to community concerns. The "When" question must be raised in terms of scheduling related to learning styles. Questions of the duration and sequence of the instruction require local attention. The question, "When?" in terms of the logistics of the individual, community, and teaching agency, requires research. When taken together, timing issues often require significant adjustments to contextualize a curriculum.

What

What should be taught? What needs to be learned? A missiological educator will raise the question of the learner rather than just the subject matter specialist. The concerns from one's own cultural perspective virtually always define and constrain what should be taught. The question is what should the learner be learning, not what should the teacher be teaching. The "what" should be informed by information from the learner, the community to be served, and the subject matter specialist, while being guided by a biblical and theological value base. The "what" of a missiological curriculum requires local information to be either appropriate or effective.

Where

Venue questions raise issues about access and relevance of the learning. Where can the learner learn best? If the learner is not yet a believer, then the venue should be where he or she is. If the person is a new believer, then the instruction and nurture should occur in the community where it can be permanently established. If the person is being instructed as an emerging leader, the venue should be with the people being led so that the knowledge, skills and relationships can be established there. Occasionally, an outside venue may be indicated as the better place to learn at least temporarily. However, to make wise and informed decisions, local information is needed. Broader venue research may serve decision makers to make wise decisions about the optimal setting for a given set of learning objectives. The question of "where" continues to be a concern when online instruction may be delivered virtually anywhere. The answer will depend on where the most effective learning can occur.

How

How should the instruction be delivered? How should the educational modes be balanced? How should the complementary teacher-centered and learner-centered approaches to education be optimally balanced in the learning situation? How should the delivery system be administered? Again, the curricular variables mentioned above must be researched locally to contextualize the curriculum and instructional approach. The delivery methods should also be conditioned by the local learning styles. To answer these questions requires local ongoing research.

Educational modes may include: 1) formal education that is highly structured, teacher centered, theoretical, content focused, certificate oriented, long term, stabilizing in terms of community standards, and resource intensive; 2) nonformal education that is highly structured, learner and community oriented, short term, functional and change oriented; and, 3) informal education that is relational based, not structured, acculturative, functional, and learner oriented.

New options for instructional technology continue to emerge. The advantages and disadvantages of face-to-face individualized apprentice or mentor model to classroom models, to a host of technology-based models present choices requiring local contextual insight. Again, the question of effectiveness in learning must be addressed through continuing research both in the context and of available and accessible methods.

How Much

How much instruction is needed? How much should be offered? How much should it cost? What are the local resources? How much can or should they be used? Key value questions arise when looking at this set of questions. Again, research in the community and in terms of establishing appropriate values for decision making.

Summary

From this brief overview at least some broad methodological concerns begin to appear. Educational research is needed in each community, with each generation and as developmental change occurs to keep the curriculum relevant and effective. Each of the broad communities identified (nonbelievers, new believers, and emerging leaders) change over time and so require somewhat different approaches in curriculum and instruction. Research is needed to inform both the perspectives to take (theory) and appropriate decisions to make (evaluation).

Distinctives

Missiological educational research, like missiological research in general, tends to range across disciplinary lines and become interdisciplinary. While some of the research subject matter in educational research is distinctive, the methods are not. Sociology, anthropology, history, theology, comparative religion, geography, economics, political science, and leadership all may contribute. Surveys, interviews, grounded theory cycling through the data, unobtrusive observations, ongoing assessment of instruction and learning outcomes, examination of historical archives and other methods all contribute to missiological education research. However, the missiological research has not as yet taken full advantage of the rigors of experimental methods. Much of the research that has been done over the past fifty years has been either descriptive research leading to theory formation or evaluative research that has aided in decision making. The "prescriptive" character of theological research presents an ongoing contextualizing challenge to educational research. Now, significant theory bases have been established; some of these theory bases would be greatly improved by the use of experiments to test and refine them.

Data Collection and Analysis

The data collection and analysis procedures for educational research resemble other forms of social research. Whether the primary methods are descriptive, experimental or evaluative, qualitative or quantitative, the same concerns emerge.

Missiological researchers face the same basic concerns of describing the population, selecting an appropriate sample and developing the means to elicit reliable and valid information as other researchers. Similar ethical questions apply. Questions of data analysis require prior planning in the data collection stage to provide useful data whether one is examining archival materials, interviewing, administering questionnaires or doing unobtrusive observation. The selection of the data analysis procedures must always be closely linked with the data collection and constrained by the central research issue at hand. One should pre-plan statistical procedures to summarize and facilitate analysis before collecting the data.

The establishment of values for use in evaluative research requires the same kinds of research rigor and methods as in other methods. For missiological educators the identification of values normally requires some biblical and theological foundations.

Validity and Reliability

All of the issues related to validity described in the first part of this text apply to the missiological educational concerns. The questions remain:

- Is the right information being collected?
- Are the values that are being selected the appropriate ones?
- Are the values being used truly biblical or are they just culturally adapted perceptions?
- Are the values from the local culture really from the local culture or are they projections from the researcher?

The issues of construct validity, that is, valid theoretical explanations are required for effective planning of curricula and the application of teaching methods. For example, to explain local learning styles inappropriately (invalidly) would result in wrong choices in terms of content, timing, selection of learners, selection of instructors, and formation activities. The whole delivery system would be inappropriately skewed.

A common mistake many make when moving into a new community or across a cultural boundary is to generalize about educational needs and planning too soon. Singular anecdotal experience unfortunately leads to an application to the whole community. While what was experienced or explained may have been true, it may not have been reliable. If the same question or issue were raised again, the same experience or answer may not be forthcoming. One may discover inconsistent (unreliable) answers require the questions to be changed (a validity question).

Whatever the educational issue the problems of asking the right questions locally, eliciting the right information in a consistent replicable ways presents a serious challenge.

Contributions to Missiology

The insights gained from answering the above questions are essential in the facilitation of two great tasks of the Church: bringing people to Christ and then bringing them up in Christ. Evangelism and nurture require education all along the way. Effective communication of the gospel across cultural boundaries requires attention to these educational issues.

None of the complementary academic disciplines is static. Each one is continually expanding and testing its theory base whether it is theology, anthropology, sociology, economics, comparative religion, geography, leadership, political science, or history. The experience and insights gained in curriculum design and instructing nonbelievers, new believers and maturing believers serves to inform all of these disciplines. As each discipline is applied in missiology with these new insights, the study of and obedience to God's will in the *missio Dei* will be improved.

10

COMMUNICATION RESEARCH

VIGGO SØGAARD

This chapter introduces the principal issues in doing
missiological research in communication.

The task of the Church is primarily one of communication.[18] Evangelism is communication. It could be argued that the Christian religion itself is a religion of communication with a communicator God who is constantly trying to establish communication with mankind. Believers participate in this process. The Great Commission is then a communication commission with the aim of enhancing and restoring communication between human beings and God.

Christian communication research deals with all aspects of the task of communicating the gospel, and it is therefore a relevant topic that is needed by all involved in Christian ministry. Using established research principles and techniques for the purpose of gaining reliable information will enhance the effectiveness of Christian communication.

Many of us have often thought: "I wish I knew . . . I wish I knew how people in this community think about our church. I wish I knew who actually listen to my program so that I can make my programs relevant to them. I wish I knew the real results of my ministry. I wish I knew how I should communicate the scriptures to these people" and so on. Communication research provides the kind of information that answers such questions and then helps us reduce errors in the decision-making process.

Lasswell states the scope of communication research well in his famous sentence on the effects of communication (1971, p. 84). Communication effects depend on

18   For a description of Christian communication see Smith, (1992); Søgaard, (1993).

- Who says
- What
- to Whom
- in Which channel
- and with What effect?

Communication research therefore deals with analyzing issues related to the communicator, the content, the audience, the methods, and the results.

Principal Methodological Concerns and Distinctives

Communication research seeks to answer questions related to relevance and effectiveness by applying research methodologies and techniques that are available to us. Furthermore, communication research can be seen as an applied science drawing on other fields of study and research: anthropological, sociological, marketing, as well as media research. It may include either or both quantitative and qualitative measures.

My personal perspective is primarily a marketing research perspective, but strongly influenced by intercultural experiences. A marketing-based research concept implies a deeply involved role for research in the management decision-making process. Such a perspective suggests that one only gather the information needed for the stated objectives or decisions. This information may, for example, be the development of an evangelism strategy or the selection of relevant biblical texts for a program or printed booklet. The key will be to know what one needs to know.

Kinnear and Taylor (1992) define marketing research as the systematic and objective approach to the development and provision of information for the marketing management decision-making process. For Christian communication, the process is similar.

From the above definition, one can identify four key phrases that are important to communication research: (1) it is a *systematic activity*, that is well organized and planned. It will require a researcher who understands the methods used and is capable of carrying out the necessary activities with great care and attention to details; (2) it is an *objective activity*, that is, it is a scientific exercise where all efforts will be made to avoid bias and emotions. The researcher will need to be able to keep distance and objectivity, even when the data may show discouraging signs; (3) it is the *provision of information*, that is, it will relate to a specific situation; finally,

(4) it is *research for decision-making*, helping the organization to focus its resources on the real task and the intended audience.

Principal Ways of Collecting Data

Communication research offers a variety of methods. Each one has its specific approaches which may be readily used by Christian researchers. For some purposes a researcher needs qualitative data obtained from focus groups, and for other areas one needs quantitative data obtained from survey research. It is fairly easy to count numbers, but it takes much more refined research methods to provide good information on issues such as attitudes and feelings and to provide measures relevant to the spiritual results of our ministry.

Survey Research

A primary approach in communication research is to use survey research, which to a large extent, is based on sampling. Researchers use sampling because it is not normally possible to take a census where information is collected from everybody in a population. In a sample, the researcher chooses a representative subset from a larger group to represent the whole group. Sampling methodologies have been developed as a very refined science where error can be measured and one can make quite accurate predictions on the basis of a sample selected according to the rules of sampling.

Using Samples

Several reasons apply for using samples: sampling saves money. Economy is probably the most obvious reason. Sampling also saves time. The interviewing process itself takes time, and the difference between 400 interviews and 400,000, for example, is enormous. Sampling is more accurate. The primary reason is that a census will have more nonsampling errors. Nonsampling errors are errors related to the research process, but not part of the sampling process. Sampling avoids contamination of the study population. Avoidance of contamination is important for pre- and post-tests. If the whole group has already been exposed to the topic in a pre-test, their attitudes and behavior may have changed because of it.

Questionnaires

In communication research, researchers use questionnaires extensively. A questionnaire is a formalized way of collecting data and it functions as the link between the information needs and the respondents. Due to possible measurement errors, the one who constructs a questionnaire must have studied research methods. No series of steps, principles, or guidelines guarantee an effective and efficient questionnaire. It is both an art and a scientific undertaking. If a questionnaire is poorly made and it has a measurement error, the collected data will be useless or even lead to wrong decisions. The researcher will therefore continue to ask the questions: "Am I getting accurate information? Am I getting valuable information? And, is the question measuring what it is supposed to measure?" Both reliability and validity issues may arise.

Constructs

In order to develop accurate measures, researchers need to carefully define the constructs (theoretical bases or conceptual framework) they are measuring. As one looks at different parts of our environment and daily experiences, different kinds of special tools and techniques are needed for gathering information about them. Some instruments, like a thermometer, can be used by anybody, but other instruments and techniques need training and practice if they are to be useful. For untrained persons, a look into a microscope or telescope will tell them almost nothing. For others, numbers or economic data will make no sense. The novice needs to acquire a conceptual framework and gain additional experience before he or she can make appropriate interpretation of the data. Likewise, the communication researcher must, in addition to the basic tools and instruments of observation and measurement, have a general conceptual framework for sorting out and organizing the data received. It is important for one to master both methodologies and techniques to obtain the needed reliable and valid information.

The problem lies in the measurement of the behavior of people and of measuring concepts believed to exist in people's minds. Often, the characteristics cannot be observed directly, and consequently one needs to define such constructs as precisely as possible. Furthermore, researchers need measurable definitions if they are to study such topics as a person's loyalty to the family or to his or her church. Or, what are the observable or measurable characteristics of faith? One often hears statements like, "He is a good Christian." How does one measure that? What are the assumptions for such a statement?

Data Processing and Analysis

When the questionnaires have been filled out, they need to be tabulated and analyzed in order to provide information regarding our research objectives. The raw data need to be edited, coded, and entered into a computer program before one can begin the actual task of data analysis.

Straight tabulations are helpful in providing a general picture, but the underlying dynamics are highlighted through cross-tabulation. For example, one may want to know if a difference exists between how satisfied women are with the worship service with that of male members. Or, one may want to study different Bible reading patterns among church members.

Usually an experienced researcher or statistician is needed to assist with the selection of appropriate statistics. For example, three different measures for central tendency—mean, median, and mode—may be used. They need to be used according to the type of data available. A useful statistical procedure to test whether differences between two or more groups are due to chance variations is called the Chi-square test.

Validity

The constant question in the mind of the researcher and the decision maker will be, what do I need to know in order to answer the question at hand? Many things may be of interest, but the question is not, what I would like to know, but what I need to know. A list of specific information needs will be developed prior to proceeding with research design, sample definition, and questionnaire construction. Valid information is therefore information that is useful for meeting the needs at hand. Data can be very interesting, but if the collected data cannot be directly translated into information that will help solve our problem, it may be useless. A well developed list of information needs will assure that the data collected is valid and useful.

Furthermore, a number of technical approaches may assure validity. For example, *Construct Validity* involves understanding the theoretical rationale underlying the obtained measurements, and *Content Validity* involves a subjective judgment by an expert as to the appropriateness of the measurement. *Concurrent Validity* involves correlating two different measurements of the same phenomenon which have been administered at the same point in time, and *Predictive Validity* involves the ability to predict a future condition on the basis of a measured phenomenon.

Reliability

Clearly, not only is valid information required, but it also has to be reliable. Reliability deals with trustworthiness, consistency, and accuracy, and it will be increased as one reduces all possible areas of error in the measurement process. Careful attention to possible measurement error will help in the gathering of valid, reliable, and useful data.

Errors may creep into the research in several areas:

- Characteristics measured and data obtained may be short-term, influenced by external factors such as mood and fatigue.
- Characteristics measured and data obtained may be influenced by situational factors such as change in location.
- Characteristics measured and data obtained may be influenced by the way questions are asked and the personality of interviewers.
- Characteristics measured and data obtained may be inconsistent due to measuring factors such as ambiguous questions.
- Characteristics measured and data obtained may be changed by coding and tabulation errors (Kinnear and Taylor, 1991, p. 231).

The total error of measurement is a combination of systematic error and random error. Systematic error will be caused by a constant measuring error like the wrong speed of a stopwatch. Random error is where different stopwatches are used in a competition and one of them is not consistent.

Principal Contributions to Missiology

Communication research provides significant input to missiology by focusing on the task of communicating the gospel to others. Its focus is specific even though a wide variety of measures are involved. Communication research will ask tough questions of the communicator, focusing on key elements rather than trying to measure everything. The questions that guide in establishing parameters for communication research include:

1. What do I need to know?
2. Why do I need to know this?
3. Where can I get the information?
4. From whom do I need the information?

5. When do I need it?
6. How will I use the information?
7. What will be the result of using this information?

Furthermore, communication research helps Christian leaders to be good stewards of God-given resources. It helps us (1) measure actual results and (2) study the audience and their needs. Communication research will (3) assist in the development of strategies as research findings are phased into appropriate evangelistic or ministry strategies and (4) assist in media selection, helping the person identify the approach that is the best in a particular situation.

Principal Contributions of Communication Research to Multidisciplinary Missiological Research

Everyone needs a research perspective, a research attitude, so that one is seeking good and important information all the time. A ministering team also needs a common concern for research so that information gathering can be a joint effort. If it is just left to a researcher, the result may be research reports sitting on shelves without being used.

Contributions of communication research to a multidisciplinary perspective can be summarized in the following four points:

- Communication Research is itself a combination of methods,
- Communication Research keeps its focus on mission,
- Communication Research focuses on effectiveness,
- Communication Research has its focus on application.

Communication research is therefore a topic for all Christian leaders and not just for the media experts. Only when one has learned the principles of research design and questionnaire construction is one able to use information effectively. A primary concern is, therefore, to arrive at good involvement by both the researcher and the management or leadership. Only such close cooperation will assure that useful information is obtained and the right questions asked. And, as a result, the gospel is communicated effectively.

11

HISTORICAL RESEARCH

PABLO A. DEIROS

This chapter introduces the principal issues in conducting historical research in missiology.

A number of different concepts serve to explain history and historical research as it relates to missiology. In a general sense, history is knowledge of the past that is achieved through an inquiry of past human actions. This research follows an independent and regular method or process and then arranged in an acceptable order. In a more restricted sense, history is the present intellectual reconstruction of a specific human past through a detailed research or inquiry of human actions or facts based on the interpretation of the extant evidence and the congruent exposition of its result. Historical research is the process through which the historian tries to restore and understand past human events, to answer questions about those specific human actions done in the past. The history researcher works to reconstruct the human past, but not all past actuality. The interest of the historian is in human acts, but in socially significant actions.

Human actions have two aspects: the mere human facts (external aspect), and the thought of the agent of those facts (internal aspect). Any human action in the past—as a singular, unique, and preterit fact—"was" a reality. The task of the historian is to apprehend it in its totality and re-create it intellectually. This process explores why the event happened; and the historian identifies relevant knowledge of that event. This knowledge and understanding of past human events require specific methodological procedures. A historian follows a methodologically controlled objectivity in a well-done historical research.

History as a Science

As a science, history has a definite subject matter, a method of studying its subject matter with the purpose of knowing the truth, and an objective to achieve. The subject matter of history is unique, since it has to do with human events that happened at a certain time and place. The objective in historical research is to see the causal connections and interdependence of human events. The method in historical research is as unique as the events of the past being researched. Through the historian's methodological approach, the researcher studies subject matter to acquire knowledge of the unique human past. Interpreting the evidence, the researcher seeks to obtain knowledge that will result in the understanding of the causal connection and interdependence of human past events.

Process of Historical Research

Historical research follows four steps, each one of which has its own specific procedures and following a logical sequence.

Heuristic Step

The heuristic step finds data in the sources of information. As a technique, it deals with the establishment of rules to obtain evidence from the documents that give testimony of past events. To obtain evidence from the documents means to transform them into sources.

This step has four moments. The *bibliographic moment* consists of evaluating all of the precedent research about the research issue under investigation. Bibliographic research is the analytical survey of previous scholarship and the location of secondary literature or precedent research in the chosen field. It also has to do with the finding and identification of primary sources. This task involves selecting, ordaining, and filing the relevant source materials. This work is typically done in libraries and archives. The *thematic moment* has to do with defining and narrowing a viable topic for the research in the light of the contrasting opinions, divergent conclusions, things that are not clear, contradictions, and even issues not taken into account in the bibliography under research. The personal interest of the researcher and his or her commitment to solve the problem of ignorance or lack of understanding of a given human event is essential to the best result of the inquiry. A third moment is the *erudite moment*. A new approach to the issue becomes necessary. The researcher goes back to the sources to fill in the blanks in the investigation of others, to find new omitted or misunderstood data. The *diagnostic moment* deals with the document. The researcher has to observe its general characteristics (form, material, number of pages, conservation, calligraphy, marginal notes, and so on) and make a general description of it (record its date, general content, signatures, marks, place where it was located, and the like).

Critique Step

A second step is critique. The material obtained in the heuristic stage is summated to a qualitative analysis in all aspects. Again, four moments are expected. The *morphologic* or authenticity moment has the object of probing the testimony to be authentic or sham. Various techniques are useful to this purpose: paleography, epigraphy, calligraphy, numismatics, and so on. The *alethologic* or veracity moment has to do with the truth of a document. A testimony may be authentic but not true, or true but not authentic, or partially true. In the *hermeneutic* or interpretation moment, the researcher uses the collected evidence to answer doubts and to solve the problem under investigation through understanding. New questions may result. The *axiologic* or evaluation moment helps the researcher to see the significance of his or her new understanding of a past event. The researcher can now estimate the influence of the facts discovered in the totality of the research problem.

Synthesis Step

The third step is synthesis, which consists of the coherent ordaining of the materials collected and the resulting historic "construction" or "creation." All the elements developed through the process of research have to be put together, composed, and combined. Through this composition, the historian brings congruence to the whole, and makes the mass of evidence into a coherent unity, that can be understood. Two logic moments occurs in the *selective moment*, the researcher makes a choice of the best information available out of the mass of evidence he or she has collected. In the *creative moment*, the historian tries to apprehend the event as it was, because the evidences force him or her to do so. Then the historian understands the event and is in condition to re-create it in his or her mind. Past events become facts of history and acquire a contemporary dimension through the work of a present re-creation by the historian. This event climaxes in the historic research process.

Exposition Step

The fourth step is exposition. This step puts forward the results obtained through the historical research. The presentation may be oral or written, concise or detailed, short or extensive. The researcher must always be as objective as possible in the presentation of his or her understanding of the past. The exposition is basically a literary work. As such, matters of style, writing, footnotes, typing, and organization of the material are important.

Validity

The question on the validity of historical research is basic to an adequate approach to the challenge of reconstructing the actions of human beings in the past. Answers to this issue may vary greatly. As important as it is, self-knowledge is based on our collective experiences as they are testified by the actions human beings have done in the past. Our human past is the mirror through which we can understand the meaning of being human. What humans have done in the past is the most eloquent answer to the question on what we are. Consequently, history is not a mere knowledge of the past, but a particular kind of knowledge: it is knowledge of our human past. When one studies human achievements, institutions, cultures, civilizations, thought, and the answers other human beings have given to the problems they faced in their lives, one learns the meaning of our humanity. History certainly is a major life teacher. The value of history is somehow linked to this pedagogic orientation that history offers to the new generations.

Of all the values history provides to make human life more human, none is more relevant than the love for truth. A serious historical researcher will try to bring into light the past actions of human beings to discover the human truth wrapped in them.

The honest historian knows that his or her approach to the past through the testimony of the evidences is like looking "a poor reflection as in a mirror" and not seeing facts "face to face." It is also like knowing "in part" and not "fully" (1 Cor 13:12). Historical research is not an exact study, as is more the case with the physical sciences. Mathematical certainty and absolute conclusions are not part of the purpose of the student of history. History is not and cannot be an exact science, for its subject matter are unrepeatable human actions in the past. Any research in the field of history will be selective and, consequently, will express some level of partiality. Reliability rests on objectivity. However, in historical research, objectivity does not depend so much on the materials under research as on the attitude of the researcher and the methodology applied to the inquiry. The sources should be heard in their own terms, with the researcher interpreting them honestly, recognizing his or her own presuppositions and applying the best methodological tools.

A Resource to Missiology

Historical research is an important resource for missiology because Christianity is a historical religion. It is inseparable from the historical events, which called it forth. As the Christian faith is historical, the Christian testimony is also historical. The proclamation of the kingdom of God is performed in time and space. These events are historical facts, that is, events in the history of the nations and peoples, not special religious or sacred events out of time and space. Any past missiological event can be subject to an investigation by the ordinary methods of the historian. Such an inquiry is fundamental to achieve a full understanding of the issues studied by missiology.

History provides missiology a principle of knowledge and a rubric of truth. Conscious awareness in the present is affected by the past in all spheres of human action. This principle is also true of the historical witness of the Christian community. Historical research serves missiology as it affords an instrument in acquiring knowledge and certainty with relation to the proclamation of the kingdom of God, inasmuch as these instances of Christian testimony reside in the past. History enters missiology as the witness of the Christian community in mission. This witness is constituted of the material that emerges from the life of the Christian community in all of its historical continuity and contemporary breadth. Historical research is the tool to reconstruct that material. It is an unavoidable resource for the missiologist, since the norm by which researchers attains their knowledge and certainty consists of the totality of the events in the Christian historical witness as they appear in any present moment.

History is the terrain of human decisions and actions. However, even more importantly history is the stage of God's redeeming actions. The Church, in its missionary endeavor to proclaim the kingdom of God, creates history, that is, actions of human beings that have been done in the past. As the Body of Christ, the Christian community gives testimony of the kingdom which was set into motion by Jesus' cross and resurrection. All these missiological issues are subject to historical research. In a multidisciplinary missiological inquiry, historical research helps us to know and understand what the Church has done in the fulfillment of its God-given mission, and thus what that mission is. Knowing these issues is fundamental to an adequate understanding of what the Church itself is, since what we have done in the past as a witnessing community is the clue to understand what we are. In short, our identity as the body of Christ in mission in the world depends on our historical research on what we have done in the past to obey God's mission.

12

QUALITATIVE SOCIAL SCIENCE METHODS IN RESEARCH DESIGN

R. DANIEL SHAW

This chapter describes how qualitative social science research methods support missiology.

Choosing the right method for the desired research is essential for success when doing missiological research. A common mistake in doing qualitative research is using methods that do not match the nature of the research. The objective in any research project is to collect data, analyze that data and then determine the quality of that data (its reliability) in order to ensure the validity of the findings. These findings, in turn, enable a researcher to draw conclusions and make significant recommendations based on the completed research. The entire project must "hang together," as Elliston has made clear throughout this volume. Determining which method best suits the collection and analysis of data is the initial objective of a researcher who seeks to utilize the social sciences and accomplish qualitative research.

In order to keep the focus on establishing a rationale for proper methodological selection, my delimitation in this chapter is to focus on three methods anthropologists, sociologists and, to lesser extent, psychologists commonly use. Three primary methods with numerous permutations relate to enabling the collection and analysis of qualitative data: Observation and Questions based on Participant Observation,[19] Interviewing,

---

19 This approach combines Participant Observation as utilized by anthropologists, with interviewing based on observations. Since observation alone rarely enables a researcher to determine the meaning of an activity for participants, the questions that emerge from observation will enable a researcher to expand understanding from the perspective of the people who participate. The second chapter of my book, *Transculturation*, gives details on this approach (Shaw, 1988).

including life history, and Focus Groups. These three qualitative methods are often combined in various ways to develop a case study relevant to a particular context. Case studies use a triangulation of these three methods to check and counterbalance each other in order to ensure reliable data that produces valid results.

Methodological Concerns and Distinctives

As a researcher, one must begin by assessing the nature of the data necessary to successfully interact with the variables of the central research issue and answer the research questions set out in the research design. In short, what kinds of data are needed? Steps include: (1) determine the purpose of doing this research; (2) identify one's goal for the research; and, (3) understand the interaction of the key variables as they combine to enable the researcher to clearly state the central research issue. After these steps have been completed, one is ready to ask the methodological question: "What approach will best serve to collect and analyze data in order to answer the research questions and determine the indicators of the variables?" Once one understands the nature of the data necessary for the particular research, the researcher can assess the three qualitative research methodologies to decide which one will work best for that situation.[20] However, before doing that, one must decide on whether the research is primarily inductive, with a focus on the nature of the data which leads to theory development, or deductive, with a focus on the nature of theory and how the data supports or rejects it (see Figure 6 Inductive Reasoning Process in Chapter 4).

Jim Nelson (2007), an anthropological psychologist, has developed what he calls the "Research Cycle." He developed this concept to encourage researchers to consider the nature of the data with respect to developing or testing theory. He made the point that every research project should include both in order to complete the cycle and ensure reliability and validity. A theory that emerges from reliable data needs to be tested for validity, and the validity of a theory needs to be tested against reliable data. Nelson demonstrates that every context from which data is drawn requires the broadening or narrowing of any given theory (Slife and Nelson, 2011). Again, as Elliston has shown, the interrelationship of the parts in such a model is necessary for doing credible research. It is necessary, then, to carefully choose the best research method for any given project.

---

20   See Table 11 (p. 108) for a comparison of the three primary methodologies to assist in determining which method best suits the collection of the data you need.

In assessing the best research method to procure the most reliable data, a researcher must consider the elements of the project. As Elliston stresses in Chapter 4, a direct relationship exists between the nature of the research design as expressed in the first chapter of a proposal and the methodology presented in chapter 3 of a proposal. What is that relationship? Inasmuch as missiological research is largely phenomenological in nature except for theological research, the focus is often assessing a people group or issues within a context, or developing an appreciation for a particular set of ideas or concepts that emerge from a database. Such approaches usually require data which can then be applied more broadly to other contexts where the hypothesis or theory can be further tested. Such inductive approaches require qualitative data gathered in a context often utilizing one of the three primary qualitative methods. In addition, the choice requires an understanding of how research method (with the relative strengths and weaknesses) interacts with the kind of data necessary for a given project. Once chosen, the method can then be applied to the actual collection of data, which enables a researcher to analyze that material, produce findings, and eventually write it all up. I turn now to data collection and the delineation of each method.

Data Collection

Data collection is central to any research project. It provides the material for analysis from which findings emerge. A presupposition of collecting good data is that the researcher must approach the data in as unbiased a manner as possible. As human beings, impacted by our own culture and its worldview assumptions, we tend to feel that our perspective is the best. However, every other human being on planet Earth feels the same. This common individualistic view implies a considerable amount of culture clash when doing research. Thus, it is important for researchers to acknowledge their own biases when doing research in another context (hence the need to include assumptions in chapter 1 of the proposal). By being aware of personal assumptions, a researcher can then ask what behaviors or issues in the research context mean from the perspective of those involved. Pike (1967) calls this perspective the *emic* viewpoint, determining what something means from the particularity of concerns from within an environment. This particularity, once understood, can then be compared with other contexts for the elements that give meaning in each context where similar concerns are shared, a broader *etic* perspective. What is interesting for research, however, is what can be learned about being human from the diversity of perspective provided by understanding socio-linguistic particularity.

Color is a wonderful example of this concept. As human beings created by God (I'm presenting this perspective as a missiologist), we all share the same perceptive apparatus—our eyes and their connection to the brain. All human beings have the ability to perceive color, light and dark and so much more, as part of the ability to see. However, as Berlin and Berlin have pointed out, the way people talk about their perceptions varies considerably despite their obvious ability to make distinctions of color using standard color chips (Berlin and Berlin, 1975). The English language uses the five primary colors: red, yellow, green, blue, and purple from the scientific spectrum. To these we add black (the presence of all colors) and white (the absence of any color), and an infinite variety of shades and hues to distinguish categories of color. For the Samo, living in the vast rainforest of Western Provence in Papua New Guinea, they too have five primary colors: *obusinte*, "red"; *biyete*, "yellow"; *molowote*, "green"; *begolote*, "white/light"; and *businte*, "black/dark"; to which they add *gugumana*, "pattern/design." Each color ends with the clitic "-*te*" which can be translated "soft stone." Each primary color is represented by a soft stone which the Samo dig out of the clay in their swampy terrain. These stones can then be chewed, thereby mixing the stone with saliva to make a paste or earth dye which can then be used to paint patterns (*gugumana*) on people or things. The design on a dancer, dressed to impress the watching spirits, is a typical use of these earth paints. The Samo focus on the source of color—soft stones—not the color spectrum. Understanding this perspective gives anthropologists an appreciation for different views when it comes to color or anything else that human beings categorize.

In doing missiological research one must reduce bias by looking for the perspective of the people with whom the researcher interacts. In their context the criteria people apply are what matter, and to the extent possible, the researcher, who enters their midst, should adopt those perspectives in order to best understand them and the context in which they have meaning. This approach was what Jesus did in his incarnation, he became truly Jewish and spoke to Jews from their worldview—researchers must do the same! I turn now from perspective to the nature of the primary methods in focus here.

Observation and Questions

The observation and questions approach is built on the well-known and often applied anthropological technique of observing people, taking good notes, and then asking questions based on having experienced some event or interaction within a particular society. Having seen or experienced something, a researcher can then ask questions designed to elicit the people's perspective. Mere observation is not sufficient to provide what Malinowski (1922) called, "the native point of view." When using this method, research is carried out in the context of a particular community in an attempt to appreciate the quality of life in that time and place and establish the rationale people have for preferring their own lifestyle. Observations made in the context of participation allow for a "feeling" of what it is like to be in that context. Data come out of interactive experience corroborated by questions, and responses relating to the experience (i.e., observation-questions technique). This approach to research emphasizes "the art and science of describing a human group—its institutions, interpersonal behaviors, material productions, and beliefs" (Angrosino, 2007, p. 14).

Interviews

The interview is an extension of asking questions in order to develop an appreciation for what people think about any topic that is being researched. A wide range of approach exists, extending from open-ended questions emerging from a particular experience (as in observation and questions) to formal surveys requiring only a tick in a box that most closely represents the respondent's perspective. The key distinction for interviewing, however, is that the researcher chooses the topic as well as the nature and order of the questions, rather than their emerging from the context. This places the researcher in control of the questions being asked. These questions are then administered to a sufficiently large number of people thereby ensuring a consistency of response across the corpus. The data come out of questions, interview guides or surveys designed to produce consistent responses. Ethnographic interviewing "is a key venue for exploring the ways in which subjects experience and understand their world. It provides a unique access to the lived world of the subjects, who in their own words describe their activities, experiences and opinions" (Kvale, 2007, p. 9).

Focus Groups

The focus group combines interviewing with observations of human interaction within the construct of a carefully chosen group of individuals who are knowledgeable about the research topic and understand its context. Research is carried out for the purpose of utilizing interrelationships among those in the group in order to maximize understanding. Data come out of questions posed to the group with careful attention to the way in which debate, consensus, and/or solutions characterize social dynamics on the one hand and perceptions of cultural understanding on the other. Using focus groups draws attention to "group dynamics . . . [in] forming a consensus, developing an explanatory framework, interpreting . . . messages, or weighing up competing priorities" (Barbour, 2008, p. 3). Focus groups are particularly valuable for verifying the quality or reliability of data based on observations or interviews. People are able to corroborate viewpoints and hunches a researcher has, and their debate, body language, and interaction with others in the group often ameliorate differences of opinion and serve as a means of ensuring faithfulness.

When taken together, the three methods (with their complementary strengths and weaknesses) provide for effective triangulation in research. So, for example, after observing a particular ceremony and asking various participants about their responses and feelings, a researcher may gather a group of experts to probe their responses individually and as a group. Such corroboration enhances the strengths of each method while reducing the weaknesses inherent in each one. My own ethnography of Samo initiation is a case in point. The entire book treats initiation as a case study of the interaction between ceremonialism and interpersonal relationships. It incorporates journal entries and highlights the importance of co-initiating mature men and women in a "coming out party" atmosphere (Shaw, 1990).

When doing missiological research however, it is important to select one method as primary. Data collected using that approach can then be complemented with supplementary material from field notes, a personal journal, maps, and general observations from context. The wealth of data collected during a research project can quickly become unmanageable without an effective way to keep track of information (what happened and who said what about it, as well as when and where it was said). Using some sort of filing system that reflects the organization of cultural data or a particular cultural theory can be a great help. A well-kept personal journal (in which a researcher records feelings, biases and responses) provides a valuable check and balance to detailed field notes. These tools are valuable sources of data that can then be applied to analytical approaches inherent in each methodology. I turn now to a brief look at the analytical process.

Data Analysis

The point of analysis is to understand what the data mean to people within the context. Analysis always involves coding the data in order to extract meaning. Qualitative analysis takes many forms and each method has its own focus commensurate with the strengths of the approach. A basic analytical continuum applies to any method: collect raw data and provide descriptive statements which lead to interpretation. This approach is the essence of Spradley's (1979, 1980) developmental research sequence. Properly applied, analysis reduces surprises and enables a researcher to make predictions. When one is able to make predictions based on an understanding of the data, and is right, he or she is well on the way to understanding the context. When the data are sufficient to make accurate predictions, researchers refer to this stage as "data saturation"—one has enough data.

Analyzing Observations and Questions

As researchers observe a particular event or interact in a cultural context, they may begin with anything of personal interest or of interest to the people. One reason I began my Samo research with an initiation ceremony was because that event took place within a few days of our arrival. I had no idea what was going on, knew no Samo language, and could only observe what was taking place. Those initial notes, however, were voluminous, describing what took place. Because of my total unfamiliarity, they were focused on observations which I was able to later use to ask pertinent questions. Over the next twelve years I observed seven other initiation ceremonies and participated as an initiate in one. The most important thing, after seeing that initial ceremony, was to compare it with others to see what was similar and what differed. By the time I observed the third one I was formulating ideas about what might happen next—I was looking for patterns.

All human activity is patterned, and noting those patterns is often crucial to analysis. On one occasion, the oil company was hiring Samo men to assist in a geological survey. They announced their intent less than a week before an important initiation ceremony was to take place at Sodiyobi, and said they would come on a certain day—right in the middle of the planned initiation. Undaunted, the leaders reduced the three days of a normal initiation into a twenty-four-hour period. What was left out of those proceedings was every bit as important, for analytical purposes, as what they actually did—how were the normal patterns adjusted to ensure that the critical elements of initiation were included, and what were those elements? That particular event enabled me to check hypotheses and attempt to understand the patterns I had already begun to notice (Shaw, 1990, p. 158). Some form of pattern matching across events, then, can be a very helpful analytical tool.

Researchers can analyze observations, and ask subsequent questions inductively, letting the data largely speak for themselves or deductively in order to test hypotheses. Following Nelson's research cycle, this approach can either reflect theories from other contexts or from within the context. Qualitative researchers do both, based on the nature of the research design and the particularity of the research questions they are asking. Inductive analysis leads to understanding within a context, whereas deductive analysis gives a broader perspective for comparison in other contexts where the same phenomenon is practiced. In my research on initiation, I was able to do both, focusing on Samo manifestations and then comparing them across the breadth of the Bosavi Language Family where ethnographers and linguists have done a considerable amount of research (Shaw, 1986).

Another objective of analyzing observations is to establish the reliability of the data. How do observations of one event compare to observations of other similar events? And, how do a researcher's observations reflect what actually happened? This question raises the issue of trust when doing research based on using participant observation. Did what was reported actually take place? Observing and reporting on multiple events reduce idiosyncrasy both within the context and of a researcher's reporting. Having observed eight initiation ceremonies over a twelve-year period gave me a considerable research advantage over someone who only saw one such event—recall my lack of understanding on first observing an initiation ceremony. After seeing several such events, I was able to ask increasingly focused questions which changed again when I was directly involved as a participant. Consistency across the corpus enables a degree of confidence that considerably raises the reliability of the data, and trust in the researcher. Demonstrating a high degree of reliability is important within a research project as well as across a region where other researchers can compare the material from your context with that of others. Anything a researcher can do to demonstrate the reliability of the data gives others confidence in the validity of the findings.

Analyzing Interviews

Analyzing interviews begins with an accurate and complete transcription of the full text of an interview. Without a full transcript of an interview, a researcher has no data. This task is labor-intensive work, but it is the transcribed text that provides the initial data for coding. Coding the transcribed texts is essential for analysis. Codes may come from standard external categories, such as the Outline of Cultural Materials (Murdock, 2004) or may be drawn from the interviews themselves (often repeated words or concepts across the corpus). Vocabulary reflecting ceremonial activity, for example, will be very different from responses to economic activity. In my Samo case study of initiation, a plethora of economic activity enabled the initiates to provide mountains of food to feed all those who attended the event as guests. It is necessary, then, to determine what one is seeking based on the topic of research. Finding related information in the interviews or identifying internal terms, topics, or categories repeated by informants provides the initial coding that leads to further analysis and interviewing. Once coded, the categories of material may be entered into a chart or other device appropriate for displaying the categories that reflect these data. This information can be enhanced with further increasingly focused questioning in order to determine its meaning.[21]

Interviews relating to life histories serve as a means of understanding the stories of individuals within a society. Comparing different life experience for commonalities as well as individual idiosyncrasies gives a researcher an appreciation for life in a particular context. What are the common points of transition in an individual's life? What is celebrated and what is allowed to pass by unnoticed? For the Samo, initiation is central to the use of relationship terms which provided a rationale for my own initiation—people did not know when I was initiated and therefore did not know how to place me in the complex set of interrelationships central to Samo life. Marriage, on the other hand, passes with little ceremony other than an exchange of sisters signaling two couples being married. What cultural assumptions presume a high regard for ceremony in one social domain but not another and why? Interviewing people who have experienced these life events can help to determine the meaning of these key points in the life cycle. Such information can ultimately contribute to an appreciation for the gospel message in the research environment.

Analyzing Focus Groups

As with interviews, success in analyzing focus groups begins with detailed transcriptions of each recorded session. Furthermore, notes based on observations of human interaction during each session contribute to a rich database that can be mined for information pertaining to the topic in focus. In short, transcriptions and detailed notes based on observation are the required starting point for effective analysis of data from focus groups. Coding this material is similar to what is required when observing and/or interviewing. External categories may be applied to the data in order to evaluate a hypothesis or theoretical position. Conversely, categories may emerge out of the discussion with a focus on internal logic. It is therefore, important to notice the line of reasoning and group divergence from a researcher's expectations. As in analysis of the other primary methods, similarities

---

21   Research is an iterative process; each step leads to the next with a need to repeat each step at a deeper, more integrated level until arriving at meaningful themes that reflect people's views regarding the research topic. Discovering these themes is the point of doing research.

and patterns in one group may be compared with the next. How do responses and group dynamics in one focus group further the research and suggest new questions or approaches to observation that may be more productive in other groups? In short, what emerges from the study that provides findings that may be considered valid because they are supported by a body of data and relevant analysis?

Analytical Processes

Bernard suggests using some variation of Content Analysis of the transcriptions to enable a researcher to make replicable and valid inferences about the data (Bernard, 2006, p. 505ff). An analysis of physical units such as time or space boundaries and physical properties relevant to the context may provide clarity. Syntactical units, including linguistic elements employed in communicating information (language, use of interpreter, dialectical variation, etc.) and propositional units, structured around the particular contents of each respondent, enable deeper understanding (See Søgaard's chapter in this volume). Furthermore, thematic units reflect general content and consensus within the group. Other analytical tools include free listing, frames or true/false tests, triads tests, pile sorts and the ranking of data. These tools all serve as ways to analyze qualitative data, ask further questions, and ultimately determine the meaning from the perspective of those who provided the information through the use of one of the primary research methods.

Grounded theory is another analytical approach for inductive research. As Charmaz points out, the "method stresses discovery and *theory* development rather than logical deductive reasoning which relies on prior theoretical frameworks .... Since grounded theorists intend to construct theory from the data itself [sic], they need to work with solid, rich data that can be used to elicit thorough development of analytic issues" (1994, p. 96). She goes on to define and refine the coding process in considerable detail. This approach closely relates to Spradley's developmental research sequence (1979) and Bernard's content analysis and pattern matching (2006)—the objective is to give voice to the data. To the extent possible, treat the evidence fairly, produce compelling conclusions, and rule out alternative interpretations.

All these analytical processes are grounded in reliable data. To the degree that a researcher is able to interpret the data in a way that produces valid findings and reflect meaningful themes that replicate useful information, missiology will be enhanced. Taking such an approach to research will enable one to make recommendations that reflect the actual circumstances and perspective of the people, thereby ensuring relevance of any application based on the research. In Chapter 4, Elliston provides considerable detail regarding the need for reliable data out of which valid findings may be shown to be significant. I, in turn, have demonstrated the interconnection between quality data and the resulting understanding that emerges.

Finally, Barrett nicely integrates method and theory in a way that helps missiologists understand the important interconnection between the two (1996). He, much like Elliston, maintains that the quality of research relates to knowing the major writers and their respective theories. This perspective connects a researcher to the literature with its theoretical orientations and ideas. However, as Nelson (2007) points out, that piece is only half the equation, a researcher must then be able to connect theory with corresponding methodologies—how can you apply methods to solving research problems? To solve research problems, a researcher must understand and appreciate what kinds of data the various methods produce and utilize their strengths and corresponding weaknesses to choose the method best suited for the particular research. If the research is designed properly, the findings should connect the context and respective method to theory thereby completing the research cycle. Through the findings, a researcher is able to present results that will enable others to use that research as a foundation for other investigations. With all this in mind, missiological researchers should be able to do original research that will test theory and method within a context that can be used for the sake of God's kingdom.

Contributions to Missiology

We live in a rapidly changing, interactive, and complex world. Like all other disciplines, mission too has changed and the issues in an urbanizing, globalized world are very different from missionaries of yesteryear. Increasing pluralism creates interdependence, and the impact of technology brings daily adjustment to people's lives. Given these differences, we dare not go about doing mission the same old way. We cannot continue in a postcolonial or even neocolonial mode. Rather, the Church must truly become what God intended for the context in which it presently finds itself. Therefore, a great need remains for ongoing research that enables people within the Church to be relevant to the world about them and be on the cutting edge of change. What are the current trends facing the Church in any given context and how can understanding these circumstances contribute to the ongoing effectiveness of the Church? The answer lies in research.

Through research, outside missionaries can enable church leaders to incorporate scripture into the socio-religious environment. What biblical truths will enable the Church to be relevant to the people of a context? As Van Engen notes, Christians need to encourage theology from above rather than from below. When God breaks into a context, it transforms people who are able to relate to God's expectations and bring transformation (2006). This kind of concern is the stuff of missiological research. Making it happen is the challenge. Much research is needed in the area of relevance and application of scripture to communities of believers, wherever they are found. Qualitative research can help outsiders learn much about God and the scriptures from the local or *emic* point of view. This knowledge can then be communicated through reported findings that enable other believers to appreciate the richness of God's intent for all of humanity (the *etic* perspective). As people from every language, tribe, and nation will one day stand rejoicing around God's throne (Rev 7:9), so we need now to learn from each other and celebrate the diversity God has built into being human.

My own research among the Samo has taught me the value of qualitative research and its application to the development of the Church and local theology. Understanding the intent of Samo initiation with its focus on interpersonal relationships and the need to counteract spiritual power, has brought new insight to my appreciation of Paul's letters to the Ephesians and Thessalonians. The relationship of people to God through Jesus Christ in the power of the Holy Spirit gives the Samo a sense of wonder—they can be in relationship with God who enables them to fight spiritual battles through the power of the one who now dwells within them. Such awareness enables believers to share their burdens with one another, work against the powers of evil that surround them, and know that God's protection is sufficient for them. It will enable them to overcome as they break the arrows of evil with the ironwood rod so familiar to raiding parties from precontact days. And, what of the painted dancer? How can contemporary Christians attract the attention of watching spirits and let them know their allegiance is to Christ and not to Satan? Samo Christians are asking these very questions. More research and subsequent findings are needed. The symbols of initiation provide an understanding of Samo lifestyle—living in harmony with God's power available to them as they fight against evil. As a result, not only do the Samo have a heightened appreciation for God in their midst, but I realize how God has implanted within their understanding an awareness of spiritual things from which I too can learn. He who created people in his own image implanted creativity into the human DNA. We can, therefore, celebrate God in every context. Further research is needed in order to collect and analyze reliable data from which we can draw findings that validate our human relationship with God. This kind of understanding also expands our appreciation of God's intent for human beings who in their diversity relate to God in a myriad of ways. Such awareness enables missiological researchers to celebrate all that God is from a multiplicity of contexts using a multiplicity of approaches. This kind of engagement is what missiology is all about.

TABLE 12
Comparing Three Primary Qualitative Research Methods
(Evaluation for Choice of Appropriate Method) Manickam (2008)

Observations & Questions	Interviews	Focus Groups

Submethods

Observations & Questions	Interviews	Focus Groups
1. Participant Observation	1. Questionnaires	1. Self-contained focus groups
2. Process Observation	2. Survey (mail, telephone, etc.)	2 Group interviews
3. Cultural Subsystems	3. One-on-one interviews	3. Interactive observations
4. Mapping	4. Structured interviews	
5. Demographics	5. Informal interviews	
6. Genealogies	6. Unstructured interviews	
7. Linguistics	7. Forms of sampling	
8. Time study	8. Yes/No questions	
9. Space study		
10. Micro study		
11. Macro study		

Observations & Questions	Interviews	Focus Groups

Key Features

1. Study aspects that are obscured from the "non-participant"	1. A primary feature is to produce statistics. This is done through asking questions (survey)	1. Able to collect a concentrated set of interactions in a relatively short period of time
2. Focus on behavior versus structure	2. Data collected from a sampling of the whole	2. Provide direct evidence about similarities and differences
3. Assume personal relationships	3. Control of the situation lies with the researcher due to closer communications	3. "It is the researcher's interest that provides the focus" (Morgan, 1997, p. 6)
4. Able to gather information in a "natural" environment	4. Works individual opinions, not group consensus	4. Data tend to be more emic-oriented due to its source
5. Look at broad cultural aspects	5. Can be used to form *focus groups*	5. This method "obtains perceptions on a defined area of interest" (Kruger, 1988, p. 18)
6. Descriptive in nature	6. Studies the stages of life	6. Method relies on "the researcher's focus and the group's interaction" (Morgan, 199, p. 13)
7. Focus on daily life, routines	7. Identity through stories	7. Can be used to create a *questionnaire* or a *survey*
8. Analysis and data collection move together in the process		
9. Research process is not pre-planned—determined by context		
10. The emic perspective is at the heart of research		
11. Research is shaped by research questions		
12. Methods of data collection are, for the most part, interactive		

Where Conducted

In context	Irrelevant—except to interview people from the context of research	In context

Observations & Questions	Interviews	Focus Groups

Key Authors & Titles

1. Jorgensen, Danny L., *Participant Observation* 2. Erickson, Ken & Donald Stull, *Doing Team Ethnography* 3. Fetterman, David M., *Ethnography* 4. Spradley, James, *Participant Observation*	1. Holstein, James A. & Jaber F. Gubrium, *The Active Interview* 2. Spradley, James, *Participant Interview* 3. Fowler, Floyd J., *Survey Research Methods.* Also *Improving Survey Questions* 4. Henry, Gary T., *Practical Sampling* 5. Atkinson, Robert, *The Life Story Interview*	1. Steward, David W. & Prem N. Shamdasani, *Focus Groups* 2. Morgan, D. L. *The Focus Group Guide Book*

Emphasis

1. Experience 2. To answer questions 3. To learn about context 4. To understand the "natives"	1. To answer questions 2. Answers could be ideal versus real 3. Focuses on data and numbers, not people or relationships necessarily	1. Group dynamics 2. Perceptions of cultural understandings

Questions

1. How & why 2. Questions come out of what you observe	Who, what, where, how many & how	Much the same as Interview with a group focus on the dynamics of relationship between people in the group and the research topic

Degree of Control

None—focus on what is going on	Moderate, based on the specificity of questions in the interview guide	Less than Interviewing. Reliant on the make-up of the group and people's response to the interview guide

Observations & Questions	Interviews	Focus Groups
Kinds of Data		
Responses to questions based on observation of actual experience in a context. Questions to ask emerge from actual observation	Response to questions determined by a researcher to be relevant to a context, issues, or circumstance being investigated	Response to questions posed by a researcher in order to determine the nature of relationships and situational content
Strengths		
1. Data derived from context 2. Inductive: Lets data speak for themselves 3. A more "naturalistic" observation compared to other groups 4. The use of triangulation greatly improves the validity of the data obtained	1. Shows consistency (same response to the same question(s) 2. Able to connect with many people 3. Interaction is a result 4. Results can be reproduced 5. Allows for in-depth understanding of opinions and experiences 6. Sampling is non-biased 7. Standardized measurements 8. Able to collect information that is not available through other sources	1. Room for social interaction 2. Less time consuming than participant observation 3. Researcher can ask probing questions 4. Relatively inexpensive 5. Diversity of opinions allows researcher to probe underlying values 6. Able to make observations of group interaction in a short period of time 7. Group discussions allow for less structured interview
Weaknesses		
1. Researchers may only see what they want to see. (researcher bias) 2. Can be time consuming 3. Results may not be reproducible 4. Reliability of data based on trust and relationships 5. Unless controlled, the researcher's bias can skew the data	1. Small sampling of the whole 2. Can be expensive 3. Due to researcher bias, may be asking the wrong questions 4. Data does not speak for itself. It must first be analyzed 5. Researcher's control may bias the data 6. Speaks to issues deemed important by the researcher, but not necessarily the respondents	1. Narrow focus may not represent the whole accurately 2. Researcher has little control 3. Analysis is difficult and time consuming 4. Researcher needs to develop specific skills to moderate effectively 5. Need multiple groups to avoid group bias and false data based on group dynamics 6. Unnatural social setting 7. Limited by verbal behavior

Observations & Questions	Interviews	Focus Groups
Quantity of Data		
High based on nature of observations and the time of contact	Relative to the interview guide and individual responses to it— open-ended questions vs. closed-end responses	Quantity of data dependent on nature of questions and desired detail of response. The more focused the questions the greater the response and the greater quantity of data
Quality of Data		
As high as possible for the context	Dependent on nature of response to interview guide	Based on interaction between members of the focus group
Ideal Group Size		
Varies with context	100 + until reaching saturation	6-12 persons per group/10-20 groups

Basic Assumptions:

1. Methods may be mixed and matched to meet the needs of the research in order to collect the data necessary to handle the central research issue and the research questions.
2. No one method will always stand on its own to provide adequate data. No perfect research model exists.
3. The data attained by using multiple methods (triangulation) will be more accurate then data derived from just one method.
4. Researchers must establish the type of data needed before determining the method(s) to use.

Case Studies: A case study generally employs all of the above methods into an inclusive whole that is bounded and clearly defined. Case studies answer the what, how, and why questions but do not seek to control events. See Yin (2009) and Hamel (1993).

APPENDIX A

PROPOSAL DEVELOPMENT WORKSHEET

Please answer the following questions:

1. What topic do you want to explore in your research?
2. Why are you interested in this topic?
3. What is the ministry context for the project?
4. Why is this topic important?
5. How will this study relate to your future ministry, professional goals and to missiology?
6. State the central research as a single statement, question, or proposition. Try starting the statement in one of the following ways:
   - The central research issue in this study is a description of the relationship between *independent variable* and *dependent variable*.
   - The central research issue in this study is an evaluation of how *independent variable* has affected *dependent variable*?
   - The central research issue in this study focuses around the question: What is the relationship between *independent variable* and *dependent variable*?
   - Why does *independent variable* appear to affect *dependent variable*?
   - If *independent variable* then *dependent variable*.
   - A positive (or negative) relationship or correlation exists between *variable1* and *variable2*.
7. What questions or hypotheses does this topic suggest to you to investigate?
8. What secondary sources (precedent research) have you examined which *indirectly* deal with or are *about* your topic?
9. What primary sources have you examined which *exemplify* your topic?
10. In what ways, if any, will your proposed study *resemble* previous research (answer with reference to your answer to question #8)?

11. In what ways, if any, will your proposed study *differ* from previous research (answer with reference to question #8)?

12. How will your proposed study be a contribution to this research (answer with reference to question #8)

13. What resources have you *not examined* that will be important for you to consider for your study? (Cite broad areas of research or theory.)

14. Why would these additional works be important for your investigation?

15. Write an outline of the subtopics to be treated with major work for each topic.

16. What types of data are needed for investigating your topic? Why?

17. What research strategies or methods seem most appropriate for obtaining such data?

18. Why are these methods appropriate?

19. How will the methods from different academic disciplines be integrated in your study (e.g. theology, anthropology, communication, sociology, history, political science, economics, and/or education)?

20. What skills, training, or experience do you now possess to pursue these data collection strategies?

21. What steps, if any, do you plan to take to compensate for any deficiencies in your training and/or experience in your selected research methods?

22. Where do you plan to collect your data? Be as specific as possible about archival sources, survey samples, research sites, and so on.

23. What, if any, obstacles do you foresee in gaining access to your data and/or research subjects?

24. How do you plan to overcome these potential barriers to your data collection?

25. How do you plan to finance your research?

26. What do your think will be the significance or importance of your study to missiological research?

27. How do you plan to schedule this research and its component parts?

28. Have considered the legal and institutional requirements to do your research (e.g., research permits, Institutional Review Board (IRB))?

29. Have you considered the ethical issues that will likely emerge at each stage of your research?

30. Have you selected a mentor or has one been selected for you who is supportive of the project you are proposing?

PRE-TEXT MATERIAL

Every publisher and institution of higher learning will treat the sections preceding the principal body of the text in its own unique way. Styles vary from one institution to the next. Some of the sections noted in this appendix will not be used at all by some institutions, whereas in other cases all of these sections may be used. In some cases the information contained in some of the following sections will be included in a first chapter or introduction to the text. In any of these cases, the issues raised in this appendix should be considered as they function in the individual researcher's situation. Several publications such as the American Psychological Association (APA), Modern Language Association (MLA), or others provide manuals for detailed explanations of both the style and format to use for these sections. However, this appendix provides a set of issues to be considered as one prepares a research report or publication.

All of the pre-text sections of a report serve to introduce the text in one way or another. From these pre-text sections, a reader should be able to identify the author, the title or topic of the work, and where and when the work was done. After reading through these sections, the reader should have a clear foreknowledge of the topic, structure, organization, and general perspective of the text. With the abstract, the reader should be able to identify the key issues, findings, conclusions, and recommendations. These pre-text sections should motivate the reader to read the text.

Title Page

The title page format may vary by institution, but some basic information should be included regardless of the format: title of the work, author's name, date, and the name of the organization or institution for which it has been prepared. In the case of a thesis or dissertation, the degree for which it is being submitted should be mentioned.

The selection of the title may be the first thing a researcher will do. The choice indicates the theme or topic of the work. However, after completing the research report, the title is often the last thing that is revised in order to fine-tune it to the nuances of the text. When choosing a title of a report that will be widely circulated or for a thesis or dissertation, the preferred approach is to select a title that contains the key concepts or focus of the whole document. These key concepts will then serve as the indexing guide for librarians and others who may refer to the report in various databases in the future. Clever or cute titles with obscure or double meanings will not serve the author well when the report is circulated. Such titles may generate humor in one's immediate circle, but the humor will be lost to other researchers and the broader community. If one has spent months or years on a research project, the researcher will probably want to seriously communicate what it is about to potential readers and to increase the number of people who may desire to read it and apply what is recommended.

Several constraints guide the selection of a title:

- Fifteen word limit. Many databases will accept only up to fifteen words.
- Descriptive of the text. The title should describe only what is included in the text in terms of content and theoretical approach. One should be able to know from the title what academic disciplines undergird the study.
- Not pretentious. The title should not promise generalizations that go beyond what the text delivers.
- Simple text. No complex phrases or sentence structures are allowed. Only the subject of the text. The title page serves as the subject and the rest of the text as the predicate.
- Communicative text. The title should clearly communicate to the intended audience what the subject of the text is. Technical terms may be used if they are commonly known by the intended audience. However, if the author has coined technical terms, these terms should be avoided in the title.

Abstract

An abstract should distill the essence of the whole study in a brief summary. It should condense the heart of substance of the whole into a brief synopsis or digest of the whole study. The abstract will be the most frequently read part of the document. For a proposal, an executive summary or one-page summary of the whole may serve the same function. This summary of the document, whether in the proposal or completed stage, allows the reader to quickly gain an understanding of the perspective, content, and outcomes of the whole.

The abstract should briefly describe the following issues: the background, purpose, central research issue, principal questions, major findings, and significant conclusions and recommendations. Since the abstract will likely serve as the base for searching for the research study, all key concepts to be indexed should be included.

The constraints governing abstracts vary somewhat by agency or institution. However, abstracts are normally limited by a certain number of words. Library card abstracts are limited to fifty words. Abstracts for master's level papers are normally limited to about 150 words. Doctoral dissertation abstracts are occasionally allowed as much as 300 words.

Disclaimers

Occasionally, an institution will permit or require a page with disclaimers. For example, if the target audience would be offended by the use of inclusive language, a disclaimer would be required by some institutions. In other cases if the author does not speak English as a first language, some institutions would expect that the author would insert a standard disclaimer about English style.

Dedication

This section is optional. In brief reports it is customary not to include this kind of section. In brief reports it makes the author to appear pretentious. However, in substantive reports it offers another way for the author to express gratitude.

Acknowledgments

The acknowledgment section allows the author or researcher to express gratitude to others who have contributed to the project. Care should be taken to include everyone who made a significant contribution if this section is included. The section is optional for theses, dissertations, and many kinds of research reports. However, readers know that no missiological or church-related research is done in a vacuum. Seldom does a researcher do a research project alone. An acknowledgment to the people who have helped along the way is an appropriate gesture.

One should take care in the acknowledgments section to avoid placing any responsibility for the content of the report on anyone else. In fact the author is responsible for what is written regardless of what others may have said or done. The author is responsible for what is written if others did not cooperate. This section is not to be used for shifting responsibility or blame to anyone.

Table of Contents

The table of contents provides a picture of the overall structure and organization of the whole work. It should accurately reflect the outline structure of the work. Normally, a table of contents would be expected to report all of the headings, including chapter titles, with at least two or three levels of subheadings. In longer research reports, one may have as many as five levels of headings. If one has five levels of headings beyond the chapter titles, normally one would not be expected to include more than three levels of subheadings in a table of contents.

The table of contents should accurately reflect both the wording in the text and the page numbers. While the table of contents may serve as a useful check on the outline and writing, the author must go back to double-check the correspondence between the table of contents and the final text. Often the wording of headings or the order of headings will change in the editing processes. These changes must be reflected in the final table of contents.

The table of contents provides the first opportunity for a reader to evaluate the overall structure of the report. One should be able to clearly discern the continuity, sequence, and integration of the whole work in the table of contents. While the titles of the chapters and major headings should reflect the individual study, the standard major parts of a research study should be discernible in the table of contents for both the proposal and final report. One should be able to find at least the following parts: purpose, goals, major research issue and related questions, scope, secondary source or precedent research support for the study, methods used in data collection and analysis, findings, conclusions and recommendations, and bibliography. Other sections mentioned in this text should be identifiable in the table of contents if they are included in the text.

The headings used in the text and reported in the table of contents should reflect the content of the text so the reader will know what is following. Clever, alliterated, obscure, humorous, or cute headings should be avoided. The intention should be to clearly communicate to the reader.

Other Tables and Lists

Generally, a research report will include graphics and tables. Various kinds of graphics may be used. Each type of graphic should have its own listing like a table of contents. A separate list for figures, tables, and other graphics should be included. One might have maps, photos, or other graphics to help the reader understand. These graphics should all be numbered consecutively throughout the text and labeled appropriately. The numbers, labels, and pages should be reported in the various tables of lists.

Abbreviations

Occasionally, an author will use abbreviations through a text to facilitate the reading speed. If more than ten abbreviations are used, an author should include a list of abbreviations along with the tables of lists. If the reader is not familiar with the abbreviations, a single explanation in the text may not be adequate for a rarely occurring abbreviation.

Preface

The preface is an introduction to the text and often to the author. Either the author or someone acquainted with the author, research, and text may write it. In other publications it is often written by someone else as an introductory commendation for the text. For a research report this section is optional. Customarily, it is omitted from theses and dissertations, although occasionally a researcher will write a preface.

POST-TEXT MATERIAL

Several critical parts of a research proposal or report follow the conclusion of a research study. These parts provide essential information for the reader to assess the overall worth, trustworthiness, and usefulness of the research project. Items such as appendices, glossary, bibliography or references cited, indices, biographical sketches, and the like may provide key information for the reader and will certainly provide the reader with a view of the quality of the work as an initial scan when the work is done.

Appendices

Information that relates to the study, but may not contribute directly to the text should be included in an appendix. Each document should be included as a separate appendix. Each appendix should be sequentially identified alphabetically (i.e., Appendix A, Appendix B, and so on). Several examples that may help clarify the principle—questionnaires, letters to respondents, interview guides, and interview summaries—should be included in the appendices. Extended data tables should be included in an appendix. Brief tables and graphics should be used in the main text, but the more lengthy tables should be included in an appendix. While maps, photographs, and other graphics may be used in the text, supplemental graphics may better fit in an appendix.

Glossary

A glossary defines a list of words and terms used in the document. A glossary should be provided with the expected readers in mind. Technical terms, non-English terms, and key concepts should be included in the glossary. Any term that might not be familiar to readers should be included. The definitions in the glossary should include any terms defined in the text. The definitions in the glossary should be consistent with the way the terms are used through the text. If a term is used more than one way in the text, the glossary should explain each of the different meanings.

References Cited/Bibliography

The principle for inclusion of references in the bibliography or references cited section is simple: every source, whether primary or secondary, quoted, paraphrased or cited as an authority, that is used for the study should be cited. While a bibliography in a proposal may be assumed to be a "proposed" bibliography, the bibliography or references cited in a completed report should contain only those references that are cited in the text.

Bibliographic entries should be complete, accurate, and consistent. The preparation of the bibliography is the most difficult part of the report in terms of format and style. The principle for the references is simple: all of the information that would be needed to find the reference is what is required (see the bibliography of this text for examples.) Typically for books, the following information is required: author, full title, date of publication, place of publication, publisher, and volume number. If the book has multiple authors or editors, one reference would be needed for the editor and then each chapter would be listed with the chapter title with its author. If translators are involved, they should be noted. If it is a dissertation, it should be noted along with the institution. Periodicals require the same kinds of information including author, title of publication, date of publication, title of the article, volume number, issue number, and page numbers. For downloaded documents, the Uniform Resource Locator (URL), the Document Identification Number (DIN), the Digital Objective Identifier (DOI) number, or other identifying numbers, and download date should be included.

An academic institution or publisher will specify what style(s) may be acceptable. Often institutions will provide a style sheet or writer's manual for students to aid them. Citation and bibliographic styles vary. For detailed instructions, one of the major style books should be consulted. For missiological research many institutions and agencies have adopted either the common anthropological method, MLA, Chicago, or APA style. Each style or format differs from the others. Citations from a variety of authors and publishers will present their information in differing formats requiring careful attention to the details for consistency. One simply cannot copy the citation information into a bibliography—even if it is supposedly presented in a given format. The APA, for example, style has undergone three editions since 1994. These versions not only take into account new digital sources, but incorporate subtle changes such as punctuation and spacing as well.

Index

The index should contain all of the major concepts, names, and place names in the text. Occasionally, separate indices may be included for subjects, people, and biblical texts. If many people or biblical texts are cited in the text, it may be appropriate to separate these lists.

Indexing should only be done after the whole text has been finally approved. It is the last step in the production process. It should only be done when the pagination is final and complete. Any editing of the text may change an index and so it must be the last task to be done.

Author's Vita

A brief biography will provide the reader with an understanding of the researcher as a person. The information to be included should be limited to a single page. It should include information to provide the reader with a base to have confidence in the researcher as one who is competent to do this research. Since the general concern is missiology, one's interest in and experience with the *missio Dei* should be noted.

APPENDIX D

CENTRAL RESEARCH ISSUE CHECKLIST

The inclusion and order of the following elements will vary somewhat according to the nature of the research. However, they should all be answered affirmatively if they apply.

- Is the background adequately described including the context of the study and any personal experience providing the "why" to begin the study?
- Does a single purpose state why the study is being done in terms of its intended application?
- Are the goals, that is, the general outcomes expected to be reported in the conclusions and recommendations stated clearly?
- Are all of the goals stated as outcomes rather than processes?
- Do all of the goals relate to the expected outcomes of the research questions?
- Are the areas of significance stated ("external" goals) stated? Are the completed study's intended applications clear for all of the interested constituencies and missiology in general?
- Are the objectives, that is, the specific outcome topics expected to be reported in the conclusions clearly stated?
- Does the scope justify the study?
- Does the scope lead into new areas of research?
- Is the scope feasible (in terms of time, resources, researcher's skills, and accessibility to data sources)?
- Is the central research issue stated as either a problem statement/question or thesis statement?
- Is the research issue stated in a simple statement or question without subordinate clauses?

- Does the statement of the central research issue identify the key relationships among variables (dependent, independent, and classificatory) that are to be studied?
- Does the central research issue set the scope of the study?
- Is the number of research questions or hypotheses between three and five?
- Do the research questions/hypotheses treat all of the variables and relationships required in the problem/thesis statement?
- Are the questions or hypotheses mutually exclusive?
- Are the research questions or hypotheses presented in parallel ways?
- Do the research questions or hypotheses avoid all issues that are not explicit in the problem/thesis statement?
- Are background issues avoided in the research questions or hypotheses?
- Are goals avoided in the research questions or hypotheses?
- Are the delimitations, scope, or boundaries clearly and appropriately set for the study in terms of both feasibility and significance?
- Are the delimitations consistent with the problem statement, purpose, goals, title, and the researcher's qualifications and resources?
- Are key or foundational definitions provided?
- Are all of the assumptions necessary to understand the researcher's perspective from the view of the proposed reader clearly stated?
- Do the assumptions correspond with what would be generally held by informed researchers in the areas being addressed?
- Are the key terms that would not be commonly known clearly defined?
- Is the theoretical framework clearly stated?
- Is the required information accessible?
- Are the resources for doing the study available?
- Is an overview of the whole study presented?
- Can the research be completed in the allotted time?
- Are you willing to have your future shaped by this research?
- Are the ethical issues related to the central research issue resolved?

PRECEDENT RESEARCH CHECKLIST

The following checklist provides a set of questions that a researcher should be able to answer affirmatively before proceeding to the other parts of the research design. If any of these questions results in a negative answer, a revision of the review of the precedent research should be done.

- Does all of the review of the precedent research relate directly to the central research issue?
- Has the review of the precedent research derived its categories suggested by the problem statement, research questions, thesis statement, or hypotheses?
- Are all of the research questions or hypotheses supported by the review of the literature?
- Does the review of precedent research appropriately (adequately, but not too much) treat the background of the study?
- Have all of the significant secondary sources for the problem statement, research questions, thesis statement, or hypotheses been evaluated?
- Does this section address all of the required issues (e.g., background, research questions, values, methods by concept, not by summaries of individual authors)?
- Are the original authors' perspectives interpreted fairly and accurately?
- Have all of the significant primary sources for the research within the study's delimitations been evaluated?
- Has it demonstrated the significance of the research issue to all of the constituencies interested in the research?
- Has it described all of the relevant theoretical base(s) which undergird the study?
- Do the summaries of the subsections or of the whole adequately provide a theoretical framework for the study?

- Has it identified the boundaries of the research (scope) which are relevant to the research issue?
- Is the precedent literature reviewed limited in the scope to only what is required by the central research issue?
- Has the researcher scanned, categorized, and critiqued or evaluated the literature relevant to the problem and research questions?
- Has the full range of relevant methods been evaluated?
- Has it validated the method(s) to be used in the study?
- Has it presented a way to integrate a multidisciplinary approach?
- Has it presented critique of the literature in each category of the research questions from the perspective of the central research issue?
- Has it summarized the theoretical perspective(s) that will be used in interpreting the findings?
- Has it avoided summaries of references without evaluations?
- Has it identified the values or criteria to be used for an evaluative study?
- Has every source been cited appropriately, whether primary or secondary?
- Has it included all cited bibliographical references in the bibliography or references cited?
- Has it maintained a careful distinction between primary and secondary sources?
- Have all of the ethical issues related to evaluating precedent research been resolved?

APPENDIX F

METHODOLOGY CHECKLIST

The methodology should relate directly to the problem/thesis statement and describe the methodological approach according to the categories of the research questions. If each of the following questions cannot be answered affirmatively, then the methods section should be revised.

- Are the methods selected the most appropriate for the research topic?
- Are the resources needed available?
- Does the researcher have the required skills to conduct the research?
- Does it specifically describe the means of data collection?
- For a study involving a population from which a sample is to be selected, is the population clearly defined and described?
- For a study with a sample to be selected, does it specifically describe the sample selection process including the questions of who, how many, where, when, and how they are to be or have been selected?
- Does it describe the desired confidence level if a sample is to be selected?
- Does it describe the information needs for interviews, questionnaires, and studies of archival or printed primary documents?
- Does it describe the hermeneutical or exegetical method(s) that will be used with printed primary sources?
- Does it describe how the data are to be analyzed or treated including whatever statistical tests may be employed?
- Are the methods used for analysis the most rigorous ones available?
- Does it treat the issues of validity and reliability in ways that are appropriate to all of the methods to be used?
- Does it treat the issues of validity and reliability in ways that are appropriate to the interaction of all the methods to be used?
- Does it realistically anticipate threats to validity and reliability as limitations to the research?

- Are the threats to validity and reliability likely to be adequately treated as the proposed methods are employed?
- Does it show that the researcher fully understands the proposed methods?
- Are the methods described well enough for another competent researcher to take the proposal or final report and do the research?
- For theological research, are the issues of trustworthiness and truth adequately treated?
- Do the flow charts or conceptual diagrams clearly and adequately describe the research process and the relationship among the various methods used?
- Are all of the research instruments fully described?
- Are all of the research instruments (questionnaires, interview guides, interpretive grids, and the like) referenced in the methodology to the appendices?
- Are all pilot studies fully documented?
- Is the theoretical framework applied rigorously and consistently throughout the gathering and analysis of the data?
- If multiple methods from one discipline or multidisciplinary methods are used, have they been described well enough that the findings can be coordinated in a consistent, congruent way?
- Are the limitations clearly and honestly stated?
- Are the limitations related to the conclusions and recommendations as constraints?
- Are all of the permissions or authorizations to use the proposed methods completed?
- Are all of the ethical issues related to data collection, analysis, and the noting of limitations resolved?

FINDINGS CHECKLIST

The findings should relate directly to the problem/thesis statement and the categories of the research questions. The findings section should report all that the methods produced related to the central research issue and nothing else. If each of the following questions cannot be answered affirmatively, then the findings section should be revised.

- Do the categories in the findings chapter(s) relate directly to the categories in the central research issue?
- Do the categories in the findings chapter(s) relate directly to the categories in the research questions or hypotheses?
- Does the proposal project categories only, but not specific findings which would bias the final report?
- In the proposal, are the means for reporting the findings presented such as charts, tables, figures, and categories for prose descriptions?
- In the final report, do all of the means for reporting the findings relate directly to the central research issue, research questions, and only present what emerged from the methodology?
- Do the findings completely avoid reporting what was evaluated from the secondary sources or precedent research?
- Do the findings completely avoid reporting any opinions or conjecture of the researcher?
- Are the findings reported in terms of the theory, perspectives, and categories suggested by the precedent research?
- Are all of the findings that are relevant to the central research issue presented in either the findings chapter(s) or the appendices?
- Are all conclusions and recommendations excluded from the findings sections?
- Are the findings presented in a way that they can be easily related to ongoing research in the same subject areas?

- Are the findings presented so that the relationships with the precedent research and theoretical perspectives are clearly seen?
- Are both negative and positive results reported?
- Is the target audience for the findings clearly identified?
- Are the findings written with the expected readers in mind so that they may be able to understand?
- Are the findings presented in a way that the conclusions and recommended actions will be clear?
- Is the information presented in the findings chapter(s) presented so as not to be overwhelming? Does it communicate clearly with figures, charts, graphs, photographs, and tables as needed?
- Have the less relevant tables been moved from the findings chapter(s) to the appendices?
- Has the reporting of the findings avoided the inclusion of recommendations and/or conclusions?
- Have all of the ethical issues related to the reporting of the finding been resolved?

PROPOSAL SUMMARY, CONCLUSIONS, AND RECOMMENDATIONS CHECKLIST

The summary, conclusions and recommendations in the proposal should be brief, but closely related to the purpose and goals section. All of the following questions should be answered affirmatively.

- Does the summary adequately treat the central research issue, research questions or hypotheses, methods, and major expected findings in less than two pages?
- Do the categories of conclusions and recommendations correspond with the stated goals?
- Are the categories of conclusions and recommendations consistent with what may be expected when the methods are completed?
- Are the categories of the conclusions and recommendations strictly based on only the findings?
- Have all specific conclusions and recommendations been avoided in the proposal? (The proposal should come to no specific conclusions or recommendations since they would indicate a set of invalidating biases.)
- Have all of the specific conclusions and recommendations in the final report been moved to the appropriate chapter?
- Have all of the ethical issues related to the proposed summary, conclusions, and recommendations been resolved?

COMMON RESEARCH ERRORS

Many kinds of common errors serve to discredit research. The new researcher should work through such a list to double-check issues of validity and reliability across the whole design. If theological research is a part of the methodology, the questions related to trustworthiness and truth presented in the chapter about biblical theology of mission should be reviewed. All of the problems mentioned below threaten validity. Or, they threaten the reliability of the research and then weaken the validity. Any one of these errors will discredit and weaken the potential conclusions, recommendations, and applications of a study.

Missiological research faces the same range of research problems as do the social sciences and theology. The difference is that missiological research often combines research methodologies from multiple disciplines, including theology. When more than one discipline is involved, the research issues of each discipline arise. Additionally, the appropriate integration of a multidisciplinary approach raises issues. While the combining of history and theology is commonly done, complications arise when methods from anthropology, sociology, economics, comparative religion, geography, political science, education, or communication are used. The social sciences provide new and powerful tools for research that empower one to discern more clearly. However, the issues of trust and truth remain as critical issues from theology.

Common missiological research problems or errors emerge at every stage of the design process and continue during the process of doing the research, analyzing, and reporting it as well as seeking to apply it. Some of the common errors include the following:

- Ethical errors
- Errors of design
- Errors in the use of precedent research
- Errors with research methods premature closure of the inquiry
- Errors in research method integration

- Errors in reporting the findings
- Errors of conclusions and recommendations
- Errors of spiritualizing or mystifying the issues

Ethical Errors

Errors related to lapses in integrity may occur at any stage of the research design process. Along the way, one needs to be concerned about doing the "right" thing. Ethical behavior is required in the design, in the collection of data, in the analysis of data, in reporting the findings, in the drawing of conclusions and recommendations, and in the applying the study after it has been completed. Integrity both within the study itself and with every constituency involved is expected, including sponsors, research subjects, research recipients, and fellow researchers.

Plagiarism constitutes one of the most common ethical errors along the way. People too often succumb to the temptation to steal another person's ideas in a variety of ways. In doing so, their own work is undermined and loses credibility. By giving credit to others for what they have done and contributed, one only builds personal credibility and the credibility of the research being done.

Errors of Design

Design errors can emerge in every part of the design. Whether one is looking at the background, the central research issue and its attendant parts, the review of precedent research, the methodology, reporting the findings, or drawing conclusions and recommendations, each part is subject to errors.

Ambiguous Central Research Issue

Defining the central research issue may be the most common design error. It causes untold grief for a researcher. When the research issue (problem or thesis statement) is left fuzzy (underdeveloped) and the researcher moves on to other parts of the design, the whole design becomes increasingly ambiguous. When the design is unclear, it is very difficult to do the research or to write a dissertation or thesis that makes any sense.

Inappropriate Research Questions/Hypotheses

Several common errors occur as one begins to write either the research questions or the hypotheses. They may not be limited in scope to the central research issue.

They may overlap, that is, they may not be mutually exclusive by addressing the same issues. They may raise questions that cannot be answered and may require research in the future. They may raise issues that belong as background issues or as goals for the study. There may simply be too many of questions or hypotheses to address in a single study. They may not address all of the issues required by the central research issue. They may address background issues, goals, or significance. They may simply restate the central research issue.

Not Stating Goals

Occasionally, a researcher may fail to identify the expected recommendations or the goals expected to emerge from the study. The link between the intended outcomes and the recommendations or conclusions is often missed in the design stage. This weakness threatens the continuity and integration of the study as a whole. These goals should only be what is reported in the study or outlined in the proposal. Goals for application beyond the study should be reported in the "Significance" section.

Lacks Organization

A research design sometimes lacks *continuity* (Tyler, 1949), that is, having the same themes running right throughout the text. It sometimes lacks *sequence*, that is, it may lack an orderly logic that runs through and *integration*, that is, the whole thing does not fit together. With those kinds of concerns, it is important to think seriously as one begins to address a research topic. The organization of the design and the final report should exhibit a strong sense of organization using the following three characteristics.

Basic Misunderstanding of Research Methods

A design problem sometimes occurs when a hopeful, but naive researcher describes the methodology simply as "doing my field research" and that is the statement of the methodology. To further complicate the confusion, a budding researcher may say, "I am going to do two kinds of research: I am going to do research in the library and field research." One needs to get beyond that point to where a differentiation between precedent research in secondary sources and original research in primary sources can be made. The proposal should describe the intended methodology precisely enough in every part of the design that another competent researcher could do the research. Another competent researcher should know both how to collect and analyze the data from the proposal.

Self-fulfilling Prophecies

Occasionally, researchers will expect certain outcomes from their study and then manipulate the research environment to produce them. The result is that the methods are subtly biased to reliably produce what the researcher desires, thus invalidating the study in unsuspected ways. A self-fulfilling prophecy is a serious error that is often introduced by researchers who are familiar with a situation or who have strong opinions. When researchers are looking for something, they expect to see it; and so therefore, do see it. This risk may occur in any method. It is especially a risk in participant observation or interviewing because sometimes the researchers shape the questions and the ways they are asked. The same kind of bias may be introduced in theological or historical research as well, as one may play out the bias in the selection or interpretation of sources.

Worldview

One's worldview may inhibit some perceptions or may prevent understanding what is occurring in another culture. One's culture may see a given method appropriate whereas respondents in a different culture would not accept it or respond in an unexpected way to the researcher.

Errors in the Use of Precedent Research

Errors in the use of precedent research generally emerge out of misunderstanding of the potential uses of precedent research or abuses in the interpretation of the research that others have done. These kinds of errors may be avoided if the researcher simply seeks to be careful along the way and works with integrity.

Counting Previous Experience or Research as Present Research

Emerging researchers often believe that they can bring either personal experience or research that has been previously done into a research project without going through the rigors of working through the design procedures. This kind of practice is fraught with dangers from the perspective of every step in the design process. I have never seen this work successfully. The two largest issues obviously relate to the issues of validity and reliability. If the research were conducted in a valid and reliable way, then the present research would not likely be needed. And, if it were done well, then the purpose, central issue, and research questions would all very likely differ from the present study. If any of these elements were to differ, then the previously done research would not be entirely valid for the present one. It could serve as precedent research, but not as the research for the present study.

This kind of problem is typified by a missionary who came to work on a doctoral program during a study leave. He brought three boxes of responses to questionnaires that he had administered. He wanted to work through all the data in those responses to his questionnaires and write a doctoral dissertation. After beginning his academic program, he discovered several serious problems: 1) He had not described the research issue well; 2) He had not interviewed consistently; 3) He had neither asked the right questions nor all of the questions he should have asked; 4) He had not interviewed the right people; and, 5) He had not interviewed the right number of people. In the end he never opened his three boxes of responses. He had spent several hundred hours of work that he could not use. The problem occurs when a person brings data from some research without first having carefully identified the research issues, evaluated what others may have researched about that topic, or worked out a valid and reliable methodology.

Occasionally, a student not understanding the data collection or the analysis procedures for participant observation will state that the past years of ministry experience in a situation will serve as "participant observation." Simply living and working in an area is not the same as the rigors demanded for data collection using participant observation. It would be like a person writing a historical account saying, "I lived through that era; I can simply recall all that needs to be written!"

Biased Selection of Precedent Research

Researchers often approach their research issues with a high level of commitment that borders on passion. Because of strong emotional feelings about the issues involved, researchers often select previously done studies which would fit into their biases as basis for their own research. For example, a person studying spirituality may feel strongly about what has happened in his own evangelical tradition, but fail to see the centuries of concern and concerted action in both the Roman Catholic and Orthodox traditions. Even much of the contemporary vocabulary related to spiritual formation has its roots in the Roman Catholic Church. To neglect this body of literature, both ancient and modern, would be to make this error of a biased selection of precedent research.

The selection of the precedent research may err in other ways. Some of the issues raised in the central research issue may simply not be addressed in this section. Or, the categories of the evaluation of the literature may not correspond with the issues raised in the background, research questions, or hypotheses. It may not be selected in ways that will allow the researcher to determine the appropriate scope of the study or to fulfill the other functions expected of this section of the design of research.

Occasionally, a researcher will select literature that only marginally relates to the central research issue and then wander off into the issues raised by this secondary research. This kind of error often occurs when one also errs by just summarizing the findings or conclusions of the secondary sources.

Misinterpreting the Precedent Research

The standard principles of exegesis or hermeneutics apply to the interpretation of any research document. Basic journalistic questions must be asked: Who wrote it? Was the author competent? Why was it written? What was the perspective of the author? What did the author intend to communicate? What in fact was the point of the writing? When was it written? To whom was it written? Was the design and reporting of precedent research valid and reliable?

One may misinterpret in a variety of ways. One common way is simply by "proof-texting," that is, finding quotes that say what the researcher wants to say without regard to what the original author was trying to communicate. Such out of context comments are common as some authors believe that others can better express their ideas than they can themselves. While it may be true that a given author may express an idea well, one must be careful to interpret what has been written, and not simply present quotes to support one's own ideas.

Another common way of misinterpreting another person's work is by read-ing into the other person's writing an intention which was simply not present. Anachronisms, in which one reads into a text something that was not present at the time, are common errors. A related error is the misinterpretation of figures of speech. Metaphors, for example, are culture and time specific. They always need careful interpretation.

Summarizing Rather Than Evaluating

The point of the "review of the literature" or review of precedent research is to evaluate the research done previously in the light of the central research issue. When researchers simply summarize secondary sources as their evaluation, they have missed the point and erred. Researchers should be able to summarize what others have said and done. However, a summary is not what is significant. What is important is an answer to the question, "So what?" What is important from this text or article for my research? To summarize by itself is a serious error because it misses the purpose of the evaluation or the review of the literature.

Evaluating by Author Rather Than by Concept

It is useful and often essential to know what a given author has written across several volumes as it relates to a given research issue. However, to evaluate all of the literature by author generally causes the researcher to miss the point of how the precedent research relates to his or her own research. The point of the evaluation is to evaluate these secondary sources from the perspective of the present central research issue. It is not to simply compare the authors who may have researched topics around it.

Failing to Justify the Central Research Issue

One of the central aims of the evaluation of precedent research is to justify the present research issue. Is it worth doing? Should it be done? If from a review of precedent research one cannot answer that question, then one has simply failed to derive a fundamental piece of information from the literature. Maybe little or nothing is written about the specific research issue. If that is the case, the researcher should say so. If much has been done and the research issue does not need further attention, the researcher should say so. Previous researchers in the same research arena should give guidance to the present researcher to justify the issue.

Failing to Establish the Scope of the Study

Just as one should be able to justify the central research issue from the literature, one should be able to identify the boundaries of the research that has already been done and what the remaining frontiers are about the topic. The scope should clearly emerge from what others have researched around the topic. If the scope or delimitations are not related to an evaluation of the precedent research, a serious error is present.

Failing to Establish a Theoretical Framework

Some errors become linked. If one has made the error of summarizing instead of evaluating, it is likely that the error of failing to establish a holistic or integrating theoretical framework will occur as well. The theoretical framework provides the way of explaining the phenomena under question, ways of predicting how the variables will interact, ways to control the variables, ways to observe the variables to validate the theory, and basis for action. The theoretical framework will help the researcher integrate the multiple approaches from different disciplines in the methodology and then interpret the findings. It will help provide a prospective for making conclusions and recommendations from the findings. While a research study may enlarge or develop new theory, every study begins with a theoretical framework and a set of theoretical assumptions. This theoretical framework should emerge from an evaluation of how others have approached similar issues. If their studies did not work well, then they should be critiqued for that. If they were able to explain related phenomena or similar situations, then the studies should be cited for that. If the theoretical framework is not clear in this section and especially in the summary of the review of precedent research, a serious error affecting all of the rest of the study has been made.

Failing to Validate the Methods

Just as one needs to validate the central research issue and the theoretical framework from previous research, one also needs to validate the methods. Whether questionnaires, interview, interpretation of texts, or archives, one should give attention to a validation of the methods to be used. If more than one method is to be used, not only should each method be validated, but the integration of the methods should also be documented in the literature. Not to validate one's methods suggests to the reader that the researcher is not familiar with the methods being used, which in fact may be true.

Errors With Research Methods

Every research method has potential errors in both the data collection and data analysis stages. Wise researchers will look at each method to be used to discover the potential risks involved. Different kinds of research methods will have widely differing issues to face in data collection and data analysis. The potential for these errors grows exponentially as one uses multiple methods or multidisciplinary methods. Each additional method, while potentially contributing significantly to the research, also brings its own limitations which must be considered.

Collecting and Trying to Analyze Data before Defining the Design

Often a new researcher selects and employs a methodology before defining the key issues such as the central research issue, research questions, or hypotheses and neglects a review of precedent research. To leap into data collection before carefully focusing the central research issue and research questions or hypotheses is like leaving for a trip without deciding where one is going. Or, to initiate data collection before reviewing precedent research is like embarking on a trip without a map or even a designation. The name of destination may be known, but the ways to get there would not be known. The different methods and their relative advantages or disadvantages would remain unknown. The distance to the destination would remain only a fuzzy idea. The resources needed to get there would probably not be known. On the other hand, if one were to review a map, the walking time, driving time, or flying time could easily be determined. A little more research with maps and related literature would help a person select the best method and route. When the method and route have been selected, the costs and logistics needs can then be estimated.

Confusing Correlation With Causation

Because two variables are related and even vary together does not mean that one causes the other. Naive researchers often make this serious mistake in the interpretation of their findings. In the summer, the tarmac on the streets becomes soft in Pasadena, California. At the same time the number of drownings increases along the Los Angeles County coast. One cannot conclude that because these two variables are correlated, the soft tarmac in Pasadena causes drownings off the LA County coast. Nor can one recommend that a different kind of pavement should be used to reduce the risk of drowning.

One could demonstrate that the rate of infant mortality declines with the rise of the amount of paper in a community. In this case a very strong negative correlation predictably exists. However, one cannot validly conclude or recommend that to increase the amount of paper will bring a decrease in infant mortality. The error in both examples is the same: equating correlation with causation.

Variables that show correlation may relate to each other because of a known or unknown third variable. In the first case it was the daily temperature. As the temperature increased, the tarmac softened and more people go to the beaches where the risk of drowning increases. In the second case as people learn to read and improve their general education, the amount of paper will increase in a community as will knowledge about maternal and infant care.

Interaction With Research Subjects

Researchers often generate reliability errors in their research by influencing the responses of their respondents. These influences may occur in many varied and subtle ways. With descriptive research, one may influence the respondents by explaining too much about the study to where they respond in ways they believe would help or please the researcher. Research subjects may provide biased or unreliable results by inappropriate questions on questionnaires or interviews. The influences may be subtle in interviewing. A facial expression, gesture, a change in tone, rhythm, stress, word order in the asking of a question or order of the questions may profoundly influence the respondent to where the response would differ from before. One's gender, age, ethnicity, dress style, style of speaking, dialect, proximity, fragrance/odor, gestures, manner of standing or sitting, venue of the interviews, use of a recorder, and note-taking style all influence responses. Any or all of these concerns may, in fact, differentially bias the findings with different respondents. The effects of the interviewer provide a common source of reliability errors.

A small pilot study in which one practices asking questions may help to develop confidence and consistency as well as reduce this kind of error. Not only will it help develop one's interview style, it will provide essential feedback about the interview guide. From this feedback, one can improve the questions, the order of the questions, and how the questions are asked.

Many other kinds of reactive measures are possible in doing social research. If one is doing a participant-observation study, because of the fact of being in the situation, people respond differently. I remember going to a circumcision ceremony in Kenya among the Maasai, the very fact that I was there—I was the only outsider there—caused some stir. People wanted me to do this or to do that. They wanted me to take certain photographs and not to take other photographs. They wanted me to participate in the eating of this food, but not in the eating of that. It was, in fact, disruptive to the events of the day. I was not seeking to interfere or influence any of the events, but it did in fact disrupt because I was a guest and they were trying to show respect. My notes would not provide a reliable record in which I could say, "This series of events is what happens in this kind of circumcision ceremony." Although all of the parts that were essential were done, some things that happened were different because of my presence. Researchers have to be sensitive to the reactive nature of the research that they are doing.

With experiments, one may influence both the control and experimental groups in subtle ways that would not be immediately recognizable. For example, the "Hawthorne Effect" is a perspective that comes from an experiment that failed because of an interaction with the people who were being studied. Between 1927 and 1932, Elton Mayo conducted experiments at the Western Electric Hawthorne Works in Cicero, Illinois. The employees in both the "treatment" and "control" groups increased in productivity because they knew they were being studied.[22] Experiments were done to determine which environmental conditions would produce the greatest amount of worker productivity. Levels of lighting were changed and other work environmental changes were initiated. In every case, whatever the change, productivity increased. After reflection, it was determined that what brought the changes in productivity was the interaction of the respondents, not the changes in the work environment.

People who know they are being observed will very often alter their behavior. This change in behavior will result in unreliable and invalid research results whether the research is descriptive, experimental, or evaluative. Trustworthy conclusions and recommendations will not be possible.

Random Errors

Random errors result from an unreliable measuring instrument. For example, a person might use interviews as the basic methodology of a study. If, in the process of doing the interviewing, the researcher did not ask the questions in consistently the same ways, random errors could be expected. People would answer the questions differently depending on the word order, the question order, the rhythm or stress in the questions, the gestures or even the time of day. Or, if the same interview guide were used in a different subculture, random errors could be expected because people would interpret the nuances of the questions differently.

Constant Errors

Constant errors refer to the kind of error that is generated by a research instrument that gives consistent, but wrong results. If a person were measuring weight and the standard was in pounds, a constant error would occur if the response

---

22   *Hawthorne Effect.* The Hawthorne Effect-Mayo Studies in Employee Motivation, http://www.envisions software.com/articles/ Hawthorne_Effect.html retrieved on 11/7/10.

were given in kilograms. Or, a constant error might be consistently measuring the wrong thing. Or, if the instrument were set wrong, consistent, but inaccurate errors would result.

Misplaced Precision

The error of misplaced precision may occur when one collects the data with great care and precision, but within a faulty framework. The faulty theoretical framework or method then invalidates the findings and any conclusions that may be made. A researcher can just carefully collect the wrong information or precisely analyze it in ways that invalidate the findings. For example, one may very carefully craft a written language test that will provide reliable—that is, consistent and precise—results. However, if the goal were to learn to learn to speak and listen correctly, a written language test would be an example of misplaced precision. The results would simply be invalid.

One might strive to have a precisely selected number of respondents in a sample, but then administer a poor questionnaire or interview. The misplaced precision would not help validate the study.

"Typical" Case Studies

Studies that are based on "typical" cases are usually biased and unrepresentative. Such cases are too often more ideal than typical. They may better fit the reporter's biases than others which might have been cited. A better way would be to select cases in a random way. Claiming to select "typical" cases is a risky business. That serious reliability limitation needs to be identified. If cases for the case studies are selected carefully and deliberately, the selection criteria should be carefully described. However, claiming that the cases are "typical" raises reliability issues that may result in invalidating the study. One must be very careful about generalizability claims made about deliberately selected samples.

Error of the Instrument

An error of the instrument occurs when a research instrument is used regardless of its applicability. One can often point to a college, university, or seminary professor who always advocates the same research method. For example, if a two-year old is given a hammer, he or she will beat on anything that comes along. Sometimes researchers do that with their instruments. Whatever the situation, one takes the particular test and applies it there. Maybe it will fit or maybe it will not fit.

Maybe the hammer does not go well with the mirror. One needs to look at the method and see if it is indeed appropriate for the issues at hand.

Many standardized tests have been published. In a research library one could easily find books about tests and measurements, tests in print, references about their validity and reliability and situations in which they would likely fit. The use of a standardized test does not automatically result in an "Error of the Instrument." This error occurs when the instrument is inappropriately applied.

Enough Is Enough

The methodology section should describe in adequate detail what methods will be used so that the study could be done by another competent researcher. The data collection and analysis procedures along with any expected limitations should be clear to the reader. The naive researcher who simply passes of the proposed methodology as doing "library research" or "field research" has simply not done the essential work.

Errors in Research Method Integration

One's methods should all fit together to provide one integral holistic approach to addressing the central research issue. Errors are likely to occur if the methods are designed from the outside to work together. It is difficult after the fact to integrate different kinds of findings.

Errors in Reporting the Findings

Findings comprise the substantive part of the study and the bases for the conclusions and recommendations. If the findings are in error, the study will not be appropriately applied. Later researchers who read the study may be misled and the errors perpetuated. Several kinds of errors commonly occur. Some of these errors are listed below.

Assuming the Findings

From time to time the findings are assumed from the outset of the study. Several times after looking at a research proposal, I have asked, "If these data or sets of information are your findings, why bother to do the research?" If one has already decided what the findings are going to be, and what the recommendations are going to be, the research is pointless.

Overambitious Proposing of Findings

Design issues also arise around the proposed findings of a research study. These design issues may arise when the student is too ambitious, that is, some findings may be proposed which are not likely to emerge from the proposed methodology. Too often a person will include the details of what is expected to be found and recommended, thus seriously biasing the study. Such a flaw may be fatal to the study. This kind of bias may blind a researcher to what may in fact be found from the proposed method, as well as lead into the error of misrepresenting the findings after completing the study.

Not Reporting All the Findings

If a researcher does not report all of the findings related to the central research issue, a significant error may result. Some researchers, wanting to validate their theories, will report only the findings that support what they seek to demonstrate. Such reporting shows a significant lapse in one's integrity and will discredit the whole study.

Reporting Findings from Outside the Methodology

Occasionally, a researcher will attempt to add information to the reporting of the findings that were not produced by the methodology. Such additions reflect a serious breach in integrity. Some researchers may not intend to deceive thinking that some respondents "should have responded" in a certain way or they will fill in blanks in questionnaires thinking that no one will know. No one may discover this breach in integrity, but adding information that was not honestly produced by the methods constitutes a serious error.

Again, some unscrupulous researchers will report their own opinions and prejudices as findings. This kind of error may appear in subtle ways of biased reporting.

A related error relates to the reporting as findings what was in fact discovered and reported in precedent research. When researchers confuse primary and secondary sources or when researchers try to evaluate secondary sources (precedent research) throughout their whole research report, this kind of error is almost inevitable. This kind of error again leads to serious ethical questions as well as the potential charges of plagiarism. Researchers simply cannot claim the findings of another study as the outcomes of their own study!

Misleading Graphics

Often when researchers are just learning how to report their findings, they are less sensitive to the ways that graphics are interpreted than they should be. Graphics create impressions before the details of the figures are interpreted. Graphs, for example, can be manipulated using the same data to create very different impressions by changing the scales or the type of graph. The researcher will need to be aware of the intended audience so that the graphics can be appropriately presented.

Errors in Making Conclusions or Recommendations

Errors in the conclusions and recommendations are more often noticed because many readers will skip to this section to read it first. If this section is faulty, the mistakes of the study are likely to spread to the community and infect others. People may actually believe and act on faulty conclusions and recommendations. If we are concerned about the *missio Dei*, people may be acting inappropriately to carry it out. As with the other sections the following errors are simply suggestive of common errors that do occur. Researchers should take these as warnings.

Misplacement of Conclusions and Recommendations

Frequently, new researchers think about the implications of both the secondary sources and their own findings as they work through them. They should be thinking about these implications and the inferences they can draw along the way. However, if they report the conclusions or recommendations anywhere outside of the conclusions and recommendations chapter(s), the readers may very well miss them. Recommendations and conclusions should only be found in the appropriate sections or chapters. Readers will often skip through a research report to read the conclusions and recommendations. If they are strewn through the whole report, the reader will likely miss most of the implications of the researcher outside of the final chapter(s).

Based on Something Other Than the Findings

A researcher will need to take care not to draw conclusions on anything outside of the findings. Occasionally, I have read conclusions based on the secondary sources used in a research study. At other times I have seen conclusions and recommendations based solely on the opinions or intuition of the researcher, but not justified in any of the findings presented. Such errors should be avoided.

Faulty Reasoning

Faulty reasoning may appear in many ways. Two common errors frequently occur: equating causation with correlation and post-hoc[23] circular reasoning. The use of logic should not be suspended along the way. Both deductive and inductive approaches to critical thinking require rigor and integrity. In any given research study, both approaches may be employed.

Overgeneralization

Every researcher wants his or her research to be applied as widely as possible. Researchers often err by seeking to apply the conclusions and recommendations more widely than the external validity of the methodology will permit. Overgeneralization is a serious error and will discredit both the researcher and the research. Cautious application is to be preferred. While the theory produced in a study may indeed apply more broadly, the researcher must carefully state the limits of the generalizability by referring back to the limitations in the methodology chapter and the considerations for validity that were treated there.

Errors of Spiritualizing or Mystifying

Many researchers conducting church-related or missiological research have theological background and training. Many have been trained as pastors and preachers. Many have not only been trained in these ways, but have served for years as pastors or preachers. They are accustomed to interpreting the spiritual dimensions of a situation. While this kind of interpretation is not an error, when this tone is brought into a research study, problems emerge. This kind of error is often found as one seeks to draw conclusions too early or to draw out spiritual implications from all of the literature in ways that do not relate to the central research issue.

Summary

As one works through the design of research, potential hazards wait at every step to invalidate the work that is to be done. A researcher may avoid most of these risks by a strong sense of integrity and commitment to the central research issue. If, along the way, one keeps the issues of validity and reliability in mind, most of the threats may be minimized. (A checklist has been provided as an appendix to

---

23   That is, after the fact.

aid in the correcting of common errors. The reader is advised to work through the checklist both before the documents are written and afterward to provide a check on what has been done.)

GLOSSARY

The following terms provide a perspective for this book and may generally be applied in research contexts. Some of these terms may be applied in other ways than listed here, but the assumption here is that all of these terms will apply in one way or another to missiological or church-related research.

Action research — Research that combines the testing or development of theory with application.

Active variable — A variable that can be directly manipulated.

Analysis of variance — (ANOVA) A statistical procedure for analyzing simultaneous comparisons between two or more means.

Assigned variable — A variable that cannot be actively manipulated.

Assumption — A belief or perspective that is taken as granted or true. An undergirding perspective for a research project about which and for which the author does not do research.

Average — Arithmetic mean, a measure of central tendency. A sum of the scores divided by the population.

Background — The context for which and out of which the research is being done. The background of a research study provides the broad reasons for doing the research and the situation in which the conclusions and recommendations are likely to be applied.

Bar graph — A histogram; a graph in which the frequencies of scores are shown as vertical or horizontal bars.

Bibliography — An alphabetized listing of all of the sources including books, articles, and archival materials such as letters, interviews, or online sources. A bibliographical entry will include all of the relevant information to assist another person find the document including such issues as full name of author, full name or title of document, date, place of publication, volume number, number of the publication, page numbers, edition, document object identifier number, database name, chapter name, translator, and the like. A bibliography differs from "references cited" in that it may be somewhat broader in scope by including references not cited in the text of the study.

Boundaries — Research boundaries are the limits of what has been researched about a given topic and the frontiers of what has not yet been researched. Knowing the boundaries provide the researcher with the essential information to make decisions about the scope or delimitations of a research project.

Case study — An in-depth study of a limited number of instances. The number may range from one to ten or more cases. Each case may number as few as a single individual to a congregation or a community.

Causal observation — Observation without planned categories or a systematic means for scoring.

Chi-square — A statistical test used with nominal data to test whether the observed distribution of scores differs from what would be expected by chance. Chi-square is useful to find the significance differences among proportions of subjects that fall into different categories. X^2 compares two sets of frequencies: observed frequencies and expected frequencies.

Cluster sampling — Sampling in which groups which naturally occur together are selected, as people in a city block, people in a given village, families, and so forth.

Coefficient of equivalence — A statistical measurement used in showing that two tests are the same to assure reliability.

Coefficient of stability — A statistical measurement used to show the level of consistent results with a test to assure reliability.

Confounding — Confusion that occurs when one cannot determine which variable(s) led to the observed outcomes.

Conclusion — The reasoned outcome or inference of a research study based on what has been discovered in the study. The necessary consequence of what has been discovered in the study. A conclusion may be based solely on what was discovered in the study.

Concurrent validity — A view of validity in which the measurement of a variable is the same as an external criterion, for example, if one can type fifty words a minute on a typing test, it would be the same as typing fifty words a minute in a job situation. Often referred to as criterion or predicative validity.

Consilience — "the linking together of principles from different disciplines especially when forming a comprehensive theory."[24]

Constant error — A consistent error which affects validity. Suggests that the measuring instrument is measuring the wrong thing.

Construct validity — A view of validity in which the variables being tested are logically and theoretically consistent with what is intended to be tested. One might ask, "Do the assumptions of the test match the assumptions of the course?"

Contemporary History — A risk to validity in an experimental study in which the subjects are exposed to other variables not being controlled over time. These variables may be expected to confound the results of the experiment.

Content analysis — A research method that systematically describes the form and content of written or spoken material.

---

24   http://www.merriam-webster.com/dictionary/consilience retrieved on 1/5/2010.

Content validity — A view of validity in which the research instrument is said to indeed describe or test the issues about which conclusions are to be drawn, for example, a test in mathematics in which students are to be evaluated about multiplication tables ranging to nine might be asked, "What is nine times eight?" The question would have content validity.

Contextualization — A process of adapting the subject at hand to the local situation while remaining faithful to the major worldview issues of both.

Continuous variable — Variables that may take on an infinite number of values, such as height, distance, and age.

Continuity — The reiterative quality of a discourse. The recurring theme or themes that link the whole discourse. For example, the recurring themes of worldview and cultural forms will occur in a discourse related to anthropology. Continuity may also be understood as the essential redundancy of a discourse that balances the information load.

Control — An essential requirement for experimental research in which all extraneous variables except the one being tested (independent variable or test variable) are held in check during the experiment to prevent any effect from them on the outcome (dependent variable).

Control group — The group in an experiment that does not receive the application of the independent variable. The group will be like the experimental group in every way except for the application of the independent variable.

Correlation — A measure of the degree of relationship between two variables.

Correlation coefficient — A statement of the relationship between two variables in which the values range from -1 to +1. A -1 is a perfect negative correlation and a +1 is a perfect positive correlation.

Criterion validity — A view of validity in which the measurement of a variable is the same as an external criterion, for example, if one can type fifty words a minute on a typing test, it would be the same as typing fifty words a minute in a job situation. Often referred to as either concurrent or predicative validity.

Data analysis — The processes by which the data generated by the application of the method are processed and examined to identify what may be significant in the research in terms of the goals of the study.

Data collection — The processes by which the methods are applied to collect information to answer the research questions and solve the research problem or validate/invalidate the thesis statement.

Definition — Statements which determine or identify the essential characteristics of terms or concepts used in the study. The stated assumptions about specific terms used in the study.

Degrees of Freedom — The number of observations free to vary around a constant parameter.

Delimitation — A statement of the scope of the study in which the limits of the extent of the study are defined. Delimitations often exclude arenas which are known to be related, but beyond the scope of the study.

Dependent variable — The subject of the investigation, a consequence to the independent variable. An expected outcome. The variable that results from the implementation of the independent variable.

Descriptive research — Research that aims at explaining a condition or a situation. It normally aims at the formation of or expanding of theory. Typically, seen in such different kinds of studies as case studies, surveys, developmental studies, historical studies, theological studies, correlation studies, and trend analyses.

Descriptive statistics — Mathematical procedures used to organize and summarize numerical data related to the characteristics of a sample or population.

Dichotomous variable — A variable with two classes (e.g., male and female).

Differential Experimental Mortality — As the subjects in an experiment are involved in the experiment, occasionally one may drop out of either the control or experimental group. By the change of the number of subjects in either group, the outcomes of the experiment are jeopardized in terms of reliability and validity. The loss of a subject is described as differential experimental mortality.

Differential selection — The choosing of samples using different criteria or not using standardized criteria. If one selects the subjects in some way other than randomly, the difference in terms of selection and the bias in terms of selection may generate the results rather than whatever the researcher does.

Double-blind procedure — An experimental procedure in which neither the researcher nor the subject is aware of the treatment to which the subject has been treated.

Equivalent forms — One may check the reliability of a test by having two forms of the test that are equal or comparable in terms of what they measure. These comparable forms are described as "equivalent forms."

Evaluative research — Research in which the outcome is aimed at providing value-based information for making judgments or informing decision making.

Experimental group — The group in an experiment that is given the treatment or exposed to the independent variable.

Experimental research — Research characterized by the control, manipulation, and observation of variables. Aims primarily at the testing of theory.

Ex Post Facto research — Research done after the fact. A research procedure used when the investigator cannot test a hypothesis by assigning subjects to different conditions in which he directly manipulates the independent variable.

External validity — The extent to which the conclusions and recommendations of study may apply beyond the sample used to provide data for the study. The same as the term *generalizability*.

Extraneous variable — A variable unrelated to the independent or experimental variable that may cause confounding or confusion with the outcomes; a source of error.

Face validity — An outsider's common sense perspective of an instrument that suggests it is measuring what it claims to be measuring.

Findings — The information that has been generated by the data collection and analysis process of a research study. Not to be confused with what may be discovered from secondary or precedent research.

Frequency — The number of times that a variable occurs in a distribution.

Frequency distribution — An arrangement of the scores in the order of their occurrence.

Frequency polygon — A line graph showing relative frequencies.

Generalizability — The extent to which the findings, conclusions, and recommendations of a study may be applied; external validity.

Goals — The expected outcomes of a study that can be reported in the study. To be differentiated from the purpose which is the broadest statement of intent for a study that normally answers the question "why?" To be differentiated from "significance" that refers to how the study is expected to be applied once the study has been completed.

Histogram — A bar graph showing relative frequencies.

Hypothesis — A subproposition of the central research issue (thesis) that is to be tested in a research study. A tentative explanation of phenomena that facilitates the extension of knowledge in the area of the central research issue. A research question stated as a proposition to be tested. A tentative answer to the research problem. Sometimes stated as an "If-then" statement (If *independent variable* then *dependent variable*).

Independent variable — The causal variable in a research study. The variable that would be manipulated in an experimental study. Sometimes called the experimental variable. The independent variable is the antecedent or cause to the dependent variable.

Inferential statistics — Mathematical procedures to make projections or generalizations from a sample to a whole population.

Interval scale — A scale that indicates the relative position on a scale of predetermined intervals (e.g., intelligence tests, the measurement of temperature). These scales may or may not have a true zero point. A zero point is irrelevant to the working of the scale.

Instrument — The tool, device, or mechanism that is used to collect data. Often takes the form of a questionnaire, interview guide, or test.

Internal validity — Any one of a number of perspectives that raise the question about whether the design of a research method will produce information about what it claims to be addressing or about which conclusions and recommendations will be made.

Level of Significance — The predetermined level at which the null hypothesis is rejected. May be tested by a variety of statistical tests such as the Chi-square test.

Likert Scale — An attitude scale in which a number of items are rated from very favorable to vary unfavorable.

Limitation — Any threat to the validity or reliability of a study either at the design, data collection, or analysis stage. Limitations of reliability or validity constrain the kinds of conclusions or recommendations that can be made from a research study.

Manipulation — The application of the independent variable (experimental or research variable) in an experiment. Sometimes called the experimental "treatment."

Maturation — The natural growth process in an experiment which may result as a threat to the internal validity of the experiment. For example, if an experiment were conducted with children who are between nine and twenty-four months in which they were given instruction about how to walk. It could be expected that the normal growth and development process through this time would influence the process more than any instruction that might be given.

Mean — The arithmetic average; the sum of scores divided by the number of cases.

Measures of central tendency — Mode, the most frequently occurring score; median, the midpoint in a distribution; and, mean, the arithmetic average.

Measures of variability — Range, the distance between the highest and lowest scores, a nominal measure; Quartile deviation, the ranking of a score in relation to the scores that are less, for example, a 50% percentile would mean that that 50% of the scores would be less, an ordinal measure. Standard deviation, a measure of variability which takes all of the scores and their distribution into account, an interval, or ratio scale measure.

Methodology — The means for data collection, data analysis, and recognition of the potential limitations of these means.

missio adventus — The in-breaking (the advent) of God, of Jesus Christ in the Incarnation, of the Holy Spirit at Pentecost, of the Holy Spirit in and through the Church.[25]

missio Dei — The mission of God. The central focus of missiology.

missio futurum — Mission as it relates to the "predictable issues of God's mission as they work out in human history and *missio adventus*; "the in-breaking (the advent) of God, of Jesus Christ in the Incarnation, of the Holy Spirit at Pentecost, of the Holy Spirit in and through the Church."[26]

missio hominum — The human dimension of mission.

missio political oecumenica — Mission as it draws from and impacts global human civilization.[27]

Missiology — The study of the *missio dei*, that is, the mission of God. Includes not only God's intentions, revealed precedents in scripture, but what has occurred and occurs in the accomplishment of this mission.

Mission — The central purpose or aim. Mission as used in missiology may refer to the central purpose of God or God's people.

missiones eccesiarum — The mission of the Church as God's people.

---

25   Van Engen, 1982, 29-31.

26   Ibid.

27   Ibid.

Missions — Agencies or parachurch organizations involved in the *missio Dei*. Sometimes refers to specific mission projects of a church or church agency.

Mode — The single score that occurs most often in a frequency distribution.

Multidisciplinary research — Research that uses methodological approaches from more than one academic perspective, for example, a missiological study might require studies in theology to understand what God has revealed, studies in anthropology to provide the means for understanding the culture and worldview of a people and history to understand what has been previously done about a particular concept.

Multivariate analysis — An analysis of the relationships among several variables at the same time. For example, ethnicity, number of years one has lived in a community, age, and educational level might all interact to influence receptivity to the gospel.

Nominal scale — A scale that sorts objects or classes of objects into exclusive categories in which there is no information about their equivalence or difference (e.g., class A, B, C, etc.).

Null hypothesis — A statement of a research question as a proposition in which states that the independent variable has no effect on the dependent variable. The opposite of the normally stated hypothesis. A statement that there is no relationship between the variables and that any relationship is only a function of chance.

Observation — The process of viewing and obtaining the results of the manipulation of variables in an experimental study. May also refer to the gathering of data as in a "participation observation" study in which the researcher participates in the community being studied. Observation may be done by either nonreactive means in which the subjects being observed are not affected. Or, observation may be done by reactive means such as "participant observation" where the person collecting the information may influence the outcomes of the process.

Ordinal scale — A scale which sorts objects according to some basis of their relative standing to each other (e.g., first, second, third, and so on).

Participant observation — An anthropological method in which the researcher joins in the community or series of events that are being studied.

Percentile — An ordinal statistic or score at which or below which a given percentage of cases lie.

Pilot study — A preliminary small scale study aimed at the same population as the proposed study with the purpose of establishing the validity and reliability of the research instrument(s).

Plagiarism — The conscious, unconscious, deliberate, or nondeliberate use of another person's idea or artistic creation without giving credit to that person. Plagiarism is the stealing of another person's ideas and claiming that they are one's own. A serious breach in ethics and integrity in the misuse of another person's ideas or artistic creation.

Point of contact — A cultural form which may facilitate the communication of the Christian gospel. For example, the sacrificial lamb of the Jews of the first century provided a means by which to explain the sacrifice of Jesus on the cross. A point of similarity in another cultural or religious system that may be used as an initial means to facilitate communication of the Christian gospel. Points of contact always contain perceived meanings that differ from the Christian gospel.

Population — The whole group or class in a given category. For example, the population of a school would include all of its students.

Precedent research — Research that has been done previously that is relevant to the present research. Precedent research should be treated as a "secondary source" because it is research *about* the topic that is being studied not the original or primary information itself.

Predictive validity — Criterion or concurrent validity in which a test is able to predict future behavior according to a given criterion.

Primary source — An original source, an eyewitness, or firsthand account. Not a study about something, but the thing itself. For example, if one were studying the missiological implications of the writings of John Wesley, his writings would serve as the *primary source* material. Any commentary about these writings would be a secondary source.

Problem — The central research issue. May be stated as a statement in which the key issue among the variables to be studied is noted. Or, it may be stated as the primary question for the research in which the key issue among the variables to be studied is raised as a question.

Purpose of study — The broadest statement of intent for a study, which describes the general outcome of the study and answers why the study should be done.

Random — Without a pattern. When applied to the selection of a sample for a research project it means without any bias in the selection process in which every case of the population being studied has an equal chance of being selected. Randomization is required for studies to be generalizable to the whole population from which the sample was drawn.

Random error — Unpredictable error which affects reliability indicating a poor or unreliable measuring instrument.

Range — A measure of variability among nominal variables. It is determined by subtracting the lowest score from the highest score.

Ratio scale — A scale that has equal intervals and has a meaningful zero point (e.g., measures of weight, distance, money).

Recommendation — The reasoned counsel or advice based solely on the findings of the research study. The necessary action to be taken based on what has been discovered in the study.

Redemptive analogy — A cultural form that appears to be similar to an aspect of Christian teaching. This kind of form may be useful to facilitate the communication of the Christian gospel. For example, the sacrificial lamb of the Jews of the first century provided a means by which to explain the sacrifice of Jesus on the cross. Redemptive analogies always contain locally perceived meanings that differ from the Christian gospel.

References cited — Refers to all of the sources that have been used and cited in a document. An alphabetized listing of all of the sources including books, articles, and archival materials such as letters, interviews, or online sources. A bibliographical entry will include all of the relevant information to assist another person to find the document, including such issues as full name of author, full name or title of document, date, place of publication, volume number, number of the publication, page numbers, edition, chapter name, translator, and the like.

Reliability — The consistency, repeatability, replicability or stability of the design and methods of a research project. A reliable research instrument will produce the consistent results with what it is intended to measure. For example, a scale in a doctor's office should weigh a hundred pound object as a hundred pounds every time it is placed on the scale. Affected by the length of a test, the homogeneity of those tested, ability to take the test, and the quality of the test.

Reliability coefficient — A statistical measure of the consistency or stability of a research instrument.

Research — A systematic way of investigation or discovery.

Research question — A question which addresses one set of variables in a research problem. Should always be a subset of the research problem being constrained in scope and the variables by the problem. Research questions should be mutually exclusive and yet comprehensive of all that is included in the related problem. They should be researchable. For example, they should avoid future issues which cannot be reliably researched.

Review of the literature — A phrase that is used widely in research circles to refer to an evaluation of what has been written from previously done research about the topic at hand. An evaluation of secondary sources about a given topic.

Sample — A subset of a population that is selected for study.

Sampling bias — A type of error in which the selection technique favors certain characteristics over others.

Sampling error — Chance variation among samples chosen from the same population.

Scope — A statement of the delimitations of the study in which the limits of the extent of the study are defined. The scope statements often exclude arenas which are known to be related, but beyond what is intended for the study.

Secondary source — A source that is written *about* the subject. To be contrasted with a primary source, which is the subject or an eyewitness who provides testimony about the subject. A secondary source from a legal perspective provides hearsay evidence rather than admissible evidence. Secondary sources are *interpretations* of the topic rather than the original documents themselves.

Significance — The *external* goals of a study, that is, the expected ways the study will be applied after it has been completed.

Standard deviation — A measure of variability from a ratio or interval scale.

Standard error of the mean — A measurement of sampling errors or the standard deviation of the means of the samples of a single population. The larger the sample size, the smaller the standard error will be. The larger the standard deviation of the population, the larger will be the standard error of the mean.

Statistical regression — A phenomenon that occurs when a sample has been selected on the basis of some extreme score and then retested. The sample can be expected to "regress" to a distribution characteristic of the population from which they came.

Statistics — A branch of applied mathematics used to design and analyze research. Statistics may be generally divided as descriptive or inferential, that is, either providing a means of analysis of quantitative data or for providing information about how collected data may be applied to the whole population from which the sample was taken. Statistics provide the means to interpret and describe the measurements taken in a research project.

Stratified sample — A type of random sampling in which the characteristics of the sample(s) are proportionate to those present in the total population. A sampling procedure by which all defined groups in a population are guaranteed representation, sometimes called proportional stratified sample.

Summary — A condensed, comprehensive interpretive restatement of a previous section. No new information is to be included in a summary.

Systematic sampling — A sampling technique in which every k^{th} is selected from a population. For example, every fifth name may be selected from a phone book or a voter registration list.

Test-retest — A method for ensuring reliability by testing a sample and then retesting the same sample using the same test. May be used when skills are involved, but may not be used when memory may be a factor.

Theoretical base — The foundational perspective(s) that are used to guide the collection of data, data analysis, reporting the findings and developing the conclusions and recommendations.

T-test — An index used to find the significance of the difference between the means of two samples. The standard error of the difference between two means.

Theory — The general abstract principles for explaining phenomena, predicting the future, providing a base for action and potential control. Theory may be stated as a set of laws, a set of well supported empirical generalizations, axioms, or a set of principles.

Thesis — The central research issue stated as a proposition to be tested. Often the term applied to the major written project for a master's degree.

Type I Error — An error that occurs when the investigator says that the null hypothesis is false and it is fact true.

Type II Error — An error that occurs when the investigator says the null hypothesis is true and it is fact false.

Validity — The quality of the design, data collection and analysis, conclusions, and recommendations of a study that it indeed does address what it claims to address.

Value — The desired state or conditions, often expressed by such words as "should" and "ought." In evaluation studies, values serve as the criteria for assessing worth, merit, or quality. It may mean the amount of a variable (e.g., the score on a particular test).

Variable — A concept that can take on different values. A factor that becomes the focus of a research project. A characteristic or quality that may differ in degree or kind. Variables may be described as "dependent" (i.e., outcomes) or they may be described as "independent" variables (i.e., causes).

Venn diagram — A figure that typically uses overlapping circles to depict a conceptual framework.

Worldview — The core shared assumptions in a community which guide and constrain the patterns of values, perception, and action in every area of life.

REFERENCES CITED

Angrosino, M. (2007). Doing ethnographic and observational research. In G. Gibbs (Ed.), *The SAGE qualitative research kit*. Woodland Hills, CA: Sage Publications.

Ary, D., Jacobs, L. & Razavieh, A. (1972). *Introduction to research in education*. New York, NY: Holt, Rinehart and Winston.

Babbie, E. (2006). *The practice of social research* (11th ed.). Belmont, CA: Wadsworth.

Baer, M. (2006). *Business as mission: The power of business in the kingdom of God*. Seattle, WA: YWAM.

Barbour, R. (2008). Doing focus groups. In G. Gibbs (Ed.), *The SAGE qualitative research kit*. Woodland Hills, CA: Sage Publications.

Barna, G. (Ed.). (1997). *Leaders on leadership*. Ventura, CA: Regal Books.

Barrett, D. (1982). *World Christian encyclopedia: A comparative survey of churches and religions in the modern world, A.D. 1900-2000*. New York, NY: Oxford University Press.

Barrett, D., Kurian, G., & Johnson, T. (2001). *World Christian encyclopedia: A comparative survey of churches and religions in the modern world volume I: The world by countries: religionists, churches, ministries* (2nd ed.). New York, NY: Oxford University Press.

Barrett, S. R. (1996). *Anthropology: A student's guide to theory and method*. Toronto, Canada: University of Toronto Press.

Befus, D. (2005). *Where there are no jobs*. Miami, FL: Latin American Mission.

Bennett, D. W. (2004). *Metaphors for ministry: Biblical images for leaders and followers*. Eugene, OR: Wipf and Stock.

Berlin, B., & Berlin, E. (1975). Aguaruna color categorie. *American Ethnologist, 2*, 61-87.

Bevans, S., & Schroeder, R. (2004). *Constants in context: A Theology of mission for today* Maryknoll, NY: Orbis.

Bernard, H. (2006). *Research methods in anthropology* (4th ed.). Lanham, MD: Altamira.

Bonk, J. (2010, January). World Christian Information: Public Freeway or Private Toll Road? *International Bulletin of Missionary Research, 34*(1). Retrieved from http://www.internationalbulletin.org/archive/all/2010/1

Bosch, D. (1991). *Transforming mission: Paradigm shifts in theology of mission*. Maryknoll, NY: Orbis Books.

Bradley, J., & Muller, R. (1995). *Church history: An introduction to research, reference works and methods*. Grand Rapids, MI: Eerdmans.

Campbell, D., & Stanley, J. (1963). *Experimental and quasi-experimental designs for research*. Chicago, IL: Rand McNally.

Charmaz, K. (1994). The Grounded Theory Method: An Explication and Interpretation. In B. G. Glaser (Ed.), *More grounded theory methodology: A reader*. Mill Valley, CA: Sociology Press.

Clinton, J., & Clinton, R. (1997). The life cycle of a leader. In G. Barna (Ed.). *Leaders on leadership* (pp. 149-182). Ventura, CA: Regal Books.

Consilience. (n.d.). In *Merriam-Webster's online dictionary* (11th ed.). Retrieved from http://www.merriam-webster.com/dictionary/consilience

Crandall, E., & Diener, R. (1978). *Ethics in social and behavioral research*. Chicago, IL: University of Chicago Press.

Creswell, J. (2003). *Research design: Qualitative, quantitative and mixed methods approaches* (2nd ed.). Thousand Oaks, CA: Sage Publications.

Creswell, J. (2009). *Research design: Qualitative, quantitative, and mixed methods approaches* (3rd ed.). Thousand Oaks, CA: Sage Publications.

Davis, G. & Parker, C. (1997). *Writing the doctoral dissertation* (2nd ed.). Hauppauge, NY: Barron's Educational Series.

Deduction and Induction. (2010, January 31). Retrieved from http://www.social researchmethods.net/kb/dedind.php

Dressel, P. & Marcus, D. (1982). *On teaching and learning in college*. San Francisco, CA: Jossey-Bass.

Eldred, K. (2005). *God is at work: Transforming people and nations through business*. Ventura, CA: Regal Books.

Elliston, E. (1981). *Curricular foundations for Christian leadership development in the Samburu Christian community* (Unpublished doctoral dissertation). Michigan State University, Michigan.

Elliston, E. (1987). Applied Research and Church Growth: A Turkana Case Description. In H. Schreck & D. Barrett, *Unreached peoples: Clarifying the task*. Monrovia, CA: MARC.

Elliston, E. (2000). Doctoral Degrees in Missiology. In A. Moreau, H. Netland, & C. Van Engen (Eds.), *Evangelical dictionary of world missions* (pp. 288-289). Grand Rapids, MI: Baker Books.

Elliston, E. (2000). Receptivity. In A. Moreau, H. Netland, & C. Van Engen (Eds.), *Evangelical dictionary of world missions* (pp. 809-810). Grand Rapids, MI: Baker Books.

Engel, J. (1977). *How can I get them to listen?* Grand Rapids, MI: Zondervan.

Forman, C. (1987, October). Response to James Scherer's paper from different disciplinary perspectives. *Missiology: An international review, 15*(4), 523.

Hagner, D. (1993). *New Testament exegesis and research: A guide for seminarians*. Pasadena, CA: Fuller Theological Seminary Press.

Hamel, J., Dufour, S. & Fortin, D. (1993). *Case Study Methods.* Newbury Park, CA: Sage Publications. Hiebert, P., Tienou, T., & Shaw, R. (2000). *Understanding folk religion: A Christian response to popular beliefs and practices.* Grand Rapids, MI: Baker Academic.

Isaac, S. & Michael, W. (1985). *Handbook in research and evaluation for education and the behavioral sciences* (2nd ed.). San Diego, CA: Edits Publishers.

Johnson, C. (2003). *IMM directory of marketplace ministries.* Pasadena, CA: Institute for Marketplace Ministries.

Johnson, C. & Rundle, S. (2010). *Business as mission: A comprehensive guide to theory and practice.* Downers Grove, IL: InterVarsity.

Johnstone, P. (2001). *Operation world—21st century edition, updated and revised edition.* Carlisle, United Kingdom: Gabriel Resources Paternoster Press.

Kinnear, T., & Taylor, J. (1991). *Marketing research: An applied approach* (4th ed.). New York, NY: McGraw-Hill.

Kirkpatrick, J. (1987). *A Theology of Servant Leadership* (Unpublished doctoral dissertation) Fuller Theological Seminary, Pasadena, CA.

Kraemer, H. (1947). *The Christian message in a non-Christian world.* New York, NY: Harper.

Kraft, C. (1996). *Anthropology for Christian witness.* Maryknoll, NY: Orbis Books.

Krathwohl, D. (1976). *How to prepare a research proposal* (2nd ed.). Syracuse, NY: Syracuse University Bookstore.

Kuhn, T. (1996). *The structure of scientific revolutions* (3rd ed.) Chicago, IL: University of Chicago Press.

Kvale, S. (2007). Doing interviews. In G. Gibbs (Ed.), *Qualitative research kit.* Woodland Hills, CA: Sage Publications.

Lasswell, H. (1971). The structure and function of communication in society. In W. Schramm & D. Roberts (Eds.), *The process and effects of mass communication* (p. 84). Urbana, IL: University of Illinois Press.

Latourette, K. (1937-1945). *A history of the expansion of Christianity* (Vols 1-7). New York, NY: Harper.

Leedy, P., & Ormrod, J. (2005). *Practical research: Planning and design* (8th ed.). Upper Saddle River, NJ: Prentice Hall.

Malinowski, B. (1961). *Argonauts of the western Pacific.* New York, NY: E. P. Dutton (Original work published 1922).

Manickam, J. (2008). Comparing three primary qualitative research methods. *Course Syllabus, MB560.* Pasadena, CA: Fuller Graduate School of Intercultural Studies.

Markman, R. Markman, P., & Waddell M. (1989). *Ten steps in writing the research paper* (4th ed.). New York, NY: Barrons' Educational Series.

Martin, A. (Ed.). (1973). *The means of world evangelization: Missiological education at the Fuller School of World Mission.* South Pasadena, CA: William Carey Library.

Miller, D., & Salkind, N. (2002). *Handbook of research design and social measurement* (6th ed.). Thousand Oaks, CA: Sage Publications.

Moreau, A., Netland, H., & Van Engen, C. (Eds.) (2000). *Evangelical dictionary of world missions*. Grand Rapids, MI: Baker Books.

Moreau, A., McGee, G., & Corwin, G. (2004). *Introducing world missions: A biblical, historical, and practical survey (Encountering mission)*. Grand Rapids, MI: Baker Academic.

Morris, L., & Fitz-Gibbon, C. (1978). *How to present an evaluation report.* Beverly Hills, CA: Sage Publications.

Murdock, G. (2004). *Outline of cultural materials* (5th ed.). New Haven, CT: Yale University Press.

Nelson, J. (2007). *Qualitative Methods and the Scientific Epistemological Cycle.* Paper read at China Conference.

Neely, A. (1995). *Christian mission: A case study approach.* Maryknoll, NY: Orbis Books.

Newbigin, L. (1986). *Foolishness to the Greeks: The gospel and the western culture.* Grand Rapids, MI: Eerdmans.

Paul, R., & Elder, L. (2006). *Critical thinking: Learn the tools the best thinkers use.* Upper Saddle River, NY: Pearson Prentice Hall.

Pierson, P. (c. 2000). Class notes from History of the Christian Mission. School of Intercultural Studies, Fuller Theological Seminary.

Pierson, P. (2009). *The dynamics of Christian mission: History through a missiological perspective.* Pasadena, CA: William Carey International University Press.

Pike, K. (1967). Etic and Emic Standpoints for the Description of Behavior. In *Language in relation to a unified theory of the structure of human behavior.* The Hague: Mouton and Company.

Plagiarize. (n.d.). In *Merriam-Webster's online dictionary* (11th ed.). Retrieved from http://www.merriam-webster.com/dictionary/plagiarize

Pocock, M., Van Rheenen, G., & McConnell, D. (2005). *The changing face of world missions: Engaging contemporary issues and trends (Encountering mission).* Grand Rapids, MI: Baker Academic.

Qualitative Measures. (2010, January 31). In *WebCenter for Social Research Methods.* Retrieved from http://www.socialresearchmethods.net/kb/qual.php

Researching world Christianity Doctoral dissertations on mission since 1900. (2010). *International Bulletin of Missionary Research with Yale Divinity School Library.* New Haven, CT: Overseas Ministries Study Center. Retrieved from http://www.internationalbulletin.org/resources

Richardson, D. (1976). *Peace child.* Glendale, CA: Regal Books.

Roth, A. (1999). *The research paper: process, form, and content* (8th ed.). Ft. Worth, TX: Harcourt College.

Rundle, S., & Steffen, T. (2003). *Great commission companies: The emerging role of business in mission.* Downers Grove, IL: InterVarsity.

Salant, P., & Dillman, D. (1994). *How to conduct your own survey.* New York, NY: John Wiley & Sons.

Salkind, N. (2008). *Exploring research* (7th ed.). Upper Saddle River, NJ: Prentice Hall.

Schramm, W., & Roberts, D. (Eds.). (1971). *The process and effects of mass communication.* Urbana, IL: University of Illinois Press.

Schreck, H., & Barrett, D. (1987). *Unreached peoples: Clarifying the task.* Monrovia, CA: MARC.

Shaw, R. (1986). The Bosavi language family. *Pacific Linguistics, A-70,* 45-76.

Shaw, R. (1988). *Transculturation: The cultural factor in translation and other communication tasks.* Pasadena, CA: William Carey Library.

Shaw, R. (1990). *Kandila: Samo ceremonialism and interpersonal relationships.* Ann Arbor, MI: University of Michigan Press.

Shaw, R., & Van Engen, C. (2003). *Communicating God's word in a complex world: God's truth or hocus pocus?.* Lanham, MD: Rowman & Littlefield.

Slife, B., & Nelson, J. (2005). Theoretical and epistemological foundations. In L. Miller (Ed.), *Oxford handbook of the psychology of religion and spirituality.* New York, NY: Oxford University Press.

Smalley, W. (1993, July). Doctoral dissertations on mission: Ten-year update, 1982-1991. *International Bulletin of Missionary Research, 17*(3), 97-100.

Smith, D. (1992). *Creating understanding.* Grand Rapids, MI: Zondervan.

Søgaard, V. (1993). *Media in church and mission: Communicating the gospel.* Pasadena, CA: William Carey Library.

Søgaard, V. (1996). *Research in church and mission.* Pasadena, CA: William Carey Library.

Spradley, J. (1979). *Ethnographic interview.* New York, NY: Holt, Rinehart and Winston.

Spradley, J. (1980). *Participant observation.* New York, NY: Holt, Rinehart and Winston.

Steffen, T., & Barnett, M. (Eds.). (2006). *Business as mission: From impoverished to empowered.* Pasadena, CA: William Carey Library.

Stufflebeam, D. (1973). Educational evaluation and decision-making. In B. Worthen & J. Sanders *Educational evaluation: Theory and practice* (pp.128-142). Worthington, OH: Charles A. Jones Publishing.

The Hawthorne Effect-Mayo Studies in Employee Motivation. Retrieved from http://www.envisionsoftware.com/articles/Hawthorne_Effect.html

Tippett, A. (1973, January). Missiology: For such a time as this! *Missiology: An International Review 1,* 25-31.

Tippett, A. (1974). Missiology, a new discipline. In A. Martin (Ed.), *The means of world evangelization at the Fuller School of World Mission.* Pasadena, CA: William Carey Library.

Trochim, W. (2006). Hypotheses. In *WebCenter for Social Research Methods.* Retrieved from http://www.socialresearchmethods.net/kb/hypothes.php

Trochim, W. (2006). Ethics in Research. In *WebCenter for Social Research Methods*. Retrieved from http://www.socialresearchmethods.net/kb/ethics.php

Tyler, R. (1949). *Basic principles of curriculum and instruction*. Chicago, IL: University of Chicago Press.

Van Engen, C. (1996). *Mission on the way: Issues in mission theology*. Grand Rapids, MI: Baker.

Van Engen, C. (2006). Critical theologizing: Knowing God in multiple global/local contexts. In J. Kraybill, W. Sawstsky and C. Van Engen (Eds.), *Evangelical, ecumenical, and Anabaptist missiologies in conversation* (pp. 88-97). Maryknoll, NY: Orbis Books.

Van Engen, C., Woodberry, J., & Whiteman, D. (Eds.). (2008). *Paradigm shifts in Christian witness: Insights from anthropology, communication and spiritual power*. Maryknoll, NY: Orbis Books.

Van Rheenen, G. (1996). *Missions*. Grand Rapids, MI: Zondervan.

Van Rheenen, G. (2006). *Contextualization and syncretism*. Pasadena, CA: William Carey Library.

Ward, T. & Dettoni, J. (1974). Increasing effectiveness through evaluation. In T. Ward & W. Herzog (Eds.), *Effective learning in non-formal education* (p. 208). Lansing, MI: Michigan State University.

Ward, T., & Herzog, W. (Eds.). (1974). *Effective learning in non-formal education*. Lansing, MI: Michigan State University.

Whiteman, D. (1987, October). Response to James Scherer's paper from a different disciplinary perspectives. *Missiology: An International Review, 15*(4), 525-527.

Winter, R. (1995). My pilgrimage in mission. *International Bulletin of Missionary Research, 19*(2), 37-40.

Wolf, T. (2010). *Lifecode: An examination of the shape, the nature and the usage of the Oikoscode, a replicative nonformal learning pattern of ethical education for leadership and community groups*. Doctoral dissertation. Andrews University, Berrien Springs, MI.

Worthen, B. & Sanders, J. (1973). *Educational evaluation: Theory and practice*. Worthington, OH: Charles A. Jones Publishing.

Yamamori, T., & Eldred, K. (Eds.). (2005). *On kingdom business: Transforming missions through entrepreneurial strategies*. Ventura, CA: Regal Books.

Yin, R. (2002). *Applications of case study research*. Thousand Oaks, CA: Sage Publications.

Yin, R. (2002). *Case study research design and methods (Applied social research methods)*. Thousand Oaks, CA: Sage Publications.

Zahnheiser, M. (1987, October). Response to James Scherer's paper from different disciplinary perspectives. *Missiology: An International Review, 15*(4), 527-528.

INDEX

A

B

R